FRANCES KRAY

The Tragic Bride

By the same author:

Bombsites & Lollipops: My 1950s East End Childhood

The Real Life Downton Abbey

Jennifer Saunders: The Unauthorised Biography

*White Boots & Miniskirts: A True Story of Life
in the Swinging Sixties*

*Bomb Girls: Britain's Secret Army: The Munitions
Women of World War II*

FRANCES KRAY

The Tragic Bride

The True Story of Reggie Kray's First Wife

REVISED EDITION

JB

JOHN BLAKE

Published by John Blake Publishing Limited,
3 Bramber Court, 2 Bramber Road,
London W14 9PB, England

www.johnblakebooks.com

www.facebook.com/johnblakebooks 📘
twitter.com/jblakebooks 📧

First published in hardback in 2014 by John Blake Publishing Ltd
This revised paperback edition published in 2015

ISBN 978-1-78418-374-5

British Library Cataloguing-in-Publication Data:

A catalogue record for this book is available from the British Library.

Design by www.envydesign.co.uk

Printed in Great Britain by CPI Group (UK) Ltd

Every attempt has been made to contact the relevant copyright-holders,
but some were unobtainable. We would be grateful if the appropriate people
could contact us.

JACKY HYAMS is a freelance journalist, editor, columnist and author with over twenty-five years' experience in writing for mass-market magazines and newspapers in the UK and Australia.

A Londoner who has spent many years travelling, her feature-writing career was launched in Sydney, Australia, where she wrote extensively for the *Sydney Morning Herald*, *Sun Herald*, *Cosmopolitan*, *Rolling Stone*, *Good Housekeeping*, *New Idea*, *Clio* and *The Australian Women's Weekly*. Returning to London, she spent several years as a women's magazine editor on *Bella Magazine*, followed by six years as a weekly columnist on the London *Evening Standard*.

Her memoir, *Bombsites and Lollipops: My 1950s East End Childhood*, and its follow-up, *White Boots & Miniskirts: A True Story of Life in the Swinging Sixties*, were published in 2011 and 2013 respectively, both by John Blake Publishing. She is also the author of *The Real Downton Abbey*, a brief guide to the Edwardian era (John Blake Publishing, 2011) and *The Female Few*, a study of the women Spitfire pilots of the Air Transport Auxiliary, while her most recent book is *Bomb Girls: Britain's Secret Army: The Munitions Women of World War II* (John Blake Publishing, 2013).

CONTENTS

INTRODUCTION

She was beautiful, intelligent and innocent. Yet while growing up in the fifties in London's East End, neither she nor Frances Shea's family could ever have imagined that her entire life would be tragically destroyed because she caught Reggie Kray's eye when she was just a teenager...

At the time, the Kray twins were already notorious around the East End, poised to kill men and laugh in the face of the law for years to come. The 'Two Ones' wanted fame, celebrity above all else and, in the end, they got it, twin souls locked into an obsessive and eerie relationship with each other. Cockney gangsters from London's East End, with all its traditional associations with crime, poverty, dark deeds and extreme violence, they garnered a huge reputation as crime lords of their era – the iconic fifties and sixties.

Reggie Kray died, in a blaze of ghoulish publicity, his second wife Roberta at his side, in the year 2000. His twin,

Ronnie, died in Broadmoor hospital, a psychiatric institution for the criminally insane, in 1995.

Yet their mythical status is, if anything, more powerful than it ever was when they were alive.

A huge part of that myth is the imagery that lives on, the photos they gleefully commissioned, posed for, used as tools in their thirst for fame. Criminals were supposed to live in the shadows, weren't they? Not the twins. They used extreme violence to intimidate and extort, stuck two fingers up at authority – and turned it all into celebrity gangster dollars.

There they were, glamour boys, dripping cashmere and gold, at a time when most Brits could just about afford the hire-purchase repayment on a telly, rubbing shoulders with sleek, good-looking movie stars, wayward politicians, sporting heroes of the time. Big fluffy hairdos. Nightclubs. Movie premieres. Slick, beautifully cut suits. And, of course, very public good deeds, craftily engineered into the pages of the newspapers, all geared towards showing their warmly philanthropic side. Generous, big-hearted East Enders – who happened to kill people, too – but only 'their own'. It was a compelling story. Yet it was a pack of lies. The reality, as Frances Shea discovered, was quite different – and unbelievably terrifying.

Back in 2013, while pondering some of those iconic images taken so long ago, one big question struck me: Why, with so much already said, written, scripted, documented and delivered to the public gaze about the Kray twins, had so little been told or revealed about Frances Shea, briefly at the centre of it all, the beautiful young girl whose image literally shimmers off the page or screen in the midst of this oft-repeated history?

In 1965, Frances had married Reggie Kray in a blaze of

tabloid publicity, left him after a matter of weeks – and killed herself just over two years after the marriage.

Even close to half a century on from her suicide at the age of twenty-three, total strangers flock to her grave, place flowers and ponder the power of her beauty. Mostly, though, they wonder about the tragedy of her short existence.

Who was Frances Shea and why did she die? This became, for me, a compelling question. Many theories abounded, naturally, because this story was about the Kray twins and the tales told about them are legion, especially those concerning the crimes they are rumoured to have committed yet never stood trial for.

Many of the people in their story are no longer around, of course. Both sets of parents, the Krays and the Sheas, are long gone. Yet it seemed to me that despite the complexities of revisiting the past, going back over Frances Shea's brief lifetime, here was a significant story. Her acknowledged status, as 'arm candy' for Reggie in his bid for gangster power, wasn't really good enough. There had to be more.

I had one very small, personal advantage, in that the more I researched her story, the more I understood that my own world, growing up in the murky, battered streets of fifties Dalston within two miles of the Hoxton home of Frances and her family, might, superficially at least, offer an insider's perspective. Her father, Frank, worked for a time as a street bookie after World War Two, when street betting was illegal. So did my dad, Ginger. I'm younger than Frances but she grew up surrounded by the scars of the war in London's East End, as I did.

However, there were big disparities in our respective day-to-day lives and I was not personally familiar with the world she was to briefly inhabit as Reggie Kray's girlfriend and wife. This was mostly because even though, during the 1960s, I ventured forth into the West End of London and a life beyond the East End as soon as I could, that life had been virtually handed to me in my teens, through working each day as an office girl in the centre of Swinging London.

Frances Shea also started out that way, having an office job as a bookkeeper in London's legal district, the Strand, months before her sixteenth birthday. But beyond that, she never really had much of a working life, thanks to Reggie Kray's intense possessiveness: he couldn't tolerate the idea of Frances being exposed to any other influence, especially that of the opposite sex. And while I was certainly aware of the associations with crime in my dad's East-End betting world, I was an over-protected only child in a somewhat solitary world. Few people visited our home. I never witnessed or met anyone from my father's shady working environment; I just heard the stories.

At this point, I must say that despite this childhood, and even having written about it in an earlier book, *Bombsites & Lollipops* (2011), I am not especially sentimental about the old East End and its traditions in the way that history often portrays the area. The wave of nostalgia that has swamped the twentieth-century history of London's East End, the tales of the Cockney survivors, triumphant amidst the dust and heartache, has now emerged as a permanent part of the city's World War Two history.

There is truth in some of this, certainly. But I hope the reader will forgive me if I find it impossible to share the belief in that misty, rose-coloured glow that has somehow taken precedence over reality. As a child, I saw the post-war East End as a dark, dirty and immensely scary place.

INTRODUCTION

Yet the link to the Kray twins in my childhood is worth recording, though many former East Enders of the time are likely to offer a similar story, such was the Kray legend as we all grew up.

My dad, Ginger, was born and bred in Petticoat Lane: only when war and the call-up intervened did he take his place overseas with millions of others in the services. Post WWII he returned to 'the Lane' to work with his father Jack, a well-known local bookmaker, known as a 'commission agent'. In the thirties, Ginger had briefly left home and worked 'on the knocker' with Charlie Kray, the twins' father, travelling around the south of England, knocking on doors, buying and selling old clothes, furniture and, if they could get it, gold and jewellery. This bond – and the mutual bonding place of the Bishopsgate pub – led to my dad spending drinking hours with Charlie in those post-war years. As a consequence, sports-mad Ginger knew the twins as teenagers – 'good little boxers' – and, like so many in those mean streets, briefly got caught up in their endeavours.

Up in court for one of their juvenile crimes, the Kray brothers petitioned my dad, climbing the narrow stairs to my grandfather Jack's tiny office off Middlesex Street, home to his respectable front as a legal 'commission agent' for his mostly illegal street-betting activity. 'Can you write us a letter, for the court, Ginger?' they asked. My dad had a reputation around 'the Lane' for being clever with the pen. He obliged, of course, lying through his teeth in his neat handwriting, pointing to their good behaviour and respectability.

And that could have been the end of it. But because the twins had phenomenal memories, much later, as they prospered, they suggested Ginger join them on their payroll.

Good money. They'd keep an eye out for the missus and the little 'un. What did Ginger think?

My dad had his faults. But he was smart enough to decline – he knew all too well what lay underneath all their manipulative guile: he wasn't interested in making a living from violence or the threat of it. He worked for his dad. Jack wouldn't be happy if he left the business, he explained.

This, thankfully, was good enough for the twins. Family first. Yet my dad was on their list, as it were. So when the good times came, and the late fifties/early sixties parties celebrating their various club openings or successful tussles with the law came about, off they'd go, my mum and dad, all dolled up to the nines, my mum reeking of Chanel No 5, to the lavish Kray parties.

Nowadays, of course, it's understood that these well-known parties were all part and parcel of the Kray PR machine. The bigger the bash, the more well-known they became, mixing locals like my parents with big fish, such as celebrities, lawyers, bent coppers as well as assorted lowlife. In that, at least, they were egalitarian icons, way ahead of their time: instinctively they understood that image was all. Or rather, the status the twins thirsted for was all in the perception. Underneath it all lay a grim, sordid reality no law-abiding person would even wish to contemplate. But those stories told in our living room about the fabulous, access-all-areas parties became part of my own small family history.

Curiously, though, I didn't really follow their story very much when I left home and started the long, slow climb into journalism. Probably because I was very keen to shake off the grime of the East End with all its less-attractive associations, I more or less forgot about them at first.

INTRODUCTION

Back in the seventies I'd read *The Profession of Violence*, John Pearson's detailed and amazing history of his time with the twins just before they were imprisoned for life at the end of the sixties, and had been mightily impressed with what he'd revealed.

Pearson's eye was forensic. He was the fly-on-the-wall observer of the Krays, the outsider scribe given a unique peek into their world in the late sixties, just months before they were sent down for good. Already a successful journalist and author, he analysed not just their propensity for violence, their twinship, their guile, but also their talent in manipulation. He also hinted at what might have been. To me, on reading it, it was a revelation that Reggie Kray had first-class skills that could have made him a highly successful businessman.

Of course, what no one could have truly predicted then was the twins' success at reinforcing their image throughout the thirty-odd years of their incarceration. That in itself was a marvel of media manipulation and gave them the fame they craved way beyond the senseless murders and Ronnie's mental illness. They gave the interviews. They sold the stories. They married while serving 30-year prison sentences. A feature-length movie was made while they were still around. The media attention just went on and on. Yet even now, nearly two decades after their demise, with a new, big-budget movie about them on its way, the fascination with them still remains.

For me, the Frances question around her relationship with Reggie seemed, somehow, to be at the very core of the Kray history, despite her premature death. Buried at Reggie's insistence at Chingford Mount Cemetery, just outside London, alongside the entire Kray clan, she remains permanently linked to their myth, way beyond her own and her family's imaginings or wishes.

This, in itself, was a terrible injustice. And what I found, slowly, as I examined her short history, revealed a strange, tangled and tragic tale of one man's desire for total possession and a young woman's rapid descent into unending despair.

It is also a story of an ordinary East End family finding themselves trapped fast, helpless and without the power or means to escape the consequences of their involvement with two local crime lords. Both Frances's father, Frank, and her brother Frankie worked briefly for the Krays around the time that Reggie's fascination with Frances started to impact on their lives.

Aware of the Krays as local post-war 'employers' via my dad's association with them, I knew this was commonplace. If, like most people living around the area, you came from a household where money was always in short supply, you'd be hard pushed to refuse the offer of Kray cash to drive them around or work in one of their clubs. This was so even if you'd already heard the stories about the terrible things they did to people who crossed them. The mantra was: keep in with them, take the money, stay shtoom. That threat of what the twins could do was there all the time. It didn't even diminish once they were locked up.

Fortunately, people like my father didn't need their cash, in his case because he had his own business on his dad's ticket. The Shea men, father and son, weren't quite so lucky. Money, in a world of betting, boozing, ducking and diving, where you picked up cash wherever you could, ignoring the law, was, in a sense, the trigger for what was to eventually happen to Frances Shea.

INTRODUCTION

Even before Frances died, her family's lives were already blighted by guilt and blame. The guilt and the blame were to overshadow everything afterwards, while the publicity the Krays garnered for three decades continued to heap attention on the twins, attention they relished and encouraged all the time.

How it must have hurt the Sheas to have to relive their pain and loss year in, year out, through the newspaper pages read by millions. In discovering their story, it became obvious that Frances's loved ones suffered a great deal. In silence. It was a haunting too far.

Today, bereaved or stricken families can, if they wish, be a focus of media attention following a bitter injustice to a loved one. It was so different back then. The Sheas, of course, were not the only family to suffer as a result of the Krays' attentions. Yet how much consideration was given back then to the grief or feelings of the families of the two men whose murders the twins were convicted for, George Cornell and Jack McVitie? Cornell's wife suffered openly: she smashed windows at the Kray home in bitter frustration. McVitie's wife was the first witness in court when the Krays were eventually brought to trial for her husband's murder. She told the court how McVitie had told her he was meeting the twins for a drink but never returned. Then, without warning, she let rip at the twins, broke down in tears calling them 'murdering bastards'.

It was a sensational outburst at the time. The family of Frank Mitchell, whose killing was ordered by the Krays, surfaced too many years afterwards. But essentially, the families of Kray victims had limited visibility at the time the Krays were convicted. Back then, people remained fearful, in the shadows. This fear of Kray retribution around the East

End went on for decades. Even recently, in my research, I heard, more than once: 'Nah, luv. Best not to talk about it. Don' wanna dig up all that stuff.'

As for Reggie Kray, did he carry any long-term remorse for Frances's demise to his own grave? This, I discovered, was not a straightforward question. In prison he remained, as he was when younger, a complex individual with a personal charisma that never quite left him. Both sexes fell for him. Even as he died his wife and his long-term former boyfriend sat on either side of the bed.

Yet even after concluding this book, I struggled to believe that he truly loved Frances.

He certainly believed he loved her. That idealised love became an important part of his image, his myth. But the love between man and woman and obsession – or an overwhelming need for possession – are not the same thing. And Reggie made sure that even in death, Frances was his possession, so determined was he to own her, body and soul.

Photos of him kissing Frances's headstone at the funeral of his twin in 1995 seemed staged, yet another good photo opportunity. They perpetuated the myth of the caring, bereaved beloved husband. And as for the legendary and persistent Kray myth, that the Krays only harmed 'their own'– that is, other criminals from their fraternity – Frances's story clearly refutes this.

Frances Shea was no criminal. She wasn't a cynical gangster's moll. She was a beautiful innocent, one reason why Reggie was so drawn to her. At one stage before the marriage, she started seeing other men. But Reggie stalked her every move.

Late in life he admitted to his second wife, Roberta, that 'her memory and how she had died was like a weight that he always carried'. Yet if he regretted the shocking way he treated her family in the aftermath of her death, I could not find any record of this.

One word sums up Frances's emotional state during much of her relationship with Reggie: fear. Fear was the tool the Kray twins used in creating their myth, propelling them beyond the post-war wreckage of the East End to the upmarket worlds of Mayfair and Knightsbridge, to the USA – and the respect of the Mafia. Fear of their violence, of what they were capable of as a fighting, slashing, murderous duo was the dominant propellant in the explosive mixture of blackmail, manipulation and street cunning they deployed during their days of freedom. That they succeeded in maintaining this fear of their legendary violence throughout their lives gives you some sense of the utter powerlessness that Frances Shea must have experienced: one woman, caught up against all that, via sheer circumstance.

Possessive, violent men remain, to this day, a terrible threat to any woman involved with them. Reggie Kray was both. And when he was blind drunk, as he was frequently, he was emotionally abusive in the extreme. But of course, it wasn't just Reggie's behaviour that was creating the complicated and scary situation that Frances found herself in.

Much of her terror came from the fear-inducing persona of Ronnie Kray, even before the marriage. The twins were intense and possessive by nature. (Their older brother Charlie, who died in 2000, was quite different and didn't have the same criminal, violent traits.) Ronnie's extreme possessiveness towards his twin, his jealousy of any 'intruder' – which matched Reggie's possessive attitude towards Frances in its power – meant that Frances was also enmeshed in a vicious power struggle as Ronnie fought to steer his twin away from her.

The story of Frances Shea is a tragedy in three acts: an outwardly glorious courtship, conducted in exotic locales, engineered by a boyfriend who showered her with gifts, jewels, lavish attention and introduced her to a lifestyle only the wealthy and privileged were able to experience at that time; a very brief marriage which revealed the true hidden ugliness of that same world and the overwhelming power of her husband's twinship, both of which left her in the throes of breakdown and drugs to ease the nightmare; and finally, her sad ending and the troubled legacy of her death which continued to haunt her loved ones over the years.

In writing this story, I wanted to bring her a little bit closer into the light. She merits that. Not just because she's part of the Kray history. But because, as I hoped when I started to look at her story, underneath the smoke and mirrors of the Kray facade, there was a thoughtful, aware young woman, someone who looked as good as a sixties movie star but was, in fact, an ordinary girl who only hoped for the normal things: marriage, security, children, a pleasant home in a leafy suburban street.

Reggie Kray, for his part, fantasised about achieving those things but couldn't escape his destiny: the bond with his other half, his twin. He had caught Frances in a deadly trap. Yet he was equally trapped, too: by blood ties and violence.

In telling this story, so as to relate Frances Shea's story in context, it was essential to give an overview of the Kray twins' background, rise to prominence and crimes for which they were eventually convicted in 1969.

However, Frances Shea remains the focus of this book.

INTRODUCTION

The stories of all the multiple gangland feuds, the frauds, the characters who engaged with them in the time before and after they went to prison are not included. These stories have already been told on the pages of the many books written about the Krays.

Finally, it would not have been possible to write this book without a certain amount of external support and enthusiasm for the task in hand. So I would like to give due thanks to John Pearson, whose knowledge and insight into the Kray story remains, as ever, both compelling and invaluable. Anyone new to the Kray genre will find Pearson's trilogy of Kray books a fascinating and revealing compendium of their history.

Thanks are also due to the helpful staff at the Hackney Archives, Tower Hamlets Archives, St Bartholomew's Hospital Archives and Museum, the National Archives at Kew, Brighton's Jubilee Library, the Edda Tasiemka Archive and my ever supportive friends Danny and Saskia at West End Lane Books, West Hampstead.

This story is historical. Yet the lives of those who unwittingly find themselves trapped by violent, possessive partners remain under threat, all around us, every single day.

So if there is any dedication for this book it should be to all victims of domestic abuse – and in particular to the memory of those whose lives ended in tragedy, cut short by their relationship with an unstable, violent partner.

JACKY HYAMS
East Sussex, July 2014; May 2015

CHAPTER 1

WAR BABIES

Blackout. Dim street lamps, the occasional car out on the Kingsland Road crawling along with muffled headlights. Behind the dark main road lie streets of wreckage, the inhabitants clinging to everyday life in the little two-up, two-down Victorian terrace houses that were still standing after the bombing raids, their windows blacked out with material; even the briefest chink of light will bring an ARP warden to bang noisily on the front door, and the threat of fines and penalties for anyone ignoring the strictly enforced blackout regulations. A few windows in these darkened streets are criss-crossed with sticky tape or wire net – a precaution against flying glass as a result of yet another bombing raid.

Tonight it's quiet. Yet no one around here can ever be too sure when it all might kick off again. If it isn't the terrifying 'crump crump' sound of the bombs raining down from the planes overhead or the booming explosions, it's the sirens wailing night and day, summoning the people to drop everything, dash to an underground shelter or stumble down the road to home and the damp garden shelter – if home itself hasn't already been reduced to ash and rubble.

Brutal, relentless, chaotic wartime. Throughout the land, millions of lives turned inside out, personal tragedy of the nigh unthinkable kind being a daily event. Get on with it somehow. Feed the family with whatever you can lay your hands on. Barter. Listen to the radio. Spot the telegram boy on the bike coming down your street, close your eyes and hope with all your heart, as your neighbours do, that he won't be heading to your front door with bad news about a loved one serving in the forces. In the cinema, study the newsreel with intense concentration, crane your neck to peer at what surely looks like a familiar face: a son, a brother, a husband of just six weeks out there in the enormous jumble of massed troops. Queue for ages to swap a few coupons for a pathetically tiny bit of meat. Or sod the rationing, use the black market to glean a 'little bit extra' off a market stall, the extra coming from God knows where; no questions asked, a few precious coins slipped into the pocket of the stallholder's apron.

A combination of hope and humour kept them all going through these war years, families and neighbours looking out for each other, helping out when needed, sharing the worst, though their stoicism meant that tears were more likely to be shed alone, in snatched privacy. The ciggies helped the shattered nerves – half the women of Britain were confirmed smokers by the mid-1940s. Even with the worry, the waiting, the wanting, everyone knew they had to hang on, believed they'd get through this somehow, with their sanity – and family – intact when it all ended. The only trouble was WHEN would it end?

This was the bewilderingly upside-down world that Frances Shea was born into at her family's home at 57 Ormsby Street, Hoxton, in London's East End in September 1943.

At that point in the war, the news came through that Italy had done a volte-face and switched sides. They'd formally surrendered to the Allies, and the Allied troops were embarking on the long, bloody slog of liberation through Italy, while the German enemy began their march on Rome. Was this the beginning of the end? Public bar optimists around the shattered streets peered at the headlines, shrugged, sipped their pale ale and said well, it was good news, wasn't it? That effing bastard Jerry was now on the run. The Yanks would make sure of that.

But of course, not everyone blithely accepted what they were being told, the official version of events. There was too much secrecy around everything, grumbled the cynics, what with the government poking their nose into every aspect of people's lives, telling everyone what they could and couldn't do, saying things like: 'Where's your ID card?' 'Be like dad, keep mum.' 'What's in that bag you're carrying, missus?'

When censorship and state control seep into everyday routine for years, it's easier to remain blinkered, stumble on, not question anything. Yet here in London's East End, the territory of the renegade, the petty crim and the poorest of the poor teetering on survival's edge, authority's sweep was never going to be accepted. War or no war.

In the blacked-out, bombed-out streets around Hoxton, Haggerston, Shoreditch, Bethnal Green and Hackney, it remained pretty much business as usual: them versus us, look out for yourself and your family, shun authority at any cost, they're not interested in you, anyway. In this place, in one sense, it had always been war – of a different kind.

Law-abiding citizens these East Enders might not be. But the people's spirit of survival, born out of centuries of rough, tough living, had never been stronger than it was now, four years into the war. Too many exploded bombs, lives lost overseas, homes in ruins, families wrenched apart, and kids sent off to live with total strangers, where ten shillings (50 pence in today's terms) per child was paid to families willing to accommodate other people's children... It had all been going on for far too long.

Yet the default setting here is tenacity: an iron grip on survival amidst utter deprivation. By sheer instinct, they understood resilience, even now, when the only world they'd known was literally crumbling all around them. Tenacity, you see, was part of their cultural heritage, as much as crime and violence had been for a long, long time.

Not every family in the area lived as outlaws, of course. Many people here had usually survived through working in poorly paid, often casual work – the 'working poor' – finding jobs whenever they could, struggling to get by on a pittance but staying relatively straight. And, of course, keeping quiet about what they knew about those living outside the law. There was always talk about what so-and-so had been up to, who'd gone inside, who was out, who'd run off and deserted. Yet if authority started stickybeaking (making enquiries), there'd be scant chance of anyone dropping their neighbour in it. Omertà (the traditional Mafia 'code of silence'), East London style. Stick together. Social glue.

Frances's parents, Elsie and Frank Shea, had been married

for nearly four years when they moved into the tiny terraced house in Ormsby Street, which lies just behind the long, meandering Kingsland Road, the main thoroughfare running some two and a half miles from Shoreditch Church up to the leafier surrounds of Stoke Newington. With a four-year-old son, Frank, born just a month after war had been declared and a new baby on the way, for the couple, who'd both left school at 14 to seek employment in the many thousands of factories and workshops that crowded the nearby area, it was a relief to be rehoused in the tiny, shabby little house. It had nothing much to commend it, though – other than that the bombs had missed it.

Like many young courting couples facing the 'will it, won't it happen' uncertainty of the looming threat of war with Germany, Frank and Elsie had married hastily in July 1938 at Shoreditch Register Office.

Elsie Wynn was a twenty-one-year-old skilled seamstress and Frank Shea a woodworker aged twenty-six when they opted to join forces. Both had always lived in the locality; Frank grew up in Hoxton, the youngest of a big Irish family, headed by his dad Joseph, a shoe salesman.

Hoxton today is one of central London's most fashionable areas, with trendy new loft apartment blocks and smart cafes and bars. Yet for much of the nineteenth and twentieth centuries it was one of the roughest areas in Britain, overcrowded, crime ridden, its tiny streets of pubs and pickpockets virtually overwhelmed by the huge number of small factories and workshops that had been set up there in the late nineteenth century.

Elsie's family had lived in nearby Shoreditch, a shade closer to the heart of the city itself, and slightly less rough than the mean streets of Hoxton. Elsie's father, Robert, was a driver. 'Always tell people you live in Shoreditch, not Hoxton, it's much nicer,' Elsie would frequently remind her kids as they grew up – low-level postcode snobbery that she'd probably absorbed as a child, but which at the same time hinted at her yearning for respectability and social acceptance. Tragically, this was destined to elude her in ways she could never have imagined.

Elsie had come from a broken home. Her father left the family for another woman, a source of much family bitterness amongst the Wynns in later years. Yet by the time she fell for Frank Shea, a quiet, good-looking young man, Elsie was a very smartly turned out, attractive dark-eyed brunette, who was a good physical match, at least, for the equally sharp-suited, slightly built Frank.

Once married, the young couple lived briefly in Hemsworth Street, Hoxton, then found themselves on the move again to nearby Malvern Road, Hackney, after baby Frank arrived in October 1939. Then came the devastating effects of the German bombing raids of the Blitz in 1940, when London and the East End were continuously bombed for fifty-seven nights from September through to November. This ferocious attack on Londoners was followed by even more continuous bombing raids, from March until mid-May 1941, which left a pall of thick smoke hanging permanently over the city. Everywhere you went, London was burning. The fear of annihilation never stopped. It just went on and on.

Many thousands of homes were left without gas, water or electricity after the bombings, and Malvern Road was right in the heart of the bombing of Hackney, so at around the time Elsie discovered she was pregnant for a second time, the Sheas considered themselves lucky to be rehoused in Ormsby Street.

This was to be their family home for nearly thirty years, right up until the time when the houses in the area were finally demolished in the late 1960s as part of the major-slum clearance programme that took place in parts of East London. At that point, the Sheas were moved, along with their neighbours, to new homes nearby.

By then, however, moving to a brand new home with all mod cons held little comfort for the Sheas. The fabric of their lives had been torn asunder by a gut-wrenching emotional wrecking ball as powerful as the worst of the Luftwaffe's assaults on London: their only daughter's brief life as the girlfriend, then wife of Reggie Kray was over. And the tiny Hoxton thoroughfare where she'd grown up, just less than a mile away from the Kray family's home, 'Fort Vallance' in Vallance Road, Bethnal Green, had been the setting for some of the strangest, most poignant scenes in the history of Frances Shea's troubled relationship with Reggie, the twin who was so determined to claim her as his own – in life and then beyond.

Elsie was hardly a social climber by today's standards. But even as a young wartime mum, she always clung to her hopes and dreams, even though she was desperately struggling to cope with rationing, bombs and looking after little Frank – a good looking child with melting chocolate brown eyes and an endearing manner – as well as having a husband away in the services (Frank Senior had signed up to join the Fleet Air Arm just after war was declared). Somehow, her dreams helped her through the worst times.

She was aspirational, at a time when day-to-day aspiration was in very short supply. Elsie desperately wanted a better, cleaner, brighter world for her family when the war finally ended. What mother didn't allow herself the occasional dream of better days ahead in the midst of all they were living through?

Elsie had been lucky enough to give birth to Frank, named Frank Brian, in a proper maternity ward, at the City of London Maternity Hospital in City Road, a hospital later to be destroyed by bombing raids in 1940. As the war went on and medical/nursing resources had to be deployed elsewhere around the country for the war effort, home births became the norm, with overstretched midwives on bikes wobbling their way through the rubble-strewn smoky streets. They were shakily coping with the ever-present threat of death or injury, helping bring life into the world right in the midst of the war, sometimes to the accompaniment of gunfire, explosion or falling debris. And there were times when even the home birth became impossible – history records that some women even gave birth while sheltering in the London Underground during air raids.

Frances arrived at Ormsby Street on 23 September 1943. There is no record of bombing in the area around Kingsland Road for that week, and by then everyone was fervently hoping that the worst of the bombing was over. In fact, the intermittent bombing of London, day and night, was far from over: the Luftwaffe dropped 30 tons of bombs over Battersea, Ilford, Hampstead and Woodford, Essex two weeks later on 7 October and the following day, killing thirty-five people and injuring many more.

Bombs or no bombs, Elsie wanted her baby daughter baptised. With everyone living with death and destruction all around them, baptism was popular for newborns. Not only did it mean a church marriage in adulthood, it also meant burial in consecrated ground. And so the three-week-old baby, named Frances Elsie, was baptised at St Chad's Church, Nichols Square, just round the corner from Ormsby Street on 17 October 1943 by Father Henry Wincott, who presided over St Chad's parishioners throughout the war years.

It was a happy day for the Sheas; the baby gurgled contentedly in her mum's arms throughout the short ceremony. In fact, just forty-eight hours after she was born, Elsie noted with some satisfaction that her little girl was smiling up at her: a moment in time she'd often proudly recall in the years ahead.

Frank's period in the services saw him working as a veneer preparer (helping to make wooden propellers for aircraft) in the Fleet Air Arm and fortunately he didn't wind up being sent off to serve overseas. Yet there were still periods of separation for the couple, with Frank returning briefly on forty-eight-hour leave to find his wife just about coping with the demands of a small baby and a lively four-year-old son running around.

Money, of course, was tight: Elsie, as a mum of two small children, was not compelled to register for war work, and she could work from home as an outworker, making clothes on the kitchen table – if she could manage it. But the news in 1943 that servicemen's wives were eligible to claim for a weekly War Service Grant of £3 a week would have been very welcome in Ormsby Street. Frank's Fleet Air Arm pay would have been less than this, around £1–2 for a seven-day week, after deductions.

Like the other families living in cramped housing that didn't boast a cellar or basement area, the Sheas had to keep an Anderson air-raid shelter in their tiny backyard. Named after Sir John Anderson, Home Secretary during the first year of the war, the six-foot six-inch by four-foot six-inch shelter, which measured just six feet at the highest point of the roof, was made from curved sheets of corrugated iron, clamped together and bolted to steel rails, and then dug into the soil to a depth of four feet. Frequently, neighbours got together to help each other put up these shelters, provided free by the authorities to families of modest means (those living on less than £5 a week) to shelter in when the air-raid warnings started.

The shelter was damp, cold and cramped. Elsie grew to hate it. Even if you attempted to heat it by using a lit candle underneath an upturned flowerpot, it was still dank and uncomfortable.

She hated it so much that there were times when the air-raid warning went and Elsie, little Frank and baby Frances remained inside their tiny house, sheltering under the sturdy wooden kitchen table until the all-clear siren, with the baby snugly wrapped up inside the little case that contained the much-loathed – and fortunately never used – gas mask, issued to everyone in Britain just before war was declared. During World War One, mustard and other toxic gases had been used against troops by both sides, causing terrible casualties, and there were initially considerable fears that in Word War Two the Germans would try to attack civilians in this way.

People always said: 'Oh, things 'ave to get bad before they get better.' And by the time little Frances reached her first birthday, it looked as if they were right: D-Day, the Allied landings in Europe in June 1944, meant that Hitler was on the run.

Yet despite this, as well as the constant rumours that the war would be over later in the year, the war from the air continued, giving Londoners more even more grief than they'd have ever believed possible. This was thanks to Hitler's secret weapon of terror, the buzz bomb, or flying bomb, a very early version of what we now call a cruise missile. A pilotless super powerful aircraft, called the V-1, it was launched from the French or Dutch coasts with over one ton of explosive power. This could be devastating in urban areas, ripping off roofs, blowing out doors, wrenching out windowpanes and shattering glass in every direction. People's ears would nervously be attuned to their arrival, initially heralded by a distant humming sound, growing ever louder to become a distinct rattling noise. But then, chillingly, the engine would cut out and there would be total silence – for just fifteen seconds – before a massive explosion wreaked havoc and destruction all around. Even worse, these weapons weren't at all predictable. Sometimes one could be heard getting closer and closer, only to inexplicably veer away, then to return just at the point people believed it had gone. It played hell with people's nerves.

Many Londoners insisted that the effect of these weapons was worse than the terrible times they'd already experienced during the Blitz. This was because these lethal unmanned robot planes were so much harder to accept than an aircraft with a man inside, who was risking his own life in order to destroy yours.

The first V-1 struck London just a week after D-Day, on 13 June 1944, landing in Bethnal Green's Grove Road and making 266 people homeless. At first it was believed the damage was caused by a piloted plane that had crashed, but where was the pilot? A few days later the Home Secretary, Herbert Morrison, reluctantly made an announcement that London was being attacked by pilotless planes. During that summer of 1944, a million Londoners left for the country for a second time. Many had only recently returned to the city, believing the worst of the bombing to be over. Now they were on the run once more.

Deeper bombproof shelters opened at Underground stations in north and south London. What people didn't know, thankfully, was that the government feared these new weapons of horror might be used to deliver chemical or biological charges.

Then, between September 1944 and March 1945, more than 1,300 lethal V-1s and V-2s (a supersonic guided rocket with a two-ton warhead, against which there was no practical defence) rained down all over London, killing 2,500 and seriously injuring nearly 4,000. When they stopped – if you'd come through without loss – the April spring mornings had never seemed sweeter.

Elsie was tempted to flee the city. Not surprisingly, morale had plummeted in London to previously unknown depths. People's spirits were at their lowest ebb. Yet they all stayed put, Elsie gratefully taking the free cod liver oil and orange juice supplied by the authorities for the children's health, queuing each day outside what was left of the local shops with the baby, with a supply of newspaper in her basket to wrap up her purchases. Stoically, the Sheas and their neighbours struggled through those final months of the war. They were longing for an end to the rationing of everything (including soap), having to use the tinned powdered eggs, and the meals of kidney, hearts or liver that so often turned up on the table (offal was never rationed, so women cooked it frequently).

By the time VE Day came, in May 1945, people were

relieved but totally exhausted. They'd got through intact. You could envisage a future without bombs, noise and the terrors of war. Elsie wondered if perhaps there would be work for her in a local factory once the kids were a bit older. Little Frank was scheduled to start primary school that autumn.

Frank Senior was due to be demobbed, and like all those other ex-servicemen pouring out of the armed forces, he'd have to find something, somehow. The demob payment of £60 was welcome – but it only went so far. Life in Ormsby Street was still tough in every way. But peace of a sort had arrived.

Under a mile away, in Bethnal Green, the day-to-day lives of an extraordinary pair of twelve-year-old identical twins also settled down somewhat after the upheavals of war.

The Kray home at 178 Vallance Road, into which the family had moved in 1939, wasn't very different to the Shea home in Ormsby Street. It was a cramped but slightly bigger, four-roomed house in a row of Victorian terraces, a home without a bathroom, with an outside lavatory in the little backyard, and an alarming propensity to shake as the trains heading for nearby Liverpool Street Station went past the bedroom windows.

This was the home of Violet and Charlie Kray, their oldest son Charlie Junior and their twins, Ronnie and Reggie, idolised and doted on by their cheerful blonde mother and nearly all their family virtually from the moment they arrived in the world in 1933.

Theirs was a very tightly knit family. Violet's parents John Lee (known as 'the Southpaw Cannonball' because he'd been a good boxer at one stage) and Helen lived just around the corner, as did her sister Rose. Her other sister, May, lived next door but one; Violet's brother John ran a cafe across the street. At one point, locals called the area 'Lee Street'.

When war broke out, Charlie Senior was called up like everyone else to do his duty for King and country. Until that point he'd earned a decent living as a 'totter', buying and selling gold and old clothes around the country, though he was rarely home, either away on working trips or in the pub, and his influence on his children was somewhat limited.

However, the free and easy life he'd led, 'on the knocker', held too powerful an allure for him to give it up, and he went on the run from the police, becoming a deserter with an established penchant for gambling and drinking. At one point, Charlie hid from the police in the Vallance Road house in the coal cupboard under the stairs. He remained a fugitive from the law for over a decade.

When the Blitz started, Violet, the twins and Charlie Junior had joined the hordes of evacuated London families in the countryside, initially in Hampshire, then with a family in Hadleigh, Suffolk. There, the twins ran wild for a time and developed a passion for the English countryside which remained with them throughout their lives. But it wasn't long before the family missed life in Vallance Road and they went back. Despite the bombs.

By the time war ended, the twins had developed a local reputation for fighting, not at all surprising given the influences of both boxing grandfathers, Canonball Lee and Jimmy Kray. At age ten, the inseparable, uncannily alike pair had discovered boxing, via a boxing booth at a Bethnal Green fairground. This was sited on a local bombsite, where so many of their early violent escapades took place.

The 'Two Ones' (as they were sometimes known, from

their cousin Rita's childhood term for twins) were already imbued with the love of violence that was to define them and were enthralled by the fighters on the stage in their boxing boots and dressing gowns. So they leapt at the chance to step into the ring when onlookers were invited up to fight for a few shillings during a break in the contests. They'd regularly scrapped fearlessly with other boys on the bombsites amidst the debris and the rubble, and also often fought each other with an astonishing ferocity – although they made sure that when their mother was around they were always well behaved and polite. Their utter devotion to her was cemented by the prolonged absence of their dad.

But on one particular occasion in 1943, they donned the battered, torn boxing gloves for the first time and fought three furious rounds, earning themselves seven shillings and sixpence for their efforts. This launched them into what could have been a long-term career as professional fighters, encouraged by brother Charlie, who was also an accomplished boxer and who had made sure he taught them all the right moves.

Certainly, this call to fight was an established way of life where they grew up. There was nothing unusual about it at all. But their two-for-one power as vicious twin street fighters, who could always take on much older boys and prove themselves again and again, saw the early dawning of their legendary reputation for ruthless violence.

And so 'The Terrible Twins', the cute, identically dressed, dark-eyed, pretty babies in the angora hats and coats that Violet had pushed around in their pram so proudly along the streets of Bethnal Green, were now approaching adulthood. And infamy. Their schooling interrupted by the war, they started their secondary education at Daniel Street School, Bethnal Green, at the age of twelve. Here their boxing talents were encouraged, and they spent three fairly unremarkable years there until they left, aged fifteen, to work briefly at Billingsgate Fish Market as trainee porters for six months, the only full-time jobs they ever held down.

Elsie Shea and Violet Kray, two wartime mothers living in an unrelentingly tough world, both loved their kids to bits, though Violet's slavish devotion to her twins had not left much room for attention to Charlie, seven years older than his brothers. And these women had one other thing in common: a powerful, driving desire for respectability and social acceptance, a fairly common trait amongst those matriarchs of the East End who understood all too well that there was a better world out there for them and their families – if only you knew how to get it.

Elsie and Violet may have ignored the finer details of what was being promised to the British people by the politicians after the war. No one knew it in 1945, but the ten years immediately ahead still held much deprivation and struggle for ordinary people, with terrible winters and food rationing that continued until 1954.

The women's husbands may have returned to post-war life with a concern for the betting slip or the public bar above all else, yet the promise, at least, of an improved existence was unquestionably all around them once the sirens stopped. A brand new free Health Service was launched in 1948, and there were major changes to the education system, making it possible, for the first time, for working-class children to be educated, via a streaming system, to university level. These were bold new ideas for social change, designed to sweep away the squalor of the past once and for all and to build a leafier, sunnier existence in the safer confines of the suburban streets. Bigger and better horizons for all.

In Violet's case, that desire to 'be someone' would be fulfilled, to a greater extent, by the ultimate celebrity power of her 'Twins', the showcasing of their own unquenchable yearning for fame, which allowed her to rub shoulders with – or even, incredibly, make cups of tea in Vallance Road for – some of the big showbiz names of the era. Her sons' violence, manipulation and reputation turned out to be a golden pass for entry into the dazzling world of the movie star, the nightclub maître d' and the starched white tablecloth.

Yet it is one of the less acknowledged tragedies of this story that by the time the twins' outwardly glittering world started to impinge on the Sheas' modest lives, the truth behind the Krays' cleverly constructed façade of respectability – the charity events, the write-ups in the papers, the 'country squire' living and what was, effectively, an illusion of social acceptance – would be revealed to them in the starkest terms. Because underneath the glitter was an ugly, blood-drenched and repressive world of madness, violence, alcohol, manipulation and control gone haywire.

Ronnie and Reggie Kray, born minutes apart, were inseparable but also locked into an impossible love-hate relationship with each other. This meant that a wholly separate identity for each of them, a normal life removed from the madness of one twin, could only ever be a dream, since their lives were so inextricably linked thanks to the overwhelming power of their bond as twins.

Fame didn't just happen to these men. They set out, right from the start, from the time of their very first local newspaper picture as teenage boxers, to be the engineers of their own astonishing notoriety.

Without question, the Kray twins instinctively understood how public relations worked long before the words slipped into the everyday language of the twentieth century. Yet those that innocently got caught up in their slipstream, as the Shea family did, amongst others, couldn't possibly have had any idea of what they were really getting into. Until it was far too late.

CHAPTER 2

A SCHOOLGIRL
READING
TENNYSON

They were itchy, burning little red swellings on your toes, fingers and earlobes. You got them from being too cold, too wet or sometimes if you ran inside from the freezing cold street and immediately rushed to warm up in front of the fire. It didn't help if your shoes were too tight because you'd grown out of them. Or if your feet weren't encased in decent socks or stockings.

Many growing up in the immediate aftermath of World War Two can recall chilblains: their most vivid memory of childhood would often be the biting cold. Britain experienced cruel, freezing-cold winters after the war finally ended, and the winter of 1946/7 was the harshest. Across the country huge twenty-foot-high snowdrifts, floods, coal shortages and endless power cuts and blackouts made for very hard times indeed.

It was a dark, stricken time of struggle for millions who'd

hoped for so much with the war ending, only to find themselves enduring years of more hardship. Rationing continued. Some foods that weren't even rationed in wartime became rationed after the war ended. Basic staples such as bread went on the ration book in 1946 for two years. Even potatoes were rationed for over a year, when heavy frost and the biting cold destroyed potato stores.

For millions of mothers like Elsie Shea and Violet Kray the endless rationing and the hardships in feeding a family were definitely tougher after 1945. This didn't feel like any kind of victory: surely they all deserved better. The devastated streets, the rationing, the queues and the damaged, bomb-scarred houses remained as they were. There was no swift rebuilding programme in this grey, bleak post-war world.

Theft, burglary and crime soared, with men pouring out of the armed forces and jobs being as hard to find as a decent meal. A hard core of risk-takers with cash – developers, as we now call them – snapped up some of the wrecked, barely habitable buildings with a beady eye on the future. Wherever possible they let them out, which was not difficult because so many had been made homeless or had returned to the capital, thus creating sub-standard, semi-derelict housing all over the city. The country itself was bombed out, knackered – and bankrupt. The capital was shockingly drab, dirty and, some believed, facing decline and decay. Peacetime: the worst of times.

In Ormsby Street, the struggle for survival in the late 1940s must have seemed like an endless curse. But, as in Vallance Road, people were used to being resourceful. Poverty was all around, yet black-market trading, especially in food, remained consistent, given the East End's many street markets and the 'nudge nudge, wink wink, off-the-back-of-a-lorry' traditions of the area. Such was the popularity of the black-market clothing trade, for instance, that clothes rationing ended in 1949, before it finished for other items, such as petrol, meat and sugar.

If homes were spartan and threadbare in the little two-up, two-down terrace houses, most, despite the bomb damage, would have been seen as spick and span in any cleanliness contest. Being neat and clean was a bit of an obsession, especially to Elsie, to whom a grime-free respectable façade meant so much.

Heating in these homes came from coal fires in tiny grates. Fitted carpets were unknown; floors were usually only bare wooden boards covered by thin rugs. Walls were covered with faded wallpaper, while furniture was of the very plain 'utility' type, often purchased with rationing coupons. The two downstairs rooms tended to be used as a front or living room with a bedroom at the back; then there was a step leading down to a scullery, which doubled as a kitchen, with an all-purpose sink and a tap in the corner. After climbing up the narrow stairs from the cramped hallway there would be two small bedrooms, one overlooking the road.

Some houses in these streets boasted an ancient open range in the ground floor back room, good for heating water, since there was no supply of running hot water here until two decades later, by which time the houses were marked for demolition. Few families could readily afford to install an 'Ascot', a small gas water heater, ignited by a pilot light inside a white enamel box, which became increasingly used in homes throughout the fifties.

Until white goods became more affordable on the 'never

never' – hire purchase schemes of the mid-fifties, where families paid off small weekly sums for household appliances – there were no fridges, just a downstairs larder for food storage. Washing machines, dishwashers and microwaves were unknown. Inefficient carpet sweepers or brushes, rather than vacuum cleaners, helped you to clean the threadbare rugs. It was not until after 1953, and the televised broadcast of the coronation of the youthful Princess Elizabeth, which everyone wanted to watch, that the TV set started to filter into everyday British life. This accompanied, and sometimes eventually replaced, the big brown Bakelite radio (or wireless, as it was known), the sole source of news and entertainment in the home throughout the war years. A phone was, at that time, still regarded as an expense too far by most, although a few families opted to install a less expensive 'party line', meaning that they would share the line itself with another home.

Outside these houses there was a cold water tap in the tiny backyard with a mangle in a lean-to sheltered area for wringing clothes out on washing days. A tin bath usually hung outside too. Bathing itself was mostly limited to a once-weekly visit to the local baths, price sixpence; the rest of the time families made do with a 'strip wash' of water heated up from a kettle or on a range.

As for the detested Anderson shelter in the backyard, it lived on, mostly because it was handy to store precious coal supplies for the small fires lit each morning to heat up the front room and back bedroom.

Today, if you talk to former residents of the Ormsby Street area they nostalgically recall families keeping chickens in their gardens – or even pigeons. They talk of the two men who would knock on every door each week to collect the rent on behalf of the landlord, usually between twelve and fourteen shillings a week. They remember with great affection the horse-drawn carts that continued to deliver bottles of milk in the area for many years, and the rag-and-bone man, collecting any unwanted household junk. Or they tell of the chilly outside toilet with its wooden seat, with newspaper neatly cut into squares and hung on a hook as a substitute for proper toilet paper, such as Izal, which was also considered something of a luxury item in the early post-war years (paper was rationed, too). At weekends, the newspaper squares might be replaced with much-prized tissue paper, used to wrap the bread that was purchased from nearby Hoxton Market.

Most of all, though, they remember the long-lost spirit of those poverty-stricken surrounds, the neighbourly camaraderie, the open front doors, the kids happily playing outside, the bonding, if you like, that had helped them all get through the war years and beyond.

The Sheas and the Krays didn't exactly prosper but they managed somehow. Frank Shea Senior, like many men in his somewhat unsteady post-war position, found it convenient to work on the fringes of the law as a street bookie, picking up betting slips and cash from people placing bets on the gee-gees or the dogs, usually in local pubs or out on the street.

Street betting continued to be an illegal activity across the country for many years after the war, with heavy fines for anyone caught organising it or 'running a book' on the street – until the gambling laws eventually changed in 1960 and betting shops began to proliferate across the land. Legal or not, being a street bookie meant ready cash and, given the national passion for 'having a bet', something akin to a steady 'wage' by Frank's standards, those of a Hoxton lad.

Elsie, alas, was never going to feel happy or secure with this lifestyle. The family needed every penny and by the late 1940s, once her two 'war babies' were at school she could earn again at the sewing machine. There was a lot of nagging going on in the Shea household about Frank 'getting a proper job', though it would be many years before he relented and found a respectable clerical occupation.

Okay, the bookie money was there, on the kitchen table with its oilcloth, regular as clockwork. Big, crisp white fivers, ten-bob (ten-shilling) notes, carefully counted out. There was enough to make sure the kids were properly clothed and fed, the bills paid. But it wasn't a respectable way of life, was Elsie's beef. Oh how she wanted to be decent – and being a street bookie's wife usually meant you were stuck, just like most of the women she'd grown up with, with a husband who was happy with the ducking and diving – and she was always aware that the law, or unexpected circumstances, could trip you up and send you sprawling.

Yet like so many women then, Elsie had no option other than to accept her lot in life. Where could a woman with children go, without money or resources? Violet too accepted her lot, put up with Charlie's absences, his feckless ways and his boozy violence; she had her twins, and they were the sole focus of her life.

In Elsie's case, though, this trim, smartly groomed woman with ideas of a better life never stopped resenting her husband's preference for easy money with no strings attached. She too poured all her love and ambition into her kids, sitting up long into the night, using her skills as a first-rate seamstress to make most of their clothes, driven by pride, and the knowledge that her two were going to be the most smartly turned out, well-shod kids in the street.

It worked. By the time Frank and Frances were attending primary school – Frank at Laburnum Street Primary (now the Bridge Academy) a five-minute walk away from Ormsby Street and, four years later, Frances at Randal Cremer, a big Victorian building and conveniently just across the street from the Shea home – it was generally acknowledged by everyone in Ormsby Street that the Shea children were always well turned out. In fact, they looked as smart as any 'posh kids' you might see in the newspaper advertisements for Start-rite shoes. Elsie could walk tall around the area, clutching the hands of her two, one either side, and be proud of them, these pretty children who had inherited their mum's big dark eyes and thick, lustrous brown hair.

This focus on appearance and looking smart wasn't that unusual for the times, when people tended to wear outfits they'd made themselves – or, if they could afford it, had specially made for them. Men always wore hats. Long before the days of man-made fibres, winter overcoats were made of pure wool – or trimmed with real fur. Shoes were shined and buffed. And, of course, many East Enders were renowned for their love of looking sharp and well dressed when the occasion demanded – and for using their well-honed entrepreneurial skills in trading with each other to get the best.

But what is most interesting about Elsie's determination for her children to look well dressed is that both Frances and Frank 'learned' the importance of a smart appearance and looking good. As they grew up, both became quite fixated with their appearance, how they showed themselves to the world. This trait never left either of them.

Certainly, they inhabited a world where by tradition, 'street' people tended to strut their stuff in their finest clothing, irrespective of their humble surrounds. But for these two mothers, the importance they placed on making a good impression, looking utterly respectable, raised their kids way above the lawless crowd around them. Thanks to their mothers, these children grew up with very clear ideas about behaviour and good manners. In the twins' case, though, their demeanour was totally schizophrenic: before their elders they were impressively polite. Behind the scenes, as it were, it was a very different story.

Much later, one theme of the oft-repeated stories about Frances and Reggie Kray's relationship was how Reggie was always buying Frances expensive clothes, gold jewellery, anything she wanted. It was perfectly true. With his talent for control, Reggie liked to have considerable influence over the way Frances looked – for instance, he preferred her with the high, upswept hairdos, so fashionable at the time. Yet Frances already lived as part of a fashion-conscious clan: had Reggie had been less interested in appearances, it's unlikely she'd have looked anything other than the stylishly dressed, superbly coiffed young woman seen time after time in the photos taken at Reggie's side.

As for the Kray family, they too were imbued with the 'looking good' gene. Looking superbly immaculate and expensively sharp-suited became a major factor in the twins' ability to impress and impose, an attitude they struck to fantastic effect. They wore cashmere, vicuna (a very fine, expensive wool) or camel hair overcoats, handmade suits, whiter than white shirts, pressed to perfection by Violet, and slimline ties – at a time when much of the world around them remained shabby and down at heel.

'We're vicious, elegant bastards,' Ronnie Kray would boast, many years on, after they'd been locked up for good. This was a truth they revelled in. The smart expensive clothes were part of their armoury – not quite as effective as the collection of weapons they stashed in their bedroom as teenagers, for use when heading off to the Tottenham Royal dance hall for the night: knuckledusters, Bowie knives, coshes, Gurkha knives, cut-throat razors, even a surgeon's scalpel.

The Kray twins hadn't exactly shone in the classroom, though Reggie was the more alert of the two. Elsie's children were bright. Despite the big, mixed classes of forty or more, the ready distractions outside the classroom of the local Saturday kids' cinema club, and the boys' endless 'playing out' on the bombsites, recreating the furious battles they'd already lived through, collecting shrapnel or swapping cigarette cards, both Shea children did well at primary, especially when it came to reading and writing. Frances had an aptitude for arithmetic, too.

By the early fifties, changes to the education system were in place. The minimum school-leaving age had been raised from fourteen, as it had been in Elsie and Frank Senior's day, to fifteen. New types of secondary school were created to follow the Eleven-Plus exam, which streamed kids according to results into grammar school, secondary modern or technical colleges. Frank, to his mum's delight, passed the exam and was offered a grammar-school place. Frances too already seemed to have an excellent aptitude for the written word, so Elsie's hopes were high that Frances would also be bright enough to pass the exam to get her to a good school.

But what was she like in childhood you wonder? Photos of Frances in Randal Cremer days show a cheerful, chubby little girl with a happy grin.

Paulette Jones grew up in the area. She was in the same class as Frances at Randal Cremer at one stage when they were both aged eight. She vividly recalled, most of all, Frances's abundant mass of hair.

'She was quite plump with longish dark curly hair,' Paulette recalled. 'We always called her Franny or Fran. After Randal Cremer we went off to different grammar schools. I went to Central Foundation at Liverpool Street and Frances went to Dalston County, a girls' school in Shacklewell Lane, off Stoke Newington Road.

'I can still see her in my mind's eye in a dark belted raincoat and a hat perched on the back of her head, because of the amount of hair she had. The coat and hat would have been part of the uniform for Dalston County. I wanted to go with Franny and some of the others to Dalston County but my mother said Central Foundation was a better school.'

The discovery that Frances was a grammar-school girl, taking the mile-and-a-half bus journey each day up the Kingsland Road to Dalston County, paints a different picture to the way Frances has usually been portrayed. Iconic and immaculate as her appearance became in adulthood, the general assumption was always that she was not especially intelligent, more of a good-looking clothes horse or 'arm candy', as many people suggested when I first started researching Frances's story. But this low-roofed modern building with tennis courts and gardens was a school where the emphasis was on academic achievement rather than sporting ability.

As I started to realise when I contacted those who had 'known' Frances as an adult, the men who had met her socially, although they wouldn't admit it to me, would never have had any real conversation with her anyway – because she was on Reggie's arm. This was one very good reason why the 'arm candy' theory had prevailed down the years, with its consequent implication that Frances was a bit dumb.

This lack of conversation was not simply because of any shyness or reticence on her part, but because in those days, especially in the East End pub and club environment of the late fifties/early sixties, real conversation between the sexes was limited when couples stepped out to socialise. It involved little more than pleasantries.

Wherever these men sat within their own social pecking order – the well-respected local publican, for instance, or the host or club owner – social talk with other men's wives or girlfriends tended to be brief. Polite. Respectful. But brief. In this macho environment where a wrong word or look could develop, quickly, into a punch-up or a furious fight, everyone understood the rules: men didn't even attempt to chat freely to someone else's bird, whatever the circumstances. 'Allo Frances. All right, love?' That was the limit.

This, I began to realise, had as much to do with the social mores of the times as the well-documented fear of incurring the wrath of Reggie Kray, though sadly this fear would prevail continuously throughout Frances's life – and even beyond.

There were other factors that made the grammar-school girl discovery a fascinating insight. I too attended a grammar school in the area in the fifties and well remember it as a strict, disciplined 'old school' place of education, with considerable emphasis on preparing girls for A-level passes and university. It had a curriculum that included languages (French or German), Latin, English Literature and Art, with school outings to places like Paris and big evening events at the school, such as Speech Day. At that point, the grammar-school education offered opportunities that had never ever been available to bright working-class youngsters, wherever they lived. These post-war changes were created, specifically, to give ordinary children a chance in life via education.

If it was all a far cry from what my own family had known in their personal East End working-class background, what would it have meant to Elsie, a girl reaching adulthood in thirties Shoreditch, where 'travel' usually meant a train trip to the Kent or Essex seaside – if you were lucky?

Imagine a young Frances in her navy blue blazer, matching heavy wool skirt, blue-and-white striped shirt, orange tie and summer boater hat among a crowd of other chattering, lively grammar-school girls, boarding the bus going down the Kingsland Road, just as I did (though I travelled in the opposite direction). This image places the context of her early teens somewhat in contrast with the historical, somewhat dismissive, assumptions made about her because of her association with the Krays.

This girl was never a brainless bimbo or a simpering dummy. Far from it.

By the time Frances reached her early teens, life in the Shea household was starting to improve, as it was for many millions. After a decade, the scars of war were starting to fade away. Consumerism, heavily influenced by what was happening in the USA, was on its way from across the pond. Nineteen fifty-five saw the launch of fish fingers, TV advertising (Britain's first ever TV ad was for Gibbs SR toothpaste), a brand new passenger terminal at London's Heathrow Airport, and an overall increase in people's wages. There was full employment too. Moreover, the first generation of post-war kids were starting to spend their pocket money, albeit modestly at first, on pop music records.

The term 'teenager' was coined around 1955, at the time of the hit single, 'Rock Around the Clock' by Bill Haley and the Comets, taken from the movie *Blackboard Jungle*, and the following year, rock 'n' roll was on its way across the world with the cultural explosion that was Elvis and his first UK hit, 'Heartbreak Hotel'.

Screaming, frenzied young teenage girls erupting into screams every time Elvis wiggled his hips had been seen before in the US, during the short reign of forties idol the young, skinny Frank Sinatra, worshipped by the bobby-soxers (his fans, so named because of their youth). But in Britain, teen power was a relatively – and startlingly – new phenomenon that grew with every month that passed. Frances couldn't help but soak up the magazines, hear the music, admire the clothes – and, of course, she was starting to be aware of the opposite sex.

An interesting letter to her from a friend called Sylvia living in Scawfell Street, Shoreditch and dated 31 July 1956, revealed that Frances, two months off her thirteenth birthday, was holidaying at the seaside in Hastings.

The short letter gave Frances all the local gossip: Sylvia, an older girl, informed Frances that she was going to try for a holiday job at Woolworths in Dalston Junction. The pay was £3 a week, she wrote. Another local friend, Pat, was in hospital, having her tonsils out.

'And how are the boys?' Sylvia's letter concluded. 'Don't pretend you don't like them, because you do.'

This indicates her friends had noticed that twelve-year-old Frances was already extremely attractive to the opposite sex.

The late Tony Lambrianou, a Bethnal Green boy eventually imprisoned for fifteen years in 1969 for his part in the murder of Jack 'The Hat' McVitie, remembered meeting Frances for the first time one day in 1956. He already knew Frankie Shea from primary school.

'One day I came out of work and saw Frankie Shea at the junction of Hackney Road and Weymouth Terrace, which is near where his family came from. His sister Frances came along. She would have been about twelve or thirteen, very quiet and very beautiful with big eyes,' Lambrianou recalled in his book, *Inside The Firm*.

The power of Frances's dazzling allure to men was already there, right from the start.

The shift from teen to adult is rarely easy, an emotionally confusing, even fraught time for families. For fifties East End families with teenagers it was an unusually precarious time because while the memory – and evidence – of wartime was still there, all around them, the powerful popular distractions of those mid-fifties years were completely unlike any that previous generations had known.

Post-war dads had never known what it was to be a teenager, as such, or what it was like to wear clothes specially aimed at youthful fashion tastes, or to be courted by the powerful forces promoting the music, the movies, the new fashions for youngsters. They'd grown up in an era where fathers alone ruled the household, often with an iron rod. Young people back then did what their parents told them to do, and tended not to question their authority, regardless of their circumstances.

Yet their offspring, now with their own money or spending power, even before they reached their twenties or marriage, didn't see this authoritarian style of the past in the same way. And they didn't see why they should listen. Phrases like 'teenage rebellion' entered everyday language for the first time.

There's no reason to believe that out-and-out rebellion was the order of the day in the Shea household. But there were certainly domestic ups and downs. Elsie had to work at the sewing machine, in the local factory, as long and hard as she could, but her husband, while often out of the house taking bets or in the pub, wasn't as dedicated to the concept of hard slog as Elsie wished. And Frankie Junior, as attractive as his sister and perfectly capable of passing his exams if he concentrated and took it all seriously, wasn't very interested in the opportunities Elsie cherished for her kids. Frank had the ability to learn, there was no question of that. But education didn't suit him and he left school at fifteen.

Not one to give up, Elsie persisted: she even found Frank an apprenticeship as a setter with a local print firm, a distinct step on the ladder to what she rightly believed was a decent living. The apprenticeship was definitely a bit of a coup, since career opportunities locally for Hoxton boys leaving school early either meant working in the street markets – pretty much a closed shop because market stalls were run by families – or finding work in a trade like tailoring or French polishing (cabinet making). As a consequence, if a youngster could manage to get into printing it was seen very much as a chance in life. The only other options were boxing, illegal betting – or villainy.

Unfortunately, Frank had inherited his dad's attraction

to gambling, not such a great idea, especially while the laws around illegal gambling remained draconian until the early sixties, although the local constabulary was quite frequently accustomed to getting a 'drink' or a good 'bung' to look the other way. But teenage boys generally are not usually as savvy or clued up as they should be when it comes to running with the pack, ignoring the hazards – and are especially vulnerable to coming unstuck.

On Friday nights after work at Frank's print firm, a small group of his workmates would covertly gather in the men's toilet to play dice, placing bets for modest sums fresh out of their weekly pay packets. Unfortunately, a manager caught the group gambling. Frank was holding the dice. End of job and potential print career.

Viewed today, this seems like an unfair punishment for an innocent after-hours pastime, especially since they weren't exactly high rollers. But the incident serves to highlight the very different black-and-white world that existed back then.

With hindsight, if this relatively minor incident had never taken place and Frances's brother had kept his job and remained with the printing firm for some time, events might just have taken a different turn for the Sheas.

Sadly, there are several 'if onlys' in this story, not just those involving the actions of the individuals involved but many involving the historical and very important social changes that affected millions of lives in Britain during the fifties and sixties. This was just the first.

The loss of her son's job fuelled Elsie's slow-growing fear that somehow, despite the indications that her bright, pretty kids might have had reasonably good prospects in life, it would all go wrong and they'd be stuck, all of them, where they'd started. This was at the bottom of the heap, still far too close to the soot, the dark and the dodgy deal, rather than embarking on a gradual but steady ascent towards a respectable, honest sort of life in the clean, green suburbs.

Perhaps the tensions around Elsie's fears for their future had a direct impact on Frances's feelings or moods in her early teens. Elsie's resentment that her husband wasn't a steady provider gained momentum over the years, certainly. And the atmosphere in Ormsby Street would have been soured by Elsie's disappointment when her son lost the job she'd resourcefully obtained for him. There is another important point to consider: teenagers can be prone to dramatic mood swings during puberty, including varying degrees of depression. Frances would have been around twelve years old at the time of the sacking. Given that it was revealed, much later, that Frances had suffered from depression even before her relationship with Reggie started, this could have been the point when Frances's 'bad nerves', as her problems were later described, started to affect her. This factor may have put her in an even more vulnerable place emotionally than may have been commonly understood.

There is one startling piece of evidence that this was in fact Frances's state of mind in her younger years, though the precise date when this was written down is not known. It takes the form of a section of a well-known Victorian poem, neatly handwritten and copied down by Frances, into the back pages of a lined notebook. Copying out a much-read poem or a section of a book was, back in the pre-electronic era, very popular with youngsters in the fifties and it is likely that Frances copied down this poem before the time when she started seeing Reggie Kray.

The poem is called *Maud*, written by the Victorian poet, Alfred, Lord Tennyson, in 1855. *Maud* is a very long poem in three sections. Frances had copied out three fairly short sections from the poem into her notebook. Here are the extracts from *Maud* that Frances copied. Given the tragedy that unfolded, they make for chilling and prophetic reading:

> Courage, poor heart of stone!
> I will not ask thee why
> Thou canst not understand
> That thou art left for ever alone
> Courage, poor stupid heart of stone:
> Or if I ask thee why,
> Care not thou to reply:
> She is but dead, and the time is at hand
> When thou shalt more than die.

> O let the solid ground
> not fail beneath my feet...
> before my life has found
> what some have found so sweet!
> Then let come what come may
> No matter if I go mad
> I shall have had my day

> Dead, long dead,
> Long dead!
> And here beneath it is all as bad
> For I thought the dead had peace but it is not so;
> To have no peace in the grave, is that not sad?

But up and down and to and fro,
Ever about me the dead men go;
And then to hear a dead man chatter
Is enough to drive one mad.

Frances's first passport described her as a bookkeeper. Yet her studies, though cut short, had exposed Frances to poetry, literature and language itself. Here was an intelligent, articulate young woman, someone who sought comfort or solace in words.

No matter how dark or disturbing the thoughts or ideas behind those words in *Maud*, the discovery of Frances copying down poetry from Tennyson is a very poignant and revealing indication of her thinking. It also indicates a degree of literacy you might not associate with a young Hoxton girl from that time.

Frances turned sixteen in September 1959. By this time, according to a letter written to Frances and their parents by her brother Frankie in August 1959, Frances was already working in the Strand in a clerical job.

At the time he wrote the letter, Frankie was nineteen. He sent it to his family while completing a stint in a young offenders' institution called Blantyre House, in Cranbrook, Kent. (Today it is a Category C resettlement prison: an open prison.)

In the letter, he referred to a family visit, for which he thanked them, saying he was looking forward to the following month when he hoped to see them again.

'In the meantime, you all dress well and look well,' he wrote. As for Frances, he went on, 'Well, Franny, you are a proper Italian rebel now, especially now you have a job in the Strand.'

Frank told his dad he was looking younger without his son around: '...suppose this is because you've got no worries who looks smartest.' As for his mother, he suggested she cheer up a bit, saying, 'You take too much to heart. Same as me.'

Why did Frances opt to leave school at fifteen? One can only guess why she didn't continue her studies or aim for university. However, given the fast-moving social changes of the times, the most likely reason was probably the desire to go out into the world and earn, given the household tensions around her parents' relationship to money, as well as the huge, ever increasing demand for office staff in London at that time.

With Frances now out working in London's West End, and despite her disappointment about her son's behaviour, Elsie must surely have been happy about her daughter's progress. After all, as a mother, she still had every reason to hope that Frances, rapidly evolving into a well-groomed beauty with a wonderful smile and those bewitchingly penetrating eyes, would be well placed to attract the right man to lead her to the altar and the respectable family life her mother dreamed of.

What Elsie didn't know, however, was that at that point in the autumn of 1959, there was a man who was already seriously smitten by the charms of her pretty, big-eyed daughter. And like Elsie, this man also harboured big dreams.

The trouble was, this man, already in his mid-twenties, wanted it all, anything a man could possibly desire in the whole wide world: money, travel, expensive cars, beautiful clothes, a lovely home, a beautiful wife and children. He wasn't quite there yet. But partly because of his own growing confidence and partly because his mum had always insisted he was part of something 'special', he saw no reason why he shouldn't take whatever it was he wanted. Everything was ripe for the taking.

And so began Reggie Kray's obsession with a beautiful, innocent young teenage girl. She wasn't the first person to capture his possessive eye for beauty and innocence, not by a long chalk. Yet in the wake of this intense, unrelenting obsession lay emotional turmoil, fear – and destruction. There would be no escape for the heart-rending emotional turbulence that lay ahead for the Shea family. Nor would there be any escape for the man that instigated it all: Reggie Kray.

CHAPTER 3

THE MAN ON THE DOORSTEP

But who was Reggie Kray, other than an East Ender in his mid-twenties whose entire life revolved around crime, extortion and violence – and the intense relationship with his twin brother, his other half?

Driven by an unquestionable talent for manipulation – via the ongoing threat of bloodshed and aggression – and a fervently cherished desire to be respected by all as serious underworld players, by now the Kray twins were already local heroes: by the late fifties you'd have been hard pushed to find anyone in the East End of London who hadn't heard of them – and what they were reputed to have done. The twins made sure of that.

The fifties marked their inexorable rise to notoriety from local bombsite gang warfare to heavy-duty gangster chic. Though along the way the brothers' own somewhat chaotic relationship with each other had started to shift. Physically, since childhood they had fought each other with astonishing ferocity. Ronnie would goad, taunt; Reggie would react. As a two-headed beast they were capable of extreme violence and brutality. Yet their personalities were at odds: Reggie was more controlled and calculating, less prone to fantasy and irrational, explosive impulse. His twin was delusional, irrational, untroubled by boundaries.

At sixteen, they had turned professional boxers, winning every bout they fought – known around the streets of Bethnal Green as the wildest of street fighters among the local gangs they already ran. In secret.

They would have been just like the thousands of other street-fighting teenage thugs in their taste for violence – except for their penchant for truly vicious attack, sometimes cutting or slashing rather than punching. Ronnie preferred cutlasses, knives over razors – more power in the slashing. Nevertheless they were cunning in their ability to get off the hook.

A brutal beating and kicking of a local Hackney boy, involving a bicycle chain, saw the two sixteen-year-olds briefly remanded in custody, though the subsequent Old Bailey trial was eventually dismissed due to lack of evidence. (A lead witness was quietly informed that giving evidence against the twins would result in a razor attack.)

Another teenage court appearance for assaulting a policeman resulted in probation – mostly thanks to the court appearance of the twins' long-term champion of their respectability, their kindness to their elders, Father Hetherington. He was the long-term vicar of St James's Church in Bethnal Green Road and knew the twins as polite, helpful, caring youngsters. They never went to church but could impress with their good manners and polite ways.

In December 1951 when the three Kray brothers fought, with star billing, at London's Albert Hall, the promise of a professional career as sporting champions peaked – and promptly faded.

Everyone knew by then that Ron was too vicious, too undisciplined, to make it big time in the profession. That night, he lost his temper and was disqualified. Reggie, far more calculating, had everything a man required to be a boxing champion. He won. Their brother Charlie lost.

Yet the twins' growing reputation for excessive violence outside the ring meant their career prospects dwindled right there and then: the boxing authorities rejected them, thanks to the twins' assault on the policeman referred to above. Reggie was never going to seek out a solo career, anyway. The bonds of twinship were far too tight.

National Service came next: in peacetime Britain from 1947–59, men between seventeen and twenty-one were required to sign up in the armed forces for eighteen months. The twins' National Service record from 1952–54 proved to be 'a catalogue of disaster – for the army', as Reggie Kray once described it.

True to family custom, their National Service history saw them going on the run for several months until they were caught and court marshalled, imprisoned for nine months in a military prison at Shepton Mallet in Somerset in the south-west of England.

In the end, it was a dishonourable discharge. The duo merely used the imprisonment as a career opportunity – to establish contact with other criminals, and to enhance their own reputation.

Within weeks of freedom, the twins, now twenty, had

sorted out an operations base, a shabby, run-down billiard hall: the Regal, near Bethnal Green in Eric Street, Mile End. The place was a wreck, already marked down for closure.

They simply moved in, established their presence and within days the word got round: this was where to find the twins. After a few weeks during which the Regal mysteriously became the scene of a series of violent outbreaks and nightly troubles, it all went quiet again. The owner, a sensible man, had accepted an offer from the twins: £5 a week rent and the Regal Billiard Hall went into operation: a well-run refreshment bar and HQ for their varied activities, it became Kray Central.

This, then, was their launch pad, the place where they started to gather around them a group of villains of all ages, an early fulfilment of Ron's lurid and ever increasing fantasies of forming an all powerful criminal 'firm', headed by the twins, men who relished playing the genial hosts, the ringmasters, pushing everyone's buttons and reaping the benefits of fear. The billiard hall was their first stage, if you like, for the 'actor crims'. It set them on the road to power.

By 1956, they had established themselves as a distinct force to be reckoned with, running various kinds of protection rackets in their 'manor', the areas around Hackney, Mile End and out to Walthamstow, moving beyond protecting illegal bookies and gaming clubs – an income they dubbed 'pensions' – extending their remit to 'protecting' other places, such as used car lots. Any car dealer daft enough to refuse to pay up would get a night-time visit from the twins' gang members, armed with sledgehammers and spray-paint cans.

Absolute loyalty was demanded from those who worked for the twins. The rewards were 'pensions' for those families of the 'aways' (men serving prison sentences) and a helping hand for these people when they came out of jail. Word soon got round the criminal fraternity: the twins, ran the legend, looked after their own. There was some truth in this. But it was a devious ploy. The more you owed them in loyalty, the more they could ask in return. This way, they didn't even have to dirty their hands by thieving or conning people themselves, because they got others to do it for them. In the end, such requests would extend to murder.

Reggie was by far the more businesslike of the pair. As far as he was concerned, it wasn't just about creating a reputation of fear of their violence: he saw it as a chance to make real money from the gambling clubs, pubs and businesses that paid them for protection.

As a clearing house, the billiard hall was a cover for many things: locked cubicles for thieves' tools, stolen goods stashed around the back, transport arranged for robberies, percentages taken on other crims' activities. All highly lucrative. And Reggie was well organised. Ronnie schemed over the battles and gun warfare, weaponry being his major obsession, becoming a powerful criminal leader in the style of Al Capone his sole desire. He even dressed like his hero, wearing a floor-length belted cashmere overcoat and adopting slicked-back hair.

His twin, however, could see bigger and better times ahead with the lifestyle that only money can buy. Ronnie was increasingly violent, just for the fun of it. Initially, he'd been viewed as the dominant force, with Reggie spending much time trying to restrain his twin's excesses – or clearing up after him. But then, one night, Ronnie went too far. There was a row with a rival gang at a local pub where Ronnie and two others set about a man and nearly killed him in a psychotic attack; as a consequence, Ronnie was given a three-year jail sentence in November 1956.

This was a turning point. For the first time since they were three years old, when a bout of diphtheria separated them in hospital, the twins were apart. (Diphtheria is reputed to have changed Ronnie for good, making him much slower and more awkward than his twin.)

Reggie, troubled by concern for his twin, did everything he could to ensure Ronnie got whatever he needed while he was in prison. But he also started to focus more clearly on his idea of himself as an individual – and what he wanted. It was Reggie Kray's first taste of adult life as a separate identity: real freedom.

It was a turbulent time. After a year in prison, Ronnie was moved to Camp Hill Prison on the Isle of Wight – and went completely crazy. Paranoid and psychotic, he wound up in a straightjacket and was certified insane. Then, at the beginning of 1958, he was transferred to a mental hospital, Long Grove, in Epsom, Surrey. At one point he insisted his twin was not Reggie at all, but a Russian spy impersonating his brother.

This, sadly, was just one of Ronnie Kray's many fantasies. Yet there was a tiny kernel of truth in the madness. Because Reggie, no longer in daily contact with his twin, had started to become much more confident, less worried or suspicious of everyone around him. More his own man.

In 1957, the business-minded Reggie had spotted a golden opportunity to make more money by creating something quite different from the billiard hall. His idea was a drinking club in the East End in the Bow Road, Bow, named after the twins, 'The Double R'. Yet again, a semi-derelict building was transformed. Only this time, the clientele weren't all East End villains and crims; the majority of the regulars were smart couples, local celebrities, journalists, people in the know, who were all looking for a good night out, without any trouble. That was the point: Reggie could see that in order to attract the 'right' people, you had to remove the element of violence and menace.

Reggie, as the slickly dressed genial host, clad in immaculately tailored double-breasted suits, revelled in this smart club life. He positively relished all the celebrity contacts that eventually started to come through the doors. There was Reg, from humble Vallance Road, on first-name terms with gorgeous young women such as Jackie Collins, Barbara Windsor, Diana Dors, even Richard Burton's first wife, Sybil Burton. The Double R became the hot new place in the East End for a good night out. It positively thrived; Reg's confidence soared.

Cannily, he started to make even better contacts beyond the local villainy, men with real money to invest in criminal activity. He also started to enjoy life more in areas further away from his manor, going to upscale West End nightclubs or spending time in the countryside at weekends.

Alone, he was a catch, a local lad made good. A twenty-something with cash to splash. He was good looking. Immaculately dressed. Drove expensive cars. He had a playboy image, and women wanted to be around him.

It was a distinct sea change in the life of Reggie Kray. Because up until that point, women or girlfriends didn't really feature in Reggie's life.

Certainly, it was a man's world back then and the twins' day-to-day life, nurtured by their adoring and adored mother, revolved around a very male, East End bar room environment. Yet Ronnie, always excessively jealous and obsessive when it came to the unbreakable bond with his twin, had always made sure that he steered his twin away from any involvement with women beyond superficial polite exchanges.

Up to this point, while both twins had been sexually active as homosexuals since their teens, Reggie had never openly shown any sign of being interested in other men. Any indication or hint of attraction to a woman had, of course, been immediately stamped on by Ronnie. Women, he would tell Reggie, 'smell and give you diseases'. Reggie was being a cissy looking at women.

At this time, homosexuality in Britain was still illegal: it was not until 1967 that it was decriminalised. Before that there was no such thing as 'coming out'; men could be sent to prison for homosexual behaviour. Lives could be ruined by exposure of a same-sex relationship. Certainly, the world of gay people existed, as it always had. Yet it was very covert, underground, and there was a huge social stigma attached to being gay.

In a macho environment like the East End, it really was the love that dared not speak its name.

Ronnie wasn't exactly shy in his younger years about preferring men as sexual partners. So once the word was out that the laws would be changing, he made no attempt to hide his sexual preference for men, mostly younger men in their late teens or early twenties, ideally straight or heterosexual men whom he'd claim to 'turn'. Later on, conversely, he claimed to be bisexual, eventually marrying and divorcing two women whilst serving out his thirty-year sentence, though the reasons for these marriages were more to do with his understanding that marriage itself might improve his image – or even the remote chances of release.

As for Reggie, towards the end of his life he admitted to his second wife, Roberta, as she wrote in her book, *Reg Kray: A Man Apart*, that 'although he had experimented (as many young men do), he had never perceived himself as even bisexual until he was almost fifty.'

One rather startling example of this 'experiment' was described in *Villain's Paradise: A History of Britain's Underworld* by Donald Thomas: 'A gruesome story in Michael Connor's biography of the South London protection racketeer Billy Howard describes the twins in their car picking up a youth at night from the so called "meat rack" of male prostitutes outside the Regent Palace Hotel, near Piccadilly Circus.

'According to Howard, they broke into a house near Sloane Square and made use of the rent boy simultaneously, choking him to death in the process. They put the body in the boot of the car and, according to Howard, disposed of it in Norfolk. Howard was employed to pay the owner of the house for the damage caused by a "wild party" at a mistaken address and to persuade him not to complain.'

It's an ugly story and one of many of the twins' 'crimes' that they would never be called to account for. Yet whatever Reggie's sexual history, when he and his genial married brother Charlie were running The Double R, while Ronnie was inside, Reggie was not only increasingly drawn to the good life. He had also started to see the appeal of a more 'normal' existence, involving a woman, and a nice home with marriage and children to complete the picture. Respectability, in other words, versus criminality and violence. So at that point, without his twin goading him and dominating his existence,

Reggie was beginning to think outside the box: success and money, he started to reason, should also be bringing him the 'reward' of this other, more acceptable, outwardly stable way of life.

Professor Dick Hobbs is Professor of Sociology and Director of the Criminology Centre at the University of Essex. He told me that this thirst for social acceptance was a hallmark of the way the Kray twins ran their lives: 'They seem to have craved respectability, courting, getting married, one side of the coin being the traditional respectable bit, but at the same time there's all the schemes, the scams, the pill popping, the hidden bisexuality. Yet they won't let go of the respectability. It's a switch from one to the other all the time.'

This trait isn't that unknown with serious criminals, said Hobbs. 'I know people now who maintain that respectable side of their life – but alongside it they're using hard drugs, making money in all kinds of morally repugnant ways, yet the respectability goes side by side with it all. These people are not one dimensional – yet the Krays are the most extreme case of this.'

Hobbs explained that the era where the Krays flourished had a lot to do with it. 'The sixties are book-ended by two major changes in the law, the end of capital punishment [in 1965] and the decriminalisation of homosexuality in England and Wales [in 1967, between two men over 21 years of age]. Those two changes define the Krays. They nearly faced the death penalty, hanging. But the gay thing could never be overt at the time.'

'"Oh we always knew Ron was gay," their associates will tell you now. But did they REALLY know? They were nicknamed "Gert and Daisy" (after a well-known female radio double act of the forties, Elsie and Doris Waters) maybe because of their voices, which were lisping and quite high pitched, not those of gruff cockney stereotypes.

'But were people really sure of this ambiguous sexuality? It was covered up very well at the time. There was nothing effeminate or even fashionable about the way they looked. In many ways they were throwbacks to another age, old school, local hard men from the thirties East End. But visually? Warner Brothers gangsters.'

Status. Looking the part. Playing a Hollywood role. Moviemaking always needs the right props to showcase the stars, underline their affluence. And high on Reggie's list of essential props was the car, that most potent status symbol.

An expensive car remains a marker of worldly success – and the owner's desire to impress. Back in the 1950s, it was a thousand times more potent as a power trip extraordinaire since expensive cars were a rare sight on London's streets. Less than 2 per cent of Britain's total population even owned a car. And that was likely to be an Austin 7 or a Morris Minor, inexpensive and ordinary family cars.

A young man drawing up outside a humble East End two-up, two-down in an American Ford Galaxy (one of Reggie's favourite toys in The Double R days) or, later, a dazzling green Mercedes Benz 220SE two-door saloon, would have been an astonishing sight around those still-battered post-war streets.

Reggie, though mad about new cars, was a lousy driver. Ronnie didn't even bother to get a licence. And so, as they established themselves as crime lords, the twins started to hire young, pretty men to drive them around in the flash expensive cars they never paid for. Chauffeurs too were status symbols, right? In the early days of the Regal billiard hall, second-hand cars could also be bought and sold from the forecourt in the front, yet another 'nice little earner' for the twins.

Whether it was through a chance meeting with the twins at the Regal – new faces, especially good-looking young men, tended to find themselves receiving drinks sent over by the twins with increasing regularity – or, as Reggie Kray preferred to tell it, via a friendship that started because he wanted a new car, it was Reggie's association with Frankie Shea Junior that was the link that drew Reggie into Frances's life.

Already a car-crazy teenager and with a growing reputation for being 'a wheel man' around Hoxton, Frankie Shea was 'about eighteen' and already establishing himself as a car dealer when Reggie claimed he first met him. Other accounts differ: some say that Frankie knew both twins from the billiard hall when Frankie was younger, maybe seventeen.

Reggie recalled that 'first' meeting in his book, *Reggie Kray's East End Stories* – and how he had recruited Frankie Shea to work for him: 'I decided to look for a different car from the Vanguard I was driving at the time. He had a car lot in north London and although he had nothing that suited me, we struck up a friendship that led to him becoming my driver.

'He was a good-looking kid with brown eyes, dark hair and an olive complexion. As a driver he was the best I had come across, while his personality made him exceptional company.'

Frankie Shea reached his eighteenth birthday in October 1957. From correspondence (previously mentioned in Chapter 2) written to his family in August 1959, it is clear that by then, he already knew Reggie quite well. That letter from the young offenders' institution also made brief reference to Frankie Junior writing to Reggie, asking his parents to 'please post letters to Reggie and Babs [presumably a girlfriend] as soon as you can'.

At that point, judging by other correspondence from Reggie while in prison in July 1959 – he wrote to Frank Shea Senior, saying he was writing to both Frankie Junior and Frances – it is apparent that by then Reggie was already closely involved with the Shea family, and that he had recently started seeing Frances. She was then still fifteen.

So Reggie's subsequent 'official' recall of events in books – that he had met Frances while visiting Frankie at the Shea house when she was sixteen, that is after September 1959, her sixteenth birthday – does not give the true picture.

She was younger, still a schoolgirl when they first met. Indeed, in later prison correspondence to Frances in April 1961, Reggie himself recalled this, saying:

'I've known you since you were fifteen years old and have never stopped loving you all the time.'

Reggie's cousin, Rita Smith, still lives in the East End. Rita's mother, May, was one of Violet Kray's sisters. An attractive, immaculately groomed seventy-something blonde woman, just three years younger than the twins, Rita grew up next-door-but-one to them in Vallance Road. They'd pop in and out of each other's houses all the time. In many ways, she saw herself as a sister to them, more than anything else. Biased she may be, but family is family and there is no doubting the sincerity of her affection for Reggie as they grew up together.

'Reggie was so nice when he was young; he had Violet's nice ways. Charlie too was totally charming. Ron was more like his dad. But the whole family thought they were special,' she recalled.

Rita vividly remembered Reggie, then in his mid-twenties,

telling her how he'd first met and fallen for Frances whilst she was still at school. 'He used to go round to the Shea house to see Frank,' she remembered. 'That's when she would come in from school. And one day Reggie came to see me and said, "I wanna ask you something. Frankie Shea's got a sister. Oh, he's got a lovely sister. She's so nice. I do like her. But… I think she's too young for me. She's still at school."

'I said, when she leaves school, ask her out with you. And he kept on about her.

Reggie said, "She's got lovely eyes. Don't you think I'm a bit too old?"

'I'd say, "Not really. If she wants to go out with you, what's the difference?"'

Reggie's relationship with Rita was, without doubt, a very strong one: he'd confide in her frequently. She recalled her surprise when he first mentioned Frances. This, she told me, wasn't really the Reggie Kray she knew: 'I'd never seen him like that before. Women? He could take them or leave them before he met her. He'd go out with these girls and they'd stay the night with him at Violet's.

'Then he'd drop them off in my mum's house next door. And they'd wait for him to come back. Well, he wasn't coming back, was he? And he always picked good-looking girls.'

That day, on the doorstep of the Shea house, when Reggie knocked on their front door to be greeted for the first time by schoolgirl Frances, was certainly a moment in time Reggie would never forget.

Wherever his sexual tastes lay up to that point, whatever the complexity of his relationship with Ronnie or his crimes, there seems little doubt that the minute he saw the pretty auburn-haired teenager with the big eyes, he experienced something of a shock. It is what the French call 'le coup de foudre', a bolt of lightning – which some describe as love at first sight.

He recalled that moment in correspondence to Frances in May 1961. In his letter, Reggie told her he'd been thinking about the first time he saw her. He'd knocked on the door to see Frankie and she had opened it. 'You looked at me with a curious look in your big dark eyes and made me feel a little awkward. I never thought at the time I would depend on you so much, just goes to show you never can tell.'

Reggie's letter then told her that 'falling in love with you was the best thing that ever happened to me. Any time you want to put me in my place, just give me a look with your big dark eyes.'

The letter goes on to recall how he'd even conveyed the significance of that first doorstep impression to her brother. 'I said, "Your sister gave me a look and weighed me up and down and made me feel awkward…"'

Frank had quipped back and said that was nothing: 'You should talk to her.'

'I said, "She looks saucy".'

Since that moment, Reggie recalled, he knew Frances was saucy, curious, mischievous, better looking than ever, everything he dreamed a girl should be. He went on to say he had never regretted knocking at her door 'because I've been in love with you ever since and always will be.'

Whether it was Reggie's arrival in her life that led to Frances leaving school before her sixteenth birthday in 1959 or whether the decision had nothing to do with it is not known.

But the fact remains that Reggie, on that memorable day, fell so in love with a pretty schoolgirl, he could only dare discuss his romantic feelings with a woman he'd trusted since childhood. He would never have dared confide all this to his twin. He knew all too well what the response would be.

It looks like he simply took Rita's advice and waited until Frances was working. There were, indeed, other serious preoccupations for Reggie in those years from 1957–60.

His brother, for one. Once certified insane at Long Grove, and prescribed a new type of drug called Stemetil, which seemed to curb his suicidal impulses and calm him down, Ronnie started to realise, on Reggie's visits, how successful his twin was without him – and soon insisted he was 'cured' and could go back to prison, to finish his sentence.

The doctors said no. He had to wait. But that wasn't likely to mean much to the twins because what followed was the Kray twins' legendary 'switch' one day at Long Grove when Reggie came to visit.

Both were dressed identically – and, at the time, it was very difficult to tell them apart. As a consequence of a cunningly hatched plan to fool the authorities and switch places, Reggie, of course, could not be detained once Ronnie had walked out and Reggie identified himself with his driving licence. No crime had been committed. Ronnie had simply walked out of the mental hospital and into a waiting car. He was free. Then he was driven to a hideaway, a caravan in Suffolk. Without his medication. Men from 'the firm' were enlisted to look after him as best they could. But without the pills he really needed, Ronnie's madness, his paranoia, started to manifest itself again.

In the end, Reggie took his twin back to London, found a trusted doctor (normally useful for repairing slashed faces) and managed to get the drugs Ronnie needed so badly to calm him down. Then the pair enlisted the help of a compliant Harley Street doctor who saw Ronnie and wrote a letter saying he was perfectly sane – and could therefore be sent back to prison to complete his sentence. Which he did.

In the spring of 1959, Ronnie finally came out of prison. He managed to get the drugs he needed and, despite frequently drinking copious amounts of alcohol, potentially causing very dangerous situations when combined with powerful drugs like Stemetil, he was back with Reggie, both of them living at Vallance Road with their mum.

Yet Ronnie, schizophrenic, drug dependent and scarily crazy, no longer looked the same as his once-identical twin. At twenty-six he looked monstrous: fleshy and coarse featured, he was a very different man from his good-looking twin. And, of course, once he divined that Frances had caught Reggie's eye, he went into action, taunting, sneering, goading his brother, the way he always did.

Ronnie could be in love, he could be sentimental, even romantic about his affairs with his boyfriends. But as for his twin forming a romantic attachment to a dirty woman? What had gone wrong with him? Had Reggie gone soft?

All Reggie's ideas for the future of the business, carefully crafted with his more law-abiding brother Charlie, the months of avoiding trouble, making businesslike liaisons with useful allies, drawing up serious plans to get involved in the new West End casinos (gambling was due to be made legal very soon) were in danger of crumbling now that Ronnie was back. Ronnie seemed determined to destroy it all with more scheming, aggression, bloodshed and gang warfare. Reggie's plans for a more legitimate front for their activities were at risk of going down the drain.

All Reggie could hope for now was business as usual, continuing to give his all to clear up any mess Ronnie left in his wake, as he'd always done. The madman and the mopper-up. His twin was sick, no question. But he had to be there for him. No matter what went down. He wasn't about to abandon his other half.

Yet as difficult as it all was, stretching Reggie to breaking point at times, the sane brother still persisted with his fantasy of a different, respectable life with a beautiful young woman beside him to share his dreams.

He'd found Frances. She was young, beautiful and he was utterly captivated by her looks. She was bright, lively and, most importantly, virginal, untouched. And he was a young man, still in his twenties with a future before him. Whatever had happened before that moment on the Sheas' doorstep, nothing was going to keep him away from her, his dream girl, whom he vowed to convince of his love.

Yes, he had gone soft. To the world he was a tough hard nut, a criminal with a mad twin. But now he was bewitched by a teenage girl. He was crazy about Frances Shea. And he had a big advantage over other men, because he had everything a guy needed to tempt her: money, cars, travel, nightclubs. What girl wouldn't want to be treated like that? So he embarked on the pursuit of Frances.

Why did she agree so readily to go out with him at all? He was ten years older. He already had a reputation for violence. The truth was it was a time of imminent big social changes, and very few ordinary, innocent young girls would have been able to resist the lure of a good-looking, beautifully dressed older man inviting them out in his expensive car, taking them places and showing them a good time.

A local young admirer, even a law-abiding guy working in a steady job, couldn't compete with all that. As Dick Hobbs told me, Frances may have been bright and intelligent, but as far as her environment was concerned, typical of so many young working-class women in the fifties, her life options were limited.

'What could a young woman do with their life then?' said Hobbs.

When you consider the fifties landscape for ordinary women, you see exactly what he means.

Like her mother, Frances's expectations were a low-level job, followed by courtship with someone from a similar background, then marriage and kids. No travel, no career and ultimately, no financial independence once the children arrived.

Women couldn't get a mortgage, buy a car or even rent a TV unless their husband or father countersigned. Abortion was illegal. The contraceptive pill was still in the future. And as far as society was concerned, the only sex was within marriage. Divorce was out of reach too, as it was difficult, costly and usually disastrous for a woman's reputation.

'It was so unusual in those days to be wooed by one of these men, a local man who had money,' said Hobbs. 'The Krays were known locally – everything in the East End was so localised. People didn't travel, they didn't even move around London.

'So she was a local beauty – and he hadn't even stepped off his manor; he was not comfortable outside it. From Walthamstow to the West End, those were the places where the Kray twins were comfortable, their bit of the old East End.

'Frances had luminous good looks, the "look" of the time,

so for him, regardless of the ambiguity around his sexuality, she was a catch. And he had to have that.'

As Hobbs pointed out, at that time there was no limit to the the Kray twins' belief that the world was theirs for the taking – at a time when most people were still living through a period of great restraint and austerity.

'Reggie would have thought: "I can have everything, I can do whatever I like, I can have the best looking boy or the best looking girl – I've got to have the lot." Having children? You're a man therefore you have a family – he wanted that too. Why not?

'Reggie liked to present himself as a traditional East End male – don't swear in front of women – have kids, look after old people, give to charity. In reality, he wanted it all, boys, girls, money, fame, everything.

'The Kray twins were really greedy people.

'From her point of view, at fifteen, here's the most wealthy person she's ever seen in her life. Who had flash cars, bespoke suits, jewellery then? She was a child. It wouldn't take much to impress people in those days. For her, it would have all been incredibly alluring.'

But what about her family? They knew who the Krays were, their reputation, the fact that Ronnie had 'gone away' while his brothers were running The Double R. It wasn't just gossip. Everyone in the area read about them in the local paper, the *East London Advertiser*, anyway. Frances's parents already knew that Frankie had been friendly with Reggie for some time. Why were they willing to accept that this older man wanted to take their daughter out, dazzle her with the bright lights?

Elsie surely had her doubts. She understood that the Krays'

well-honed façade of respectability, their legendary generosity to charity, was a cover for the traditional compulsion of East End hard men to inflict harm by violence. Yet initially she kept her counsel. Her husband was impressed with Reggie's polite ways, his soft voice, his good manners. You could see, he argued, that Reggie was respectful, not a man to take liberties, whatever people said about the twins. Their Franny was safe with him.

But it was Frankie Junior, as attractive as his sister, as personable a young man as anyone would wish, who already knew quite a bit more about Reggie Kray than he dared to let on.

Car dealer Frankie was becoming a bit of a wide boy. He too was attracted to the good life, the flash cars, the smart suits, the West End drinking clubs. As a result, he'd gone the way of many young Hoxton boys and had not been discerning or cautious in the company he kept; he'd been in trouble with the law even after the stint at the young offenders' institution.

Frankie knew what he knew. And his sister, the tiny baby he'd cuddled as they huddled for safety under the kitchen table, was very close to his heart. But the young man stayed silent, didn't attempt to interfere with this new development or put in his two bob's worth.

It was a mistake that would go on to haunt Frankie Shea for the rest of his life.

CHAPTER 4

COURTSHIP

Reggie may have made up his mind that Frances was 'the one', yet there was a huge obstacle in the very early days of their courtship, beyond his relationship with Ronnie. It was, of course, the occupational hazard of their chosen profession. The loss of freedom.

By now, the twins were adroit at the ways and means of keeping the law at bay: expensive lawyers and barristers, intimidated and terrified witnesses who would always clam up, remember nothing, private doctors who would quietly sew up the damage, cash bribes in the right places, coppers who'd pocket them.

As with the legendary Long Grove 'switch', if it came to the crunch and either twin were imprisoned, they'd ignore the hand of authority, forget about the lock and key and deploy all their cunning to continue their activities via those working for them on the outside, while forming alliances with other criminals on the inside: prison was a nuisance, a blip in their activities. In no way was prison a deterrent. As their later history would demonstrate.

Yet in the summer of 1959, not long after he'd fallen heavily for Frances, Reggie found himself facing a two-year prison sentence for his part in a protection racket. He'd been on remand (remanded in custody) in Wandsworth prison for a few months, then he'd started taking Frances out regularly once he was out on bail for several months, awaiting court proceedings for his appeal against the conviction. Which he confidently believed he'd win.

Very soon, he'd introduced her to his family in Vallance Road. Violet was pleasant and motherly, Ronnie unnervingly polite and the twins' cousin Rita liked the young girl immediately.

'The first time we met we seemed to take to one another,' recalled Rita. 'She had shorter, quite dark hair then. Very pretty girl. Big brown eyes. She was quite shy, quite an innocent really – as you are at that age. But intelligent, you could see that.'

Reggie took to meeting Frances outside her office in the Strand after she'd finished work. They'd go to the movies. There were drives out to the country. He'd buy her clothes, jewellery, give her money. On other occasions he'd take her 'up West' to places like the Astor Club, a swish nightclub off Berkeley Square in Mayfair, though he continued, after dropping Frances off at her parents' house, to live his usual nocturnal life with Ronnie, moving around various clubs and drinking haunts, imposing order, looking after their investments, organising feuds – and boozing.

Frances wasn't keen on drinking. She'd smoke the odd

ciggy. But even then, she was bemused at the amount of heavy drinking that seemed to go on every night in Krayworld. It never seemed to stop.

Proudly, Reggie showed everyone the photos he'd had taken with Frances in the Astor club that February, 1960, the first of many photos of the couple in a glamorous setting.

'She looks like Brigitte Bardot,' said his friend Danny. Reggie was chuffed. His girl looked like a French movie star – yet she was from the mean streets of the East End, just like him. She was his trophy.

Incredibly, he also took sixteen-year-old Frances on a trip to Jersey in May 1960 in their early days of courtship. They flew there. Of course there'd be separate rooms, Reggie assured Frank Senior beforehand, and this was no lie: Frances had no intention of losing her virginity and her glamorous, free-spending older boyfriend was nothing but respectful of this.

By now, the Shea family were well and truly caught in the Kray net. Both the Shea children were already drawn into the seemingly glamorous, high-spending life of the Kray twins. Reggie had also hinted that he might be able to find work for Frank Senior in one of his clubs. So Frank Senior wasn't set against him: to the older Shea, Reggie seemed so polite, almost shy sometimes. He wouldn't do her any harm, Frank Senior kept reassuring his wife. It was fine. Everyone knew the Krays respected women. Violet had brought them up the right way.

It may be difficult nowadays to understand how dazzled Frances would have been with the world her older boyfriend was showing her. But as Dick Hobbs pointed out: 'To get on a plane and fly to Jersey at that age would have been an extraordinary experience. It was a traditional courtship that was going on there – and he had the cash to do it. People didn't take girlfriends away for trips like that then – it was unheard of.'

Yet the nightclubs and the plane trips were but a distraction from the reality: Reggie had not expected his appeal against his two-year sentence to be rejected but that is exactly what happened. Later in that summer of 1960 he was back in prison. And now that their relationship seemed to be ongoing, the separation from Frances turned out to be really painful for him.

Frances's everyday life went on. She went to work weekdays, saw her girlfriends on weekends and dutifully perched on her bed at home, writing to him, as promised, twice a week, visiting when permitted.

Reggie, in prison, unable to control his brother, had far too much time on his hands to think – and to dwell on his obsession with his teenage girlfriend. He was paranoid in the extreme. If a letter didn't arrive for a day or two, he'd be tormented with rage. He couldn't stop thinking about her, or about how, in his absence, someone else might decide they wanted to take Frances out and pursue her. Or turn her against him.

On 2 September 1960 he wrote to Frances, telling her he was in such a bad mood at not receiving any letters from her, 'I nearly choked a fella in my cell for having too much to say'. Luckily, he wasn't caught. But he was 'more mixed up than ever' he told her.

Controlling everyone was part of the Kray twins' repertoire. Indeed, at that point, business was starting to boom, sixties style: they'd achieved their goal of moving beyond the East End, into the West End of London and had taken a share in Esmeralda's Barn, in swanky Knightsbridge. Originally it had been a posh nightclub but now, with the legalisation of Britain's gambling laws, it was one of the first high-end gambling clubs in London.

This was just as well, because The Double R had already gone into decline and closed once Reggie was not around to run it. However, it didn't seem to matter, because Esmeralda's was pure gold. With its rich, upmarket clientele dining in the swish restaurant or seated beside the green baize table, focused on the roulette wheel and gambling huge sums, the move to Knightsbridge was the gift that kept on giving, earning the twins around £800 a week, a huge sum of money for the times.

Reggie was now rich. But his obsessive jealousy about Frances – locked away, unable to do little but worry and write letters – was something he'd never encountered before. Until then, all he'd really troubled himself with was the mental state of his mad twin. Now all he had were bits of paper to channel his thoughts and emotions towards Frances, to convince them both that they had a real future together.

Even in July 1960, just after his court hearing, even though Frances was not yet seventeen, his letter made it very clear he was determined to marry her, to 'take her off the market', as it were. He couldn't bear the idea of anyone else getting close to her.

His one consolation while serving the rest of his time in prison, he wrote to her, was knowing he was engaged 'to such a nice person as yourself'. Then he asked her to have a full-length photo taken in her black dress, wearing a new necklace he'd chosen for her. After he'd finished the prison sentence, Reggie said, he would make sure she'd never leave him again. He was looking forward to getting married as soon as possible.

Frances knew she was too young for marriage. But she obviously agreed to commit herself. In August 1960 she wrote to say she wanted to wait two years. 'I want to get married not next year, but the July after,' she wrote, pointing out that this would give them enough time to get a house built and organise the wedding properly. They didn't want to rush, she told Reggie, because it had to last a lifetime.

This must have given Reggie enough encouragement to feel reasonably confident about their future. In a letter written on 16 September 1960 he mentioned 'our new wedding date' and told her he was hoping her dad, Frank Senior, 'likes being called my father-in-law'.

How he envisaged their married life makes for intriguing reading too, given their respective backgrounds, where their mothers had known little but hard slog, coping with husbands who were anything but regular providers.

'Please don't look at marriage as scrubbing, cooking, and all work,' Reggie wrote.

As far as he was concerned, she would have no manual tasks. There would be a comfortable home, 'decorated nice', good furniture, lovely clothes, records to play, a car – 'and the company of each other'. He assured her there would be no worries whatsoever. If she was concerned about cooking, they'd eat out, should she wish. He was marrying for love, he told her, not because he needed a cook. Finally, he reminded her, there were six requirements for happy marriage. The first was faith. 'And the remaining five are confidence.'

When they were married, he told her, all he wanted to do was sit around cuddling her. 'Your name should have been cuddles.'

That night, the letter continued, he was going to dream of

their wedding and their married life. 'I honestly believe it will be a success.'

Reggie Kray wasn't used to being deprived of anything: if he wanted something, he just took it. Prison and loss of liberty lowered the opportunities to operate, yet crime itself could still continue to function on the outside. Yet in this situation, he worried all the time that Frances wouldn't have him, or be distracted, without the promise of marriage. Possessive in the extreme, the correspondence shows he was desperate to be legally tied to her as soon as he could possibly arrange it.

An engagement at seventeen or eighteen, making the traditional statement of commitment, was not at all unusual at that time. Some of Frances's friends at school would have been going steady by sixteen and engaged a couple of years later. Many girls then considered themselves 'on the shelf' if they weren't married by twenty. At twenty-one, you'd reached spinster status. But you have to wonder at the anxiety that seemed to be driving Reggie's obsession, the belief that marriage to a teenage girl was a springboard for long-term emotional security.

Was he also desperate to escape the bond with Ronnie? It seemed like it. Marriage then would have certainly changed everything. Separation from his twin quite recently had given Reggie an opportunity to see life quite differently; it had nourished a dream to break free from their claustrophobic twinship.

While the isolation of the prison cell day in, day out brings extreme frustration, at the same time, it can only serve to fuel a fantasy life, an ideal world to cling to. The frustration would end with his prison sentence. Yet unquestionably, he was deluding himself: separation from his twin remained a fantasy. Ronnie knew exactly how to push his buttons, reel him in, jeer at him for loving a smelly woman. Ronnie, by now, needed his twin more than Reggie needed him. Still, while the sneering and jibing might lead to furious fighting it still served its purpose for Ronnie in keeping his twin locked into their twisted relationship. So the idea that Ronnie would be there, outside, flinging abuse at him, trying to turn him away from his dream, merely added to Reggie's conflicting emotions.

In the time they'd spent together, it was a joy to adorn Frances with beautiful new clothes and jewellery. She was his doll, his toy. And although she was as keen as any young girl on doing her hair, getting made up, spending hours making herself look nice, he'd noticed that she didn't seem as wild about possessions and having new things as he'd imagined.

She didn't seem greedy for more; it was always Reggie who'd carefully wait for her to mention she liked something – then he'd rush out and get it, to surprise her. So it was sheer torment now to look at her photo and imagine other men approaching her, admiring her charms.

This correspondence with Frances revealed the truth of Reggie's obsession with her. But Frances's own responses were mature and clear thinking, given her age. And it was true, her priorities were not material. This was demonstrated in a letter from Frances to Reggie dated December 1960. In the letter, she took him to task, in no uncertain terms, about his habit of walking in front of her when they strolled down the street. As far as she was concerned, she wrote, this showed a lack of respect. Buying her presents and taking her out was fine. But walking in front of her was not – it was demeaning. She also suggested that he was not being fair in only sending the precious visiting orders for visits to her alone; his parents ought to be able to visit him too.

There's the normal day-to-day trivia in the letter: a painful visit to the dentist, the new flock wallpaper the Sheas had had put in upstairs, the Christmas gifts she'd be getting for his family, including cousin Rita's new baby, Kimmie. She wasn't sure about getting a present for brother Charlie's little boy, Gary, whom she thought was quite 'spoilt', but she'd probably get him one anyway. The letter also mentioned a Christmas works do – she thought it might be boring. But, she added, it might be fun to see the partners at her firm get tipsy.

This was the sort of letter any girl might write to a boyfriend in 1960, but the comments about not walking in front of her reveal a spirited young woman with a clear idea of appropriate behaviour between the sexes. And the mention of the visiting order also indicates a strong sense of family obligation. That was how she'd been raised, in the way of East End families then.

But this letter was unsent, addressed but not posted. Did she have second thoughts after writing it because it was too strongly worded?

Yet again, Frances's writings revealed a very different girl to the compliant 'arm candy' previously portrayed. How she squared all this with the knowledge that the man she was planning to marry was a criminal, serving a prison sentence, one half of a double act with a reputation for excessive violence, is not easy to imagine.

You can only assume that with the blithe innocence of youth, she believed Reggie when he promised her so much in the future, so much of the respectable stability her mother had always dreamed of but never found. The house in a leafy suburb. The freedom from worry about money. It would have seemed very attractive.

Moreover, the promises he gave her in this prison correspondence extended to his own behaviour. Initially, in a letter dated 15 August 1960, he promised he would stop boozing all the time and mend his ways:

'I will definitely cut out the drinking... how right you were about the drinking.'

Then, in a letter dated 5 October 1960, he repeated these promises. In this letter he claimed he realised what a fool he was to 'split our nights up' by going to clubs after taking her out to the pictures and other places – although, he added, when they first started going out he did stop drinking for a while.

Now, in his cell, he swore to her he could see how futile a lot of his nocturnal ways were. And, again, he realised that much of the advice she'd given him now rang true. Her 'wise head for her age' and her understanding, he concluded, reassured him that in the future 'you and I will be happy'.

In the light of what eventually happened, you can't help wishing that he'd been able to follow through with all this. And perhaps he did mean it all at the time. Yet the promises were hollow – once reunited with his twin, the clubbing and the nightly boozing would continue: it was part of their joint DNA.

What else is revealed by these letters? The same October letter shows a romantic side, another hallmark of the Kray twins' bizarre personalities: brutal men with a penchant for extreme sentimentality.

As a plane flew over the prison, it reminded Reggie of their night flight to Jersey and the way Frances had held his hand on the plane. Another memory he cherished was when she would come back off the beach and walk through the hotel 'with just your swimsuit and jumper on ha ha – and all the old squares would look at you.'

One of his most pleasant memories, he wrote, was the time round Frances's house when she sat on his lap and put her arms around his neck. That night, he wrote, he really felt she loved him and he felt very proud. And happy.

Yet Reggie's jealousy, his fear of losing her, was never far away. In the same letter he warned her that when she went out dancing with her friends, one of them might try to egg her on to let someone take her home, saying, 'It won't do any harm, he'll never know' and then she might be paired off with 'some Teddy Boy' wanting to satisfy his ego. (A 'Teddy Boy' was a fifties youth attired in a long-jacketed 'Zoot' suit with a slicked-down greasy hairdo, often with a quiff at the front, wearing crepe-soled shoes and a 'Slim Jim' narrow tie. To Reggie, with his social aspirations and obsession with cleanliness and neatness, gangs of Teddy Boys were a lower form of life.)

Reggie knew Frances had a mind of her own, he said. He knew people couldn't sway her. But he'd seen these things happen. So perhaps she might understand why he couldn't help worrying.

But what did she think of Ronnie, who was now beginning to really enjoy himself in charge of Esmeralda's Barn, spending huge amounts of money on beautiful clothes from Savile Row and Jermyn Street and dreaming up bizarre stunts like buying a chimpanzee from Harrods, dressing it up and sitting it at the gambling table? There is a hint in this prison correspondence in October 1960 that Frances was already wary, feeling uncomfortable around Ron. She'd obviously made this clear to Reggie.

'If you don't want to go drinking with Ron, don't go,' wrote Reggie. Yes, he knew how Frances felt – but his twin didn't mean any harm. She'd got it wrong. Ronnie was surely trying to be nice. After all, Frances was 'getting along nice with him and my family'. This was true, insofar as Frances certainly felt comfortable around cousin Rita, who'd recently had a baby girl.

Frances had eagerly taken the baby out sometimes. 'Have you been pushing Rita's pram lately, I'd have liked to have seen you,' wrote Reggie – and Frances happily posed for photos with Kimmie on her lap.

By the beginning of 1961, however, some of Reggie's worries and concerns about outside gossip reaching Frances were surfacing. In a letter dated 2 January 1961, where a friend had obviously told Frances about a girl Reg had previously been seen around with, he was quick to reassure her.

'I'm not surprised someone tried to mix it for me,' he wrote. 'But I never took her out hardly.' As for getting engaged, he wrote, until he'd met Frances 'the idea had never occurred to me.'

Yet the web he was now starting to weave around the Shea family was, by this point, increasing rapidly. In the same letter he wrote 'glad your dad is on the firm', a reference to Frankie Senior starting to work for the twins, as promised, as a croupier at the Regency Club in Stoke Newington, not a move that made Elsie dance for joy. The extra cash was needed. But that was it.

But this was how the Kray twins hooked people in: they needed money, the Krays played benevolent local guv'nors, took them on the payroll or, in some cases, dished out handouts. First had been Frankie Junior, young, cute, impressionable, in awe of the twins, thrilled to be driving Reggie's luxury cars. Now Frankie Senior was being reeled in – alongside his daughter. Control. Money. All disguised with civility, kindness and good manners. It was astonishingly effective. Unwittingly and unwillingly, so far as Elsie, at least, was concerned, they were all now involved with the Kray twins' world.

Given the intensity of Reggie's obsession with Frances, you might expect these prison letters to carry some hint of sexuality, but the correspondence seems relatively tame.

In January, Reggie had written that he'd heard 1961 was going to be a romantic year 'and short skirts are going to be the fashion again'. He reckoned Frances had very nice knees. And when he did get out, he reminded her, 'I'll be lively enough… like a tiger out of a cage, ha ha, so save some energy. Can't have you saying it's time to go home.'

Even towards the end of his sentence, the jealousy continued to dominate his thinking.

'Please don't go dancing' he wrote in April 1961.

No harm in dancing, of course, but he couldn't stand it if she were dancing with anyone while he wasn't around. Then he implored Frances to stay away from 'sordid places' like jazz clubs, saying, 'The atmosphere is not your kind. You belong in a much better atmosphere.'

By the summer of 1961, Reggie was free. Even before going home to Vallance Road, he went straight round to Ormsby Street to see his girl. She'd lightened her dark brown hair to a reddish colour and had applied for her first passport, in anticipation of the trips abroad he'd promised her so often.

In July, she received that first passport. Yet the following month, Reggie took her on a motoring trip to Devon and Cornwall. In this, and the trips that were to follow, they were accompanied by Reggie's friends, which might have initially been reassuring to the Sheas, but probably didn't leave the couple with much time alone. The truth was, Reggie needed to have his minders around wherever he went.

Yet Frances must have been delighted taking a trip to what was still a somewhat remote, very pretty part of Britain. She even carefully noted the places they'd visited in a lined notebook. There's no hint of anything other than brief descriptions of what she saw. But it was obviously memorable enough to commit pen to paper.

This is the gist of what she wrote in the notebook:

1961 CORNWALL-DEVON

They drove from Exeter to Brixham, near Torquay, where they met 'a German bookie'. At Brixham they stayed with a 'Mrs Parkington' at a place 'in a private road after the Links Hotel, Devon.' Then they took a ferry to Dartmouth, stopped at an inn for some cider, rested 'near the coastline', then drove to Plymouth and stayed at the Continental Hotel. 'Went to different hotel in the evening' Frances noted.

From Plymouth they'd driven to Looe, with its fishing harbour, and Polperro. Then they drove down to Falmouth in Cornwall, from there across to Land's End and then St Ives, which Frances noted as 'a very hilly seaside resort, rather commercialised'. They'd stayed at Mrs Davies's farm, near Polperro 'and in a guest house at Land's End'.

They'd also stayed at another farm 'near some

horse riding stables, run by a Mr Lightfoot'. They'd gone shark fishing at Looe all day long and had also taken speedboats out at Looe. They went horse riding. Then their travels took them up to Bude on the Devon/Cornwall border and then to Clovelly in Devon: 'a quaint village on the side of a hill, harbour at the bottom.'

They travelled on to Saunton where they'd stayed at a guest house, and from there to Woolacombe, Devon: 'Beautiful beaches, golden sands, v. extensive, sea is dangerous, terrific speed of waves.' They then drove to Ilfracombe where they shopped.

Horse riding. Shark fishing. Speedboats. Hotels. Nightclubs. All courtesy of an older man, a rich, attractive, immaculate boyfriend, who liked to kiss and cuddle but was 'respectful' and didn't attempt to go further. Okay, there were all these blokes around him. But they were his friends, after all.

By taking Frances on such trips, Reggie was showing off the good life, splashing around the easy money he'd now become accustomed to. This, he was saying, is how it will be: we'll go places, see everything, have the best.

It was all in the starkest contrast to everything Frances had known – or anyone she knew had experienced, come to that, all part of the fantasy life Reggie had mapped out for the future.

Frances was wise, intelligent and curious about the world. But she was simply far too young to be cynical at this point. Or even fearful. An East End girl from a very tough, bleak post-war background would never have questioned the presence of his friends on those trips back then. Younger men traditionally moved around in small groups, in the street or the pub. Or, in the case of Bethnal Green, in gangs. For now, at least, she was enjoying what Reggie was showing her. Even if he did go a bit over the top at times with his generosity.

'She was not a grabber, not at all,' recalled Rita Smith. 'She used to say, "When I go out with Reggie, I don't like saying I like anything because he goes out and buys it for me."

'They used to go up the West End quite a lot. If she would see something in a jeweller's window, he'd come in with it the next day.

'If he could have got her the moon, he would have got that too.'

Rita confirmed that Frances frequently confided in her that she was still too young for marriage: 'What it was with her, she didn't want to get married straight away, because of her age. But the plan was, they'd buy a house near Chingford, Essex and settle down. She liked it round there – and he went along with the things she liked.'

Reggie, recalled his cousin, always had very definite ideas about how women should look. 'He liked you dressing well. He taught me what sort of clothes to wear. He didn't like clothes too short. Or low necks. He liked feminine clothes, pale pink nail varnish, not bright orange.

'In the beginning she just dressed ordinary but when he started taking her out, he'd buy lovely clothes for her. He used to get them from Marlowes in Mare Street, a Hackney dress shop. I always remember one outfit he bought her, a brown cocktail dress with lace at the neck and lace sleeves. He got her a little fox stole to go with it.'

Frances may not have been greedy but she was, like many young girls, very keen on make-up and beauty routines, as

Rita went on: 'She loved make-up, doing her eyes, always having her hair done. She had very long nails, beautifully shaped. I remember her painting her nails with nail hardener. She got her hair done at Ray's in Bethnal Green Road. Her hair always looked immaculate. You'd never see her without make-up.

'She used to say, "I like to dress nice – to please him."'

Rita Smith told me that it was her belief that had Frances and Reggie been able to develop their relationship in a normal way – crucially, spending time alone together – things might have been different. But the twins' world didn't permit such togetherness.

'They didn't get a lot of privacy, really,' Rita continued. 'If they were at Violet's house, there were always people in and out; if they wanted to talk about something, they'd have to go in the front room. And Ronnie was always around, anyway.'

Ronnie was there, of course, the night Reggie first took Frances out to show her their new acquisition, Esmeralda's Barn. At the roulette table, she was encouraged to have a flutter. In the club's restaurant, they dined on fresh lobster, juicy steaks, and Frances laughed, in delight, when the maître d' wheeled out the huge dessert trolley, groaning with fresh strawberries, black forest cake and all kinds of exotic gateaux. No, she didn't want any more, she assured Reggie. Not even the cheeseboard. She'd just have her usual tipple, black coffee.

Reggie looked at his girl quizzically. He knew Frances was very weight conscious and tried to diet sometimes. But he did worry about her health.

When he'd first gone into prison, she'd written to tell him that she'd fainted one day at work. He'd told her to go and see a private doctor with the money he'd given her, and she'd written back to say she'd seen the doctor, and everything was okay. Some time later, she'd mentioned in a letter that her nerves were bad, and her hands were a bit shaky.

He'd written back that it was all that coffee she drank: 'Coffee is only a stimulant and can't do you any good,' he'd told her. But with his obsessive curiosity about everything she did, he'd wondered what else was going on. 'I hope you've not been taking any of them slimming tablets because they can make your nerves bad,' he'd written.

Frances had assured him she wasn't taking any tablets. But now, tonight, he noticed something he'd not spotted before. When she went to pick up the cup, wasn't there just the tiniest hint of a shake in her hand? Or was he just imagining it?

Then Ronnie leaned across the table, interrupting his train of thought.

'C'mon Reg, we've gotta go and talk to 'im,' he boomed. And Reggie, momentarily, brushed his concerns to one side and switched back into business mode. Frances was fine. They were raking it in and the protection business had unlimited potential, now that the new West End casinos were springing up. Any problems, he'd sort them.

He was well and truly back in control.

CHAPTER 5

THE GILDED CAGE

By the autumn of 1961 it was well over a year since Reggie had come out of prison. Yet Frances continually stalled on their wedding plans, still insisting she was too young. Reggie took her on a short trip to Rotterdam in the Netherlands early in November, perhaps in an attempt to convince her, but there was no sign of any wedding bells.

Rita Smith remembered seeing quite a lot of Frances around that time. She had sensed somehow that Frances's home life at Ormsby Street wasn't that happy. Her brother Frankie had left home for good. 'Her parents were never in and she was left on her own a lot of the time,' Rita explained. 'That's why she liked coming to our house. One day she said to me, "You're so lucky to have a mum and dad who are here for you. I have to make my own tea when I get in."'

'Sometimes, if Reggie was going out somewhere and she didn't want to go with him, he'd come next door to me and

say, "Is it alright if Frankie comes and sits with you tonight?"
Then he'd come back later and pick her up.

'She'd say to me, "Oh, I wish you'd come out with us."
But I had Kimmie, she was only a baby then. Frances loved
being with us. I think she felt more comfortable here. I got the
impression she didn't enjoy the clubs, the showbiz parties he
took her to. She wanted a quiet, ordinary kind of life.

'We used to get the chairs out in the back garden and he
would go and get jellied eels and she loved it.'

Rita noticed a distinct tension between Frances and Ronnie:
'She'd be sitting in Aunt Violet's house and he would go, "Why
don't you make a cup of tea?" and she would just ignore him.
Then Reg would say, "Leave her alone. I'll make the tea."

'She wanted to go to work. He'd give her money and
say, "There's no need to go to work." But you didn't know,
perhaps she was too scared to go to work.'

Maureen Flanagan, former 'Page Three' girl and actress,
was a regular visitor to the Kray twins' home in the early
sixties.

Maureen, or 'Flan' as she's known, was a hairdresser at
the time. At twenty, she was a newly married girl working
in a local salon. She'd go round to the Vallance Road house
each Thursday evening to do Violet's hair. Her friendship with
the Kray family became one which would eventually span a
lifetime, until the end of their lives.

'The first time I met Frances would have been around the
end of 1961,' Flan said. 'She was sitting in the kitchen, where
Violet made the tea.

'I didn't have to ask who she was, of course, because
I already knew that Reggie was going out with the Shea
daughter. Everyone knew who she was. I'd also heard that she

was very lovely. I'd got that from Mrs Kray. "Oh, you know, Reg's got a girlfriend, she's very pretty, Flan," she told me.

'I remember looking at Frances and thinking, "Oh yes, you are lovely." She was a beauty, hazel eyes, thick browny auburn hair, nice skin and a nice little rounded figure.

'But it was her face that drew you in – especially her eyes.

'Knowing the twins, and with me thinking Reggie was a far more handsome man than his twin, I did think: "Hmm... they make a nice looking couple, especially when the man looks as if he's been around a bit, like Reggie."

'That was how it worked in the East End back then, a good-looking young girl and a man several years older. And I knew Reg well enough to know that he'd want someone who was outstanding to look at. So that when he walked into a place, she was on his arm and they'd be a pair close to perfection.'

In those days, Flan, a stunning leggy blonde, was also well known as a local beauty. 'So as girls do, I checked her out carefully. And she was immaculate, just a straight pencil skirt and a sweater. But not a hair out of place.

'I went straight into hairdresser mode: "Oh you must be Frances, I'm Maureen," I said. "D'you ever wear your hair up?"

'"Yes, in a pleat," she said shyly. Well, we all had that hairdo. Upswept hairdos were all the rage.

'"Before I go, I'll put it up for you," I promised her.

'I could see she was shy. I suppose she didn't like to say no. She just nodded.

'She seemed a bit timid. But she had a lovely smile. Then I did Mrs Kray's hair, put the rollers in. When I'd finished I said, "Sit here Frances and I'll put your hair up."

'What I noticed was you had to keep talking to her to

get a response. And when you asked her a direct question, she seemed a bit cagey when she answered you. Like I'd just been to see Steve McQueen and Natalie Wood in a film called *Love with the Proper Stranger*. I'd been telling Mrs Kray how handsome Steve McQueen was, so I asked Frances, "Have you seen that film?"

'"I don't go to the cinema," she said.

'That was a bit unusual. All young girls of her age went to the cinema. I was only a couple of years older than her but it felt like I was ten years older. Later, I realised that Mrs Kray talked to her as if she was about ten.'

After a while, Flan noticed something else about the young girl.

'The other funny thing I noticed that first time was she seemed fixated on the clock.

'"What time is it?" she said after about an hour – even though she was wearing a watch. It was about 9 p.m. "What time do you think Reggie will be here?"

'This went on constantly. It was obvious she was worried about when he was coming back.

'As I did her hair, she asked again. I kept thinking, "Why do you keep asking the same question?" It was very odd. If he left her there at 8 p.m. and said he'd be gone for a couple of hours, why bother to ask? You could see that she was depending on him coming back for her. It was strange. It was as if she was worried he was going to leave her there.

'I did a lovely pleat at the back for her, with a bun on top. Lots of backcombing and lacquer of course. Then she looked in the mirror. Silence. You couldn't tell if she liked it or not.

'Then she asked Mrs Kray, "Do you think Reg will like it?"

'"Of course. It looks lovely," Violet assured her.

'I thought to myself, "What about you, do you like it?" It was all about Reg.

'To me, she seemed like a very nervous girl. I'm quite good at drawing people out. But whatever you said to her, you could see it wasn't just shyness that made her so reticent. She seemed to live on her nerves. Maybe she'd been like that before she knew Reggie, that was her personality.'

The next time Maureen went round to do Violet's hair, she asked her why Frances had kept asking about the time.

'I think she thinks once he's gone out of that door with Ronnie, he's never coming back,' Vi said.

Maureen Flanagan said she was convinced that by that time, Frances sensed danger whenever Reggie went out with Ronnie.

Which was pretty accurate. Ronnie had a very dangerous presence; there was no question of that. It was part of what made the Kray twins so charismatic, yet so feared.

An insensitive or less-thoughtful girl might have chosen to believe Reggie when he reassured Frances, time and time again, that his twin was really a lovely person underneath the scary menace. However, Maureen's account makes it clear that Frances was already troubled by the dangerous aura around Ronnie, long before they married. Instinct alone told her he was a seriously malevolent force. He scared the life out of her. And there was no mistaking Ronnie's rejection of her very existence. He couldn't hide it and didn't care to try to.

'She might have been naive and vulnerable. But she would have known straight away that Ronnie didn't like her, was jealous of her taking Reg away from him,' said Maureen. 'So every time he left the house with Ronnie, leaving her with his mum, that's what would have been what was going through her head.'

But if Frances was starting to be scared a lot of the time, Reggie too was feeling edgy. Ronnie never let up with the sneers and taunts to Reggie about Frances when he was with his twin. It all made for a very tense atmosphere at Vallance Road.

One night, Reggie took Frances to the Hirondelle cabaret club, just off Regent Street, where they had dinner and watched a floorshow. Frances wanted to go home afterwards but Reggie insisted on looking in at Esmeralda's.

It was quite late by then. Both twins were seriously drunk, Ronnie even more so than Reggie. A sly comment from his twin and Reggie, who'd managed to restrain himself until then, flipped, lost it. A vicious fight ensued, typical of the kind of scrap they'd been having all their lives, though this time they didn't hit or roll around on the floor battering each other. They just screamed insult after insult at each other. Verbal abuse of the worst kind. Frances, terrified and unused to the volley of violent abuse, burst into tears and ran into the ladies' loo. By the time she came out, Ronnie had staggered off into the night, still muttering evil threats to his twin, reminding him what a useless, sick bastard he was. He'd had it with him.

Ronnie then left Vallance Road and moved into a luxury flat in a thirties' block in Cedra Court, Clapton, but the change in their day-to-day living arrangements didn't really alter the twins' relationship very much. No matter how violent their exchanges or rows, Ronnie was always going to be able to hook Reggie in, and to push him towards extremes.

Yet witnessing the row had triggered something in Frances: it brought it home to her, in no uncertain terms, that all the smart clothes in the world, all the beautiful trinkets or the trips to glamorous places couldn't hide the fact that she had unwittingly become a part of the underworld, a hidden realm where violent men schemed, fought, swore vengeance, drew blood and where fear, that sickening terror she felt inside every time she saw Ronnie's face, was running the show.

She hadn't been completely blind to what the Krays represented, certainly. It was impossible not to know, anyway. Everyone talked about them in the East End, though she'd noticed that these days very few people asked her anything at all about Reggie or their courtship: now she was known as Reggie's girl, people were too scared to probe – in case she ran back and told him they'd been asking questions.

Now Frances was starting to see for herself where her place was within the twins' world: a pampered doll, controlled by an intense, possessive man who wanted her to be influenced only by himself.

She'd gone along with it. Hadn't she left her job, stopped work because he said there was no need for his fiancé to have to work, that he'd take care of everything? He wanted to own her – and keep her to himself at all times in a beautiful, gilded cage, someone to take out and show off, certainly, as a partner for the successful businessman he believed he'd become. Yet socially, as far as other people were concerned, she was a no-go area: Reggie's property.

She'd speak up, tell him what she thought. Then would come promises galore that they'd leave the cage, build a dream home in the suburbs, have their own life one day, away from Ronnie and all the 'taking care of business' distractions.

Reggie would do everything in his power to reassure her of all this. They'd had some lovely weekends together at the family's caravan in Steeple Bay, Essex, just the two of them. Then, Frances felt they were like any other normal couple, but most of the time Reggie inhabited that other world, the gangster world of smoky pubs, bars, nightclubs and extortion through fear, the only world he felt comfortable in. With his scary twin.

Reg knew all too well how much Frances hated the endless barhopping. Yet he continued to drink to excess, surrounded by his minders most of the time. When he took Frances out at night now, there were always the hangers-on, the people who wanted to keep in with the twins, sucking up to Reggie, wanting his approval, paying their respects. People said they had everyone in their pocket: the law, the press, nothing could touch them. 'Well-known businessmen' the press called them. The journalists didn't care to describe them otherwise.

She'd spend hours getting ready, carefully choosing her outfits, making sure her hair was perfect, on their nights out – yet it was wasted energy really, because it was impossible to relax or feel comfortable with him when they went out to pubs or nightclubs.

Reggie would be constantly jumping up all the time, moving around the place, shedding largesse and instilling fear in equal amounts. She felt isolated, shut off from the rest of the world.

The consequence of all this was the rows between them that started to be a regular occurrence. They usually began when they were on their way home from a night out or after she'd spent an evening in the kitchen at Vallance Road, waiting for Reg to come home.

That was her life: waiting for Reg to finish whatever it was. It was too much, she kept telling him. It wasn't a life she wanted. Sometimes she'd be defiant, determined: it's over, she'd tell him, and run out of the car, climbing the stairs at Ormsby Street, falling on her bed sobbing, resolute that she had to finish with him for good.

Then there'd be a day or two's silence, and he'd turn up again, all promises and apologies. Huge bouquets of flowers like she'd never seen. More jewellery. A beautiful gold bracelet. A necklace with a small diamond at the bottom, prettier than anything she'd ever owned.

Then, under the intensity of his persuasion, his insistence that they had a wonderful future to plan, she'd relent, in the way women do when, deep down, they still want to believe in their man, hoping for change – even if everything was starting to point to the contrary. And all the time, there was a nagging question at the back of her mind. Suppose she did break off with Reg for good? Who was going to dare to start coming round Ormsby Street to take out 'the Kray bird'?

It was so frustrating. Reggie insisted he loved her. He'd say it all the time. So why couldn't he see that love meant being together, sharing everything, not dumping her there at the kitchen table with his mum while he went out with his twin?

Violet, Frances sensed, wasn't really her ally. She saw no wrong in her twins. She seemed to lap up the glamour around them, thought everything her boys did was marvellous. She was so proud of them. Oh no, there was never a word of criticism from Vi's mouth. Not like Elsie, who'd make her disapproval known if she saw or heard something she didn't like.

In fact, Violet Kray was very well versed in domestic politics. To Frances, she was outwardly maternal, because that was what her Reggie wanted. Underneath it all, she didn't really think this girl was good enough for her Reg, he'd yet to find one that was. She looked good. But she didn't seem interested in cooking or doing things for her man. She just sat there. Looking nervous.

Maureen Flanagan remembered a night out at the Astor Club with the Kray family: 'Charlie Kray, the twins' brother, invited me. Vi was going too. I didn't want to come with my husband so it was agreed with Charlie that I'd accompany Vi. I told my husband I was going out with the girls.'

Maureen and Violet dressed to the nines for their night in Mayfair. Mrs Kray was immaculate in a beautiful blue dress with a fur stole, Maureen in a slim sheath with a little mink bolero. They were driven to the club in one of the twins' cars, by one of their minders.

'It was obvious Violet had been there before,' remembered Maureen. 'We all sat at a little round table. We'd been told that Lita Roza [a successful popular singer of the fifties] was going to be singing. Freddie Mills [a very well-known boxing champion who later committed suicide in highly suspicious circumstances] came over to say hello, then we were joined by Charlie with two male friends.

'Then Reggie came in with Frances. She was perfect. She had her hair swept up with a sleeveless blue brocade tight dress just to the knee and a mink stole, the kind with all the tails hanging down.

'I thought to myself, "You never went out and bought that, Reggie's got it on loan for the night, just to make sure you look as smart as his mum". Mrs Kray's stole was white mink; Frances's was dark brown. Then Lita came on and started singing: she too had the same upswept hairdo.'

About a half an hour later, Maureen said, Ronnie turned up with a driver.

'Then from nowhere Ronnie's fave boy of the time came in.

But he didn't sit with us. Everyone kept coming over from the other tables to pay their respects to Vi. That was the twins' rule. If you come to our table, you show respect to our mother.

'What I noticed about Frances before, at Vallance Road, was she was wearing these little white fabric gloves, with little stones embedded in them. The more nervous or agitated she got, the gloves would be off, on the table, but she'd be twisting them around. That night at the Astor I noticed she was doing it again. The gloves were pale blue to match the dress. The more people came to the table to say hello, pay their respects, the more she'd be twisting those blue gloves around.

'Reg noticed. At one point he put his hands over the gloves as if to calm it, his hand over her hand and over the gloves. So she'd stop twisting them for ten minutes. But if he got up and left the table to talk to someone, it would start again.

'The table-hopping was quite a Mafia style thing, going over to say hello to the other wives and girlfriends. But the minute he got up she'd be "Where you goin', Reg?"

'He'd just give her a lopsided smile and say, "I'll be back." Then he'd look at his mum as if to say, "Take care of her". Once he left the table, you could see she was on tenterhooks. The minute he was back, she'd look relieved. "He's back, everything's okay."

'I think the story was, he didn't really want her to go anywhere without him. He didn't want people stopping her, asking her questions. He was probably quite charming when they were on their own. Because his twin wasn't there. Yet he didn't want to leave Frances with her family, so it was always Mrs Kray.

'I always used to say to Mrs Kray, "Don't you think Reggie's a bit overprotective?"

'She didn't disagree with me but she said, "Look how people come up to me all the time in the street. 'Oh, Violet, how's the boys?' Frances wouldn't be able to handle that."

'I must admit, Mrs Kray was very clever at handling people. She'd turn the questions round. Charlie was the same way. He looked like a movie star and he could talk to anyone, turn it round to "'Ow's your little boy, then?" deflect the attention away from the family, what the twins were up to. Charlie and Vi both had fantastic memories. So anything anyone told them about themselves they could remember and bring it up.

'Violet knew her son was overprotective, but she also knew Reggie didn't want Frances to have friends. Anyone who might have had influence with her against him, he didn't want her anywhere near them.

'I would have gone out with her. I actually asked Mrs Kray one day if I could take her out.

'Mrs Kray said no. "What about the cinema?" I pushed. The answer was always no.'

And so Frances started to worry more and more. Underneath the fear, the nervy gestures, she was beginning to wonder what would happen to her without him. She was stunning, no question of that, her hair longer, nestling on her shoulders, making her look more luminous, especially when she gave that smile. Yet the dazzled young teenager, awestruck by the travel, the perfumed glamour of the West End clubs, the smiling, bowing maître d's had gone. For good.

Alone in her bedroom at Ormsby Street, she'd go over it again and again in her mind: how could they have any kind of life together if there were always these guys around them? Let alone even thinking about *him*, the mad twin who hated her. Well, the feeling was mutual. He was a fat pig.

As for Reggie, he veered between his attempts to placate Frances whenever they rowed and a growing conviction that Frances herself was not responsible for all these arguments and critical outbursts. Permanently suspicious of others having any influence or control over Frances, he decided it was her family, namely Elsie, who was turning her against him.

Not a man to relinquish an idea, the suspicion of Elsie soon developed into something quite sinister. Elsie Shea, he decided, was his enemy. She and she alone was poisoning his beloved Frankie's mind against him. She'd already wound him up when she insisted on him returning the engagement ring he'd bought Frances, saying she didn't like it. He'd fumed. But he'd still gone off and changed it. But Elsie didn't like that, either.

'He bought Frances a little dog, Mitzi,' recalled Rita Smith. 'But her mother wouldn't have it in the house.'

If Elsie had already made it clear this relationship was not to her taste, Frances's brother was totally distracted by his own concerns. Frankie Shea was in love. He'd met a beautiful dark-haired girl, Lily, nicknamed 'Bubbles'. She worked in a club and they'd become an item. By the summer of 1962, Lily was expecting his child. Yet though he welcomed the idea of fatherhood, Frankie couldn't seem to stay out of trouble, or avoid getting involved with the wrong people, usually in robberies. Sometimes he'd wind up in court and get off but at one stage his involvement in a warehouse break-in led to a six-month prison sentence, because the judge decided to make an example of him. For Elsie, the only good news that year was that she'd be a grandmother. Frances too was thrilled at the idea of a new baby in the family. She loved kids. Little Kimmie, Rita's girl, was a real favourite.

Frances went on three trips abroad that year. In April 1962, there'd been an eleven-day cruise, which took in Majorca, Gibraltar, Algeciras and Morocco. Then in August, a friend of Reggie's drove Frances and Reggie down to the south of France for a holiday.

According to Reggie, who recalled the holiday in his memoir, *Reggie Kray's East End Stories*, the couple had a major row while sitting outside a bistro.

At one point Frances told him: 'You're nothing outside the East End. You're not known here in France or anywhere else in the world', a retort meant to wound but a truth, nonetheless, that no one else would have dared to pass on to Reggie. This was hardly the remark of a cowed, intimidated young woman. Frances was nervous as hell within the edgy framework of Vallance Road or any place where Ronnie might appear. Away from this environment, however, she'd deliver home truths in no uncertain terms. She'd always been honest with him, right from the start. It was one of the things he'd always liked about her.

For Reggie to repeat these words nearly half a century later and commit them to print is remarkable. Though in the book he claimed his response to her remark was to spur him on towards an ambition: to be known 'in a circle much larger than my own'.

In September, Frances went on another holiday, to Spain. Rita Smith recalled Reggie sometimes paid for Frances to go on holiday to Spain with friends. 'He trusted her there. But while she was on holiday with her friends, that's when she started taking purple hearts.' These street drugs were hugely popular with young people in the early sixties, and were a combination of amphetamine and barbiturate.

According to Rita Smith, when Reggie found out Frances had been taking purple hearts he went mad: 'He found out who was supplying them and he never supplied her again. Or anyone else.'

It may well have been on the Spanish trip that September that Frances first started experimenting with drugs, though the remarks Reggie made in his letters from prison make it clear that she'd mentioned trying slimming tablets before that. Reggie, of course, knew about drugs because he took them himself: he'd pop tranquillisers such as Librium from time to time. Or take purple hearts. Such drugs were proliferating throughout London by the early sixties, easily acquired in the pubs and clubs of the East and West End by anyone.

If young people weren't smoking hashish or 'grass' (marijuana) they were popping the pills so easily bought for very little cash; in fact the idea of taking drugs as a recreational high was fast seeping into the culture. Certainly, the Kray twins had ready access to any kind of prescription drug they wanted. Yet when and where Frances first sampled illegal street drugs – and what they were – must remain open to question. Rita's assertion that Reggie couldn't stand the idea of Frances taking purple hearts is, yet again, another indication of the control he wanted to exercise over every aspect of her life. Don't do as I do. Do what I tell you to do.

Consider all the actions and words Reggie relentlessly deployed to control the woman he believed he loved above all else. In view of this, would it be that surprising if Frances did, by then, feel so hemmed in by the trap she was in that she started believing that drugs or pills were, in some way, a fairly reliable means of switching off from the increasing fear she felt so much of the time?

People use drugs to change or distort their reality, often because they can't deal with it. Alcohol can do it. Pills can do it in a different way.

For Frances, maybe it would simply have been easier at times to just blot out the reality and let the drug take over...

CHAPTER 6

PRELUDE TO A MARRIAGE

Christmas is an odd time of year; sometimes it brings out the best or the worst in people. It's a time for sharing joy, celebrating with children, loved ones, friends. Yet it can also be a point when suppressed emotions or tensions that have simmered away through the year explode unexpectedly as the year draws to an end. Rows. Recriminations. Ultimatums. Just days before Christmas 1962, Frances and Reggie had the worst fight they'd ever had.

Reggie was now spending more time than ever with his twin. Frances was distressed and angry about the way 'The Ronnie Factor' was affecting any time she did spend with Reggie.

It wasn't right, she argued. If they planned a night out as a twosome, time and again plans would be unexpectedly changed to include something involving Ronnie. They were never ever alone. Everything seemed to revolve around

Ronnie, the Firm, his friends, their mum. What was the point of them being together?

Reggie's tack, as usual, was to tell her she was completely wrong about it all. It was Frances's mother that was to blame, whispering poison in her ear, putting her against him and his family, who really liked her. Elsie, he insisted, didn't want them to be happy together, to have a good life. She was being mean, spiteful, putting her daughter off him.

Frances defended her mum as best she could.

But the nineteen-year-old, already Reggie's girlfriend for four years, knew all too well how unhappy her parents were about her seeing Reggie Kray. The frosty atmosphere at home told the story. It just hovered there all the time. Elsie could dish out the silent disapproval treatment sometimes, and somehow that chilly silence was just as bad as any talk about how she disliked Reggie or any of the Kray clan.

Frances stood her ground with Reg. She meant it. It wasn't anything to do with her mum and dad, she argued. It was her. She'd had enough of always having minders around them, let alone the endless sitting around waiting for him to finish whatever he was doing. They should break off. She wanted her own life, not this.

This time it was Reggie's turn to drive off in tears when they finally said their farewells. In his usual persistent way, he pushed her to agree they could still keep in touch. But okay, perhaps it was time they had a bit of a 'break' from each other.

Early in 1963 there was some good news at Ormsby Street: Frankie Junior's girlfriend, Lily, had given birth to a baby girl, whom they'd promptly named Frances, after her father's sister.

With all the excitement of the new arrival in the Shea

family and her own determination to stick to the break-up plans, Frances felt vaguely hopeful that some sort of happier, different future lay ahead for her. She'd seen and done a lot with Reg, but she knew, deep down, she wasn't really a person who was cut out for that kind of life, sitting around in clubs and bars. She really liked Reg's cousin Rita, who seemed to understand her, and she adored little Kimmie. But going to Vallance Road scared her, mostly because of Ron. Wouldn't it be nice, she fantasised, to be with someone who didn't have this big gang of people around them all the time? Or who had a pleasant brother or sister she could get on with?

Yet within a couple of months, the penny dropped: if she wanted a new boyfriend, she'd have to find a very brave man indeed. And she was unlikely to meet anyone who could take her out and about the way Reg did.

'At that time, most young men of her age would have at best money that would have bought a new suit every year, rent money, beer money and a week's holiday in a caravan on the Isle of Wight,' explained Dick Hobbs. 'Reg brought Hollywood. Also, what young man would have fancied following Reg? Hardly anyone actually knew the Krays. They were a rumour, a kind of vague dark threat. Sniffing around Reg Kray's ex would have been a risky venture.'

Frances liked the same things most girls of her age did. She wasn't a tomboy; she liked dancing, reading women's magazines, checking out the latest fashions, getting her hair done. She went out sometimes with her girlfriends, kept up with her shorthand studies – she'd been going to college to learn this – and tried to live her life normally without the permanent spectre of Vallance Road. Yes, he told her, Reggie missed his 'living doll' (an endearment he used after the title of the Cliff Richard hit song of 1959). He was in touch frequently. They talked. As was his way, Reggie was intense, consistent in his utter fixation with his beloved Frankie. But he didn't push too hard. Truth was, he had plenty of other things with which to occupy his time.

The twins' empire had spread beyond the West End and out into the provinces. The Barn, however, was no longer a pot of gold. It was now rapidly losing money and Ronnie, helped by their canny friend Leslie Payne, moved the base of operations for the Firm to a big restaurant called the Cambridge Rooms, on the outskirts of London. Then, in another typically flamboyant gesture, he'd gone out and bought a 1,000-guinea racehorse, Solway Cross, for their mother (a guinea was one pound and one shilling). At one gala evening at the Cambridge Rooms, Vi generously donated the horse in a raffle: cue more newspaper photos, more publicity to demonstrate the boys' generosity. (Solway Cross, alas, never won a single race.)

In private – and in complete contrast to all this craftily conceived image polishing – Ronnie's violent impulses continued to scare the life out of everyone on the Firm – and to horrify his twin.

One night at the Cambridge Rooms, Ronnie went on a vicious knife-slashing spree, slicing open the face of an associate he believed had insulted him. Doctors had to put in seventy stitches to repair the man's face. The police knew about it. They were ready to spring, to arrest Ronnie. Frustratingly, the injured man remained silent. Reggie's speedy move to warn everyone who'd been at the Cambridge Rooms that night that they'd be better off staying silent too did the trick: frustratingly, the police didn't have a case.

That autumn there was another horrific incident at The Barn

when a demented Ronnie branded a man along each cheek. Very soon after this incident, the twins quit Esmeralda's Barn for good. For Reggie, the ever-present worry that Ronnie was becoming so dangerous that he might wreck their livelihood seemed to be taking on a life of its own. It was so hard to restrain Ron.

Yet in the midst of all his woes, Reggie eventually convinced Frances to start seeing him again.

Frances's passport showed no record of any trip abroad in 1963. Nevertheless, Reggie often told everyone that they'd gone to Milan, Italy, that year, visiting La Scala, the famous opera house to see the opera, *Madame Butterfly*.

This romantic trip is mentioned in several books about the Kray twins, including Reggie's own memories of their time together.

Yet not only was there no passport stamp for any country visited in Frances's passport for 1963, there were no entry stamps for Italy at all in her travel document. (This was several years before Britain went into the Common Market, a time when all British passports were clearly stamped by any country the holder entered.)

Did Reggie simply tell everyone the romantic tale that he'd taken Frances to see the opera in Milan?

It would be tempting to believe this. But a letter written to Frances by Reggie in December 1963 contains a puzzling clue that there might be some veracity in the Milan story. This letter indicates that the on-off relationship was back on by the end of 1963.

At that point, Reggie was in eastern Nigeria, in a place called Enugu. He and Ronnie had visited Nigeria twice that year on business trips involving a housing project – the general idea was that they would invest in a development there, though the scheme never went beyond these two trips. However, while they were there they were treated like VIPs and lavishly entertained by their hosts.

In the letter to Frances, Reggie described Enugu as a 'desolate place, very lonely'. Then he informed her he'd already bought her a crocodile handbag and the following day he'd be getting her a new bracelet. He'd have phoned her at her brother's place, he said, but he didn't know whether she'd be there.

Why was Reggie calling Frances at her brother's home? Perhaps the Sheas didn't have a phone at Ormsby Street at that time. Or was the phone call to her brother's home indicative of a degree of secrecy on Frances's part: that is, she didn't want her parents to know that she was seeing Reggie again?

The letter made it abundantly clear that as far as Reggie was concerned, nothing had changed, he still wanted them to marry. He'd really missed her and thought how nice it would be once they were married, so she could accompany him to 'most places' – though he wasn't too sure about Nigeria. The letter also mentioned Milan. But there was no indication she'd been there.

'I missed you when I was in Milan too,' he wrote. 'Have you missed me? You'll have to let me know when I see you.'

The Nigeria letter also indicated that Frances was still harbouring doubts about their relationship, that she had hinted that a different type of girl might be more suitable for him (which was obviously the case).

Reggie wrote that he'd been thinking about her saying to him 'such-and-such a girl would suit you better'. But he wouldn't want her any different, he assured her. Physically and mentally, he told her, she suited him fine: 'So let's not have any more of that talk.'

The letter ended with Reggie saying how he was looking forward to seeing her. He'd be glad, he told her, 'to see your beautiful brown eyes again'.

By the beginning of 1964, the police were beginning to take a very serious interest in the day-to-day activities of the Kray twins. Scotland Yard had started to investigate their various frauds and the West End protection rackets. Then, startling information started to filter through to them about Ronnie's high-level friendships with certain politicians, in particular Lord Robert Boothby, a high-profile Conservative MP, and Tom Driberg, a senior Labour party MP who was openly gay.

Both men relished living dangerously. 'Rough trade' (a tough or violent homosexual partner) was their idea of fun, particularly for Driberg, who blithely ignored the risk of being exposed as a homosexual when in pursuit of sex, often with strangers. The two of them loved the idea of consorting with scary Ronnie, the East End thug and gang boss. In particular, they enjoyed socialising with him because of the coterie of handsome young men Ronnie always had grouped around him.

Before long, a newspaper reporter with strong links to Scotland Yard was told of the police's interest in the Krays, and on 16 July 1964, a newspaper story appeared in the *Sunday Mirror* which mentioned the police investigation (without using the Krays' names) as well as informing its readers of an existing photo 'on their files' of 'a well-known member of the House of Lords on a sofa with a gangster leading London's biggest protection racket'. For legal reasons, the article didn't actually name Boothby and Ronnie, although foreign magazines, less restricted by British libel laws, did – alongside photos of the Kray twins as young boxers. The genie was about to come out of the bottle. Or so it seemed.

On 2 August, Lord Boothby wrote a letter to *The Times* identifying himself as the politician on the sofa – and denying all the allegations of any kind of relationship with Ronnie Kray.

No, he wasn't homosexual and yes, he had been photographed with the man in question but he had no idea of the man's criminal history, even though he had met the man 'on business matters' three times in the company of others.

A few days later, the *Sunday Mirror* carried an apology to Boothby – and the paper paid Lord Boothby £40,000 in compensation, a huge sum of money for the times.

Yet the story in the paper had been true. Boothby had blatantly lied. He was bisexual, he'd known Ronnie – and exactly what he represented – for over a year and the consequence of the whole affair was a huge establishment cover-up at the highest level.

The police, who had already put a case together against the twins at the time of the *Sunday Mirror* article, promptly stopped investigating them. The press could not write about them freely because of the huge compensatory sum paid to the *Sunday Mirror* and all its implications of legal action if reporters persisted in exploring the Krays' crimes. What this all meant was that the twins, through Ronnie's friendship with these MPs, had won a form of immunity from any attempt to stop them or to write about their activities – and Ronnie's violence. This was to last for nearly four years. No one, it seemed, could touch them.

Ronnie arranged for the photographs of him and Boothby

on the sofa in the lord's flat to be passed over to the *Daily Express* newspaper picture desk.

By 6 August 1964, the world knew, without any doubt, that the gangster in the scandal was Ronnie Kray, one of the Kray twins, via the *Express* photo. Fame at last, beyond the East End. Everyone now knew who they were.

One compelling aspect of the on-off state of the Reggie-Frances relationship at this point is the story I heard, in some detail, from a man now in his early seventies. He had briefly courted Frances for a couple of months during the early part of that summer of 1964.

At the time, he was twenty-one, about six months older than Frances. An apprentice in the print trade, he lived with his family above a pub in nearby Islington, run by his father, who had various business interests. He and his brother had grown up in relatively working-class surrounds, yet they were not restricted financially. Early twentysomethings with jobs, cars and money to spend, they enjoyed the good life: back then, of course, an inner-London publican's status in the community was high and involved a very good, above-average standard of living.

The young man was, like so many fashion-conscious youngsters at that time, able to afford the £25 handmade mohair suits, Italian shoes and expensive shirts that were de rigueur for the growing numbers of working youngsters on the periphery of the huge cultural explosion that was starting to take place in the capital. He'd already taken holidays abroad. On nights out with girlfriends he could afford to splash out on posh restaurants in the West End. Yet he was no tearaway or chancer: his father, acutely aware how easy it was for young men then to 'go wrong', made sure his sons toed the line and avoided any kind of trouble.

As a result, he was a cautious young man who determinedly steered clear of any hint of violence. He wouldn't even go into a pub on his own. He'd heard of the Kray twins, such was their reputation. But he'd never seen them in person – or even in print.

He had first met Frances in a Wimpy bar on the Kingsland Road in May 1964. He'd gone in there with a friend after a drink in a nearby pub. They spotted two girls around their age, sitting at a nearby table. One was a stunner: shoulder-length blonde hair and the most bewitching pair of brown eyes he'd ever seen. His friend, bolder and a bit more outgoing, immediately started chatting the girls up.

As an opening line, the friend asked the stunning-looking girl with the beautiful eyes if her eyelashes were real or false.

No, she said, they weren't false.

The friend, eager to get something going, insisted they were.

'OK,' the stunning girl said. 'Pull them and see.'

Laughing, he duly obliged and, of course, they were real. The ice was broken. They were in. The boys moved to the girls' table.

The girl with the beautiful eyes was, of course, Frances. The young man from Islington was hooked, there and then. At the time he'd been dating a girl, nothing serious, but he was totally smitten by Frances. His friend didn't drive so it was relatively easy to offer everyone a lift home – and to drop Frances off last.

That spring night, he parked his Austin A35 around the corner from the Shea home and the pair started to get to know each other. He managed to get Frances's phone number and they stayed chatting in the parked car for quite some time.

As he remembered it so vividly, the girl with the beautiful

eyes was bright, lively and gave no hint of being nervous or shy in any way. She did briefly confide that first night that she had 'a lot of problems' but in those days, the man said, that phrase was a catch-all either for boyfriend trouble or problems with parents. He didn't probe further, mostly because he was too fascinated by this girl to ask any searching questions. He just wanted to be around her.

'Perhaps I'm your knight in a green van,' he quipped. But she said no more about her problems.

There was, he knew, a definite attraction between them. They kissed and cuddled briefly. Then, in the quiet, darkened street, they heard a car driving past them. Very slowly. As if someone was patrolling, watching the van. Sure enough, Frances sat up in her seat, tried to see outside. But, because the van had no side windows, it was impossible to see very much. When he asked her what was wrong, she brushed it off. Nothing was wrong. She'd better go. Tomorrow was a work day. He walked her to her front door. Yes, she said, ring me. They could definitely go out the following Saturday.

What followed were a series of prearranged dates, usually on a Saturday night, when the young man would drive to Ormsby Street to collect Frances and take her out to various places around London. He remembered taking her to a riverside pub in an area called Strand on the Green near Chiswick, where they lingered by the Thames, enjoying the long, balmy summer evening. On another occasion, he escorted her to the Criterion Theatre in Piccadilly to see a play called *A Severed Head*, based on a book by Iris Murdoch.

This was a sophisticated sixties hit about middle-class marriage and adultery. Frances really enjoyed the play, loved going to the theatre, he said. In fact, she seemed, to him at least, quite 'arty' in her tastes. She'd also told him she liked flamenco dancing and a black blues singer called Champion Jack Dupree.

I'd already discovered Frances's love of poetry. The man's memories of Frances tallied precisely with this: here was an imaginative young woman who appreciated creativity, the arts – once beyond her teens, was it any wonder she'd grown disenchanted with Reggie's routine of superficial nightclub glitter and celebrity-cum-criminal gladhanding? Certainly, he'd opened her eyes to the world around her with those early trips when she was still quite impressionable. But that was partly because she was a curious girl, wanting to know more about everything. Yet now, here she was at twenty, at her most stunning, lively and eager to enjoy everything sixties London had to offer – despite the ever-lurking possessiveness of Reggie. She knew all too well she was being watched, stalked. But why should it stop her from enjoying her life?

The man had been aware that they were being watched by someone in another car whenever he parked his van near Ormsby Street after they'd been out for the night. Yet he didn't talk to her about it.

Curiously enough, he said Frances had obviously wanted to 'test' him, see what he knew about her stalker. On one occasion, the Krays had come up in conversation and, eager to impress, he'd lied, told her he'd seen them in a pub one night. The next time they stepped out together, she'd produced a photo of herself with a dark-haired older man.

'Do you know who this is?' she'd probed.

No. He'd shaken his head, made a quip, saying, 'Oh, is that your boyfriend?' No response.

Frances then knew her new escort had lied about 'seeing' the Krays. He obviously had no idea what Reggie Kray looked like. So he hadn't a clue that he was in the danger zone, taking out the girl Reggie believed was his and his alone. Had the young man known, given his abhorrence of violence, he'd have run for the hills there and then. But ignorance, at that point, was bliss. Or close to it.

Another revealing insight from these memories of Frances came from the man's recall of meeting Elsie and Frank Senior, when he'd go to the house at Ormsby Street to collect Frances.

He met them a few times. They were always extremely pleasant to him. In fact, he got the distinct impression that Elsie was very keen on the idea of him as a suitor for her daughter. Back then, a man who 'came courting' a pretty young daughter, even briefly, had to run the gauntlet of parental approval, ask politely what time the parents wanted their daughter home. Chivalry still held sway in the East End. This young man sensed that he ticked all the boxes for what Elsie wanted for her child: polite, respectable, well dressed, around the same age, a hint of affluence – yet clean-living, not a boozer or a gambler. Dead straight. No history of violence.

Considering the animosity now reaching boiling point in Ormsby Street around the on-off presence of Reggie Kray in their lives, this young man must, to Elsie at least, have seemed a saviour, a longed-for safe landing far away from Kray control.

Frank Senior, the young man thought, was pleasant enough, though he didn't say much. But it was Elsie who obviously welcomed his turning up in Frances's life. So much about the on-off Reggie relationship was distressing and scary for her. Yet

Elsie Shea was still hoping against hope for the respectability she so passionately desired for her beloved daughter.

The overall impression, he told me, was of a pretty ordinary family setup. Perhaps the Sheas weren't as well off as his family – but they weren't poor, either. They kept a dog, a little black mongrel, a vicious animal that was quick to react to the presence of a stranger. Elsie and Frank, like many of their generation, holidayed locally: Frances told him that they regularly rented a summer chalet at Jaywick in Essex, a popular holiday venue for East End families in those days.

Frances met his family, too. One of his most vivid memories was the night he took her to a big family party in south London. There, she'd met his parents, his cousins, aunts and uncles, and they'd all got along famously, laughing and joking, one of those parties where everyone let their hair down, had a good time.

Frances had been a big hit that night, looking exceptionally gorgeous in a sleek outfit topped with a cute beret with her hair in a plait, Bardot style. Not only were all his male relatives agog that he was escorting such a lovely girl, everyone seemed much taken by her warmth and friendly manner. Later, one of his cousins told him he'd thought, at the time, that she was somehow quite different from other people. Not just because she was good-looking, mind you. Just different. Special.

This description, of course, sits in complete contrast to the Frances described to me previously: the socially mute, nervous and troubled young woman sitting in the kitchen at Vallance Road or the immaculate, impassive girl on Reggie's arm in the nightclub.

What is there to conclude from this disparity in these observations of the real Frances? Perhaps it is quite simple: her fear and nervousness around the Kray setup built up around

Ronnie's impossible-to-ignore aura of danger – not around Reg himself.

In another environment, away from anything relating to the twins and their relentless routine revolving around their mother, their pubs, their Firm and their club activities, she could just be herself: a warm, lively girl who relished a normal family environment, as had been already noted by Reggie's cousin, Rita Smith. Rita's family setup in Vallance Road represented that ordinary, desirable world to Frances. Yet there was nothing really 'normal' about the goings-on in the Kray house next door.

At one point at the party, the young man recalled one of his male cousins coming up to him and insisting one of their uncles urgently wanted to 'have a word' with him in the kitchen. Off he went. But there was no sign of the uncle in the packed, noisy kitchen. When he'd finally fought his way back through the throng, there was his cousin dancing away with Frances. Cheeky sod.

He never derived any impression, he said, that Frances was pill popping or taking drugs, nor did drug taking crop up in conversation. Frances, he said, wasn't even much of a drinker, just the odd glass of wine. Ciggies were restricted to one or two during an evening out. But he did recall that, at the time he knew her, she said she was going out to work each day. Despite the fact that she'd initially given up working, at Reg's insistence, during the summer of '64, Frances was working in the offices of a photographic agency in nearby Clerkenwell. It wouldn't, after all, have been very difficult for her to pick up another office job: any young, intelligent, girl who already had some experience in office work in London would easily find another job during the full employment of the mid-sixties.

There was really only one dark hint at the tragedy that lay ahead. At the time, the young man hadn't stopped to think too hard about it. Though he did think it was a bit odd. In one of their long conversations, Frances told him, quite emphatically, that she neither wanted nor hoped to grow old.

'I'm never gonna grow old,' she told him. Was this a chilling prophecy? Or was it, as the Tennyson poem had hinted, a compulsive attraction to the idea of death and suicide?

On more than one occasion, the young man took Frances out to dinner in a Spanish restaurant, Antonio's, in Covent Garden. Even here, in the busy heart of the city, he couldn't help but notice the effect Frances had on people. The first time they had gone there, the maître d' had guided them, with great indifference, to a badly placed table in a corner. Yet, the next time, he'd rushed to offer the pair the very best table by the dance floor. The staff, too, made a huge fuss of them second time around. It didn't quite add up. Only years later did he ponder this and conclude that it might, just, have had something to do with Reggie. Perhaps the maître d' thought he was 'minding' Frances for him. With the Kray reputation in London, such things were not impossible.

Usually, their nights out would end with a heavy-petting session in the car. He knew, he said, right from the off that Frances was a 'nice' girl and was unlikely to go any further than what he described as 'a bit of tit'. He figured that, like many girls of her age then, she was a virgin who expected to stay that way until marriage. Of course he tried. He wasn't an experienced guy – he'd lost his virginity a year or so before – but it had happened only once and, human nature being what it is, he would attempt to go a bit further each time with Frances, only for his hands to be pushed away.

There was one memorable Saturday night with Frances, however, that adds considerable poignancy to the story. That night, he didn't have his car because he'd damaged it in a minor accident. They'd gone out for a meal and arrived back at Ormsby Street by taxi at around midnight. Then Frances invited him into the house. It was deserted. Elsie and Frank had gone down to relax at the little chalet in Jaywick.

At the rear of the house, Frances ushered him into a small spare room. It had a bed in it, though it obviously wasn't her bedroom. For a few hours, they lay on the bed, kissing and cuddling, lost in each other, while the mad black mongrel, locked outside at the back, threw himself at the door, scratching and barking his head off.

It was late June and, of course, it started to get light very early. At which point, the young man realised he ought to head off home.

'You're only going because you can't get what you want,' Frances told him.

This was far from the truth.

'No, it's my parents – they expect me to come home,' he told her.

And so he left the Shea house and walked home through the deserted streets in the early dawn, thinking of the beautiful girl he'd been so close to, still hardly believing his luck that he'd been the one to take her out, show her the town, kiss and caress her afterwards. Yet he was ever so slightly troubled by something he couldn't quite put his finger on, a sense that, despite her welcoming parents, their happy times together, their growing closeness, he wasn't getting the full picture, that there was a presence hovering somewhere in the background, something or somebody he didn't care to know about.

Despite the smart clothes and the superficial panache, he was still quite an innocent sort of guy. It was easier for him to push those puzzling thoughts to the back of his mind. Frances Shea was gorgeous in every way. She was definitely the most charming, delightful girl he'd ever encountered. Who wouldn't want to take her out?

A week or so later, he rang her. He'd been given tickets by his boss to a West End play. Would she like to go next Saturday? Yes, she said. He could pick her up at about 6.30.

On that warm July night he had turned up dead on time at the doorstep at Ormsby Street, spruced up, primed for Saturday night out. Yet she didn't open the door as usual in response to his knock.

He knocked again, puzzled. Then he could hear a lot of noise. Screaming. Shouting. Carrying on. Baffled, he stood there, frozen, not quite understanding. Could all this noise really be coming from her house? Yet, the more he listened, the more he understood it was most definitely coming from the Shea house. What to do? Go to a callbox and try to ring her? Or should he just keep waiting outside?

Yet his dilemma was quickly resolved. The upstairs window went up and a head came out. Not Frances, but Elsie.

'She's not here!' Elsie snapped. She didn't look happy.

'But we're going out!' he said, utterly perplexed by the unexpected turn of events.

'She's not here!' Elsie repeated. Then the window went down. To add insult to injury, the vicious black mongrel appeared, ready for the kill. This time it went to bite him. Hard. Later, he realised that it had managed to make a hole in his treasured Chelsea boots.

Perhaps if he'd been a different type of lad, he might have

kept trying. But he reasoned that, if Frances really was there, she'd be okay. Her mum may have lied, sure, but she was there, in the house, to protect her daughter.

Maybe, he mused, as he walked along the Kingsland Road, there really was another boyfriend and the shouting had been about the boyfriend wanting to come out and confront him. That was how his young mind worked. It was definitely best, he reasoned, not to get involved. So home he went. He was seeing another girl anyway. And he was looking forward to his holiday in Majorca in a few weeks' time.

The young man from Islington never attempted to contact Frances again. Only the following spring, when he saw the newspaper stories about her marriage to Reggie Kray, did the penny drop about her hints to him of 'problems' and about the driver who was stalking them as they sat in his vehicle. Yes, it was a terrible shock to learn that she'd been Reggie's girl all along. And, of course, when he read about what happened to her afterwards, he was utterly devastated. By that time, he was a happily married man.

Yet her memory haunted him for many years, though he kept his story to himself.

It wasn't just her beauty, her lively charm: it was her vivid self-expression. Again and again, down the years, he remembered himself in his youth, sitting in the car with her, entranced, while she told him how the bright red glow of a lit cigarette made her imagine a cosy, snow-covered cottage, its inhabitants safely inside, warming themselves before a glowing fire. She could, he said, find poetry in something as mundane as a lit ciggy. Her beauty wasn't superficial, on the outside. Not at all.

As we look back at the dates when the Kray story exploded in the national newspapers for the first time, it becomes clear that the mystery of what was happening in Ormsby Street the night of the denouement of their friendship must have been a direct consequence of those Kray stories in the nationals. Once they landed on the nation's breakfast tables, the Sheas were now confronted with the nightmare fact that everyone, not just the people in the East End, knew about the Krays.

Ronnie, of course, relished the exposure: he wanted the world to know them, now they were 'untouchable'. Reggie, despite all his efforts, couldn't stop his twin from his crazy path. Yet, that August, Reggie would have made a seriously determined effort to lure Frances back to him. Sure, he'd been unable to stop her from seeing other men. Yet, with his ever-persuasive skills, he could still hook her back in.

What is so baffling about it all is that Frances, after all previous efforts to push Reggie away, now drifted towards him again, despite all this. She had resisted. She knew all too well she could attract someone safe and respectable. Yet at this point, after the stories in the nationals, she became a luminously beautiful player on the twins' stage. Did Reg convince her that everything would be fine now, there'd be no more talk of police and prison, they were in the clear? Or was it simply the terrifying threat that the twins now openly represented that prevented her from trying to escape from their world?

But if Reg was so determined to have Frances, what of Ronnie? Tragically, his power over his twin, his ability to draw him closer, away from her company, seemed absolute by then. He was a paranoid schizophrenic whose illness was barely under control – given the huge amounts of alcohol he imbibed along with the powerful drugs he needed for his illness. Knowing that he could do whatever he wanted because he was now 'untouchable' was essentially a death knell for an unsuspecting victim.

Now, only the chance to prove himself to the world as a killer, a fearful warrior, would satisfy Ronnie's bloodlust. As his twin's murderous impulses started to take over his entire existence, Reggie remained, as ever, in the same dreadful situation: compelled by their blood ties to try to protect his brother from himself, yet still cherishing his fantasy of a life away from Ronnie. Pushed one way, then the other, Reggie still believed that he could make an 'escape', via the marriage he'd been talking about for so long.

His generosity to Frances knew no bounds. As an engagement gift he'd got her a stunning red Triumph Herald sports car, a very fashionable car in the sixties – John Lennon was seen whizzing around London in such a vehicle at one stage. Frances couldn't drive but lessons were duly booked. She had a couple of lessons, then edgy, paranoid Reg took umbrage at something the driving instructor said and Frances, quite sensibly, decided it wasn't worth the hassle. Reggie adored the idea of his Bardot lookalike sitting behind the wheel of a snazzy motor. But not the reality of another man sitting next to her, guiding her through the Highway Code. Or worse.

That November, the couple went on a two-week holiday organised by Reg to southern Spain and Gibraltar. This time, the opportunity to get away from it all and spend time together nudged Reg and Frances closer. There were still separate hotel rooms, and, just like on their other trips, guys from Reg's entourage hovered in the background. But as they wandered hand in hand around the strange, exotic narrow streets together, Reggie eager to buy Frances whatever took her fancy – especially the cute little Flamenco dancer dolls she'd started to collect on their travels – their conflicts and rows seemed to have abated. She was still very much his beautiful princess. And he was so proud of her. Once he married his Frankie, Reggie told himself, everything else would fall into place. Her parents weren't going to stop him. How could they?

But just a month later, something happened to stop everything in its tracks. Ronnie and Reggie were unexpectedly arrested at the Glenrae Hotel, Finsbury Park and remanded in custody.

A certain Detective Chief Inspector, Leonard 'Nipper' Read was determined to bring the Kray twins to justice, and to end their reign as London's most feared criminals. Then, as luck would have it, a significant, if somewhat weak, opportunity to bring the twins down came his way. This chance for Read became the catalyst to a series of events – and, effectively, these led to the sealing of Frances's fate.

It all focused on a man called Hew McCowan. He ran a drinking club in Soho's Gerrard Street. It had been called the Bon Soir but McCowan had recently taken it over, done it up and renamed it The Hideaway. He came from a classy, well-heeled background and he knew the twins. At one stage, they'd approached him for a loan for the ill-fated Nigerian project. But McCowan wasn't interested in putting money into the venture; he wanted to put his money into The Hideaway. Very soon he'd made contact with DCI Read and what he had to say interested the man nicknamed Nipper very much.

Hew McCowan told him that the twins had attempted to muscle in on The Hideaway, demanding a 50 per cent share of the profits. This was perfectly normal for the twins – but the admission to police that the Kray twins had tried to cut themselves in on the deal was an incredibly bold one for a club owner to make. Normally they were far too intimidated by the twins' reputation to report their attempts at extortion to the police.

Yet, frustratingly, there was nothing to back up McCowan's story. Until an incident at The Hideaway in January 1965, when a friend of the Krays, 'Mad' Teddy Smith, attempted to smash the place up, demanding money from the club owner. Smith wanted everyone at the club to know that he was acting on behalf of the Kray twins. The money, he screamed, was for the twins.

Police arrested Smith at the club and on 10 January, they hauled in Reg and Ronnie. The trio were accused of demanding money from Hew McCowan with menaces. No bail would be permitted.

The twins' response was to pull out all the stops to show the law they were, indeed, untouchable. From Brixton prison, they hired the best, most expensive lawyers in London. They also hired a private detective to dig up any dirt, if possible, on McCowan – and find out more about the prosecution witnesses.

Later, the twins would claim on BBC TV to have spent many thousands of pounds to prove their 'innocence' and there are stories that, in fact, Ronnie's friend Lord Boothby, flush with cash from the *Sunday Mirror* apology, had lent him money to fund their defence. Whatever the truth of this, they certainly wanted the world to know they had run up a huge bill.

With Reggie now in Brixton Prison and determined to be released quickly, Frances wrote to him almost daily. Yet again

Reggie wrote back that the time had come for them to embark on that happy married life together in the 'burbs. Yes, once this was behind them, they'd definitely get married, Frances promised Reggie.

How come he'd now managed to convince her to commit herself? They'd been more off than on in the previous year or two. She'd tasted a little bit of freedom. But she'd had her twenty-first birthday the previous September, a landmark occasion and, possibly, with that came a realisation that with no one else on the horizon, Reggie was, for better or worse, her most likely spouse to be.

By the East End standards of the times too, Frances had hit the 'on the shelf' situation. Girlfriends were already married, expecting their first child. Social pressure, in other words, must have played a significant part in her thinking. And being an aunt to baby Frances or spending time with Rita's little Kimmie had awakened a strong maternal impulse: Reggie wanted children, he'd told her so many times.

'Reggie loved children,' recalled cousin Rita Smith. 'He used to say to me, "Don't babies SMELL nice?" He would have loved kids.'

Maureen Flanagan recalled going round to Vallance Road for Mrs Kray's weekly session with the rollers and hairpins around this time. She remembered Violet being quite definite that a wedding was on the cards very soon: '"Oh, Reggie will definitely marry her," Mrs Kray would say. "When he comes out, they'll do it. She's a lovely girl, doesn't want anyone but Reggie." Mrs Kray obviously felt the wedding was inevitable.'

In Brixton Prison, the twins pulled out the stops to secure bail. They even offered £18,000 as surety and audaciously got their friend Lord Boothby to ask questions in Parliament about their imprisonment. But in prison they remained. Finally, a trial date was set for 28 February.

The jury couldn't agree. So there had to be a retrial. In the meantime, the private detectives had done their work: they'd dug up some juicy information about Hew McCowan: years before he had been involved in a number of cases involving homosexuality; there were also hints that he was a police informer. As a result, he was discredited as a witness. And the case fell apart. The jury gave its verdict: not guilty. After two months in custody, on 5 April, the Krays and Teddy Smith were free men.

Just over an hour after the twins left the dock at the Old Bailey, Reggie was being publicly greeted at the front door of Fort Vallance by Frances. As his twin climbed out of the fawn-coloured Jaguar that had transported them home, Reggie hugged Frances and told the waiting press how happy he was to be back with his sweetheart. 'All we want now is a bit of peace and quiet,' he told the *Daily Mirror*.

Soon they were joined by the proudly beaming Vi, her dad 'Cannonball' Lee, chirpy in his braces, their neighbours, relatives, friends – everyone smiling, all over the moon that the boys' innocence had been proven once and for all.

Outside Fort Vallance, Frances cuddled their little dog, Mitzi, and posed, somewhat diffident, for newspaper photos alongside Reggie. Her hair was now a reddish blonde and shoulder length, her pretty, loose Indian cotton smock-top a bang up-to-the-minute fashion statement. Yes, they were getting married. Yes, it would be very soon.

For that brief moment in the mild spring sunshine, it seemed Frances had convinced herself that somehow Reg's dreams of their golden future were becoming reality. They'd fought, they'd waited, but now they could have their happiness, her and Reg. Briefly, her fears of Ronnie and her 'bad nerves' seemed to have been put to one side. On that day, at least, Reggie Kray appeared to be her knight in shining armour. But was he? Or had Reggie merely told her that she had no choice: if she didn't marry him there would be trouble ahead for her family?

Three weeks later, she was his wife. And in a vengeful gesture so typical of the twins, they rubber-stamped their court victory in the McCowan case – by buying into The Hideaway Club – and renaming it 'El Morocco'.

Nonetheless, even in that short time before the wedding the dark storm clouds were already looming over the two East End families.

Up until then, Elsie had made no attempt to hide her feelings. Now, she was furious, already embittered at the prospect of her family being in any way linked to the Krays. No, she told her daughter, she couldn't marry Reggie Kray.

Again and again she ranted to her husband, saying she didn't want Reggie Kray, that scum of the earth, as a son-in-law. Elsie wasn't fooled by any of it, all the hypocritical, two-faced posing with film stars and celebrities such as Judy Garland, when everyone knew they went round knifing people, doing terrible things to anyone who stood up to them or got in their way. She hadn't brought up her daughter up to wind up living as the wife of a criminal with a mad twin, someone who would always be in trouble with the law, in and out of prison. Frank Senior sided with her: the wedding could not, would not happen.

Frances had heard it all long before now. She said very little, switched off, put all her focus into the big day, choosing the dress, working out how she'd do her hair. Initially she'd told

Above: Frances strikes a sultry pose: the beautiful girl who looked 'just like Brigitte Bardot'.

(© Louise Potts)

Below: Reggie and Frances on a Spanish holiday in April 1962. *(© Louise Potts)*

Above: The twins and their older brother, Charlie: jailed for his part in their crimes, Charlie never aspired to follow their path of violence and intimidation.

(©*Getty Images*)

Below: 1965: the couple pose for the cameras after the Hew McCowan trial with Mitzi, the dog Elsie Shea refused to have in the house; weeks later, they were man and wife.

(©*Pat Larkin/Associated Newspapers/P*)

Above left: April 1965: Frances arrives at the church with her best man, brother Frankie Shea. Frankie lived to regret his youthful relationship with Reggie.

(*©Daily Mail/REX*)

Above right: Just married: leaving the church in Bethnal Green. (*©Daily Mail/REX*)

Below: Outside the church, flanked by friends and family. Violet Kray is on the xtreme left and just behind Reggie are Charlie's wife, Dolly, and behind her 'sie Shea.

(*©Jack Manwaring/Daily Sketch/REX*)

Left: The wedding reception at the Glenrae Hotel, Finsbury Park.

(*©Getty Images*)

Right: Frances and Reggie on honeymoon in Athens – unhappy and tense after the wedding night that never was…

(*©Newsteam*)

Above: El Morocco, April 1965: amidst a sea of celebrity-strewn glamour, Frances (far right) stares ahead bleakly. Next to Frances are Reggie's mother, Violet, and Charlie's wife, Dolly, with actors Adrienne Corri and Victor Spinetti to the right of Reggie. Reggie, his hand on actor Edmund Purdom's shoulder, looks at his wife sadly. (© *Getty Images*)

Below: El Morocco, April 1965: unimpressed by actor Edmund Purdom's attention, Frances reaches for her cigarettes. Newly returned from Athens, she'd already told Micky Fawcett that Reggie hadn't laid a finger on her while they honeymooned. (© *Getty Images*)

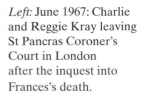

Left: June 1967: Charlie and Reggie Kray leaving St Pancras Coroner's Court in London after the inquest into Frances's death.

(*©Dennis Hart/ Evening News/REX*)

Right: July 1997: thirty years later, Reggie's second wife, Roberta, on their wedding day at HMP Maidstone, Kent.

(*©Times Newspapers Ltd/REX*)

Above left: Frances's memorial stone at 'Kray Corner', Chingford Mount Cemetery *(pictured at foot of this page)*. Her parents fought to have her remains transferred to a different resting place – to no avail.

(*©Alex Woods/REX*) (pictured at foot of this page © *Dean Houlding/REX*)

Inset: The gravestone of Frances's beloved brother Frank Shea. (© *Jacky Hyams*)

Above right: The twins' final resting place. Their legend lives on…

(*©Dean Houlding/REX*)

The doomed couple today. Frances (played by Australian actress Emily Browning) on her wedding day, and with Ronnie (Tom Hardy, who plays both twins) on the set of *Legend*, the new film about the Kray twins and their lives during the sixties.

(© *Splash News/Corbis*)

Reg she wanted a quiet do, something low-key, even modest. But as usual, he'd overruled her wishes, told her it had to be a big affair, a major event. Of course she had to be married in white, in a traditional wedding dress. Everyone in the East End would want to see 'the wedding of the year'. The Krays were famous. It had to be a big wedding, a media event, no matter what.

Her brother Frankie kept quiet but he knew his mum and dad were right. His kid sister was bright and lively, she wasn't on the take all the time, in it for the glamour, what she could get. He knew that.

But he also knew all too well you didn't cross Reg or Ron or get in their bad books. They had incredible memories, both of them. The twins never forgot a bad word spoken against them. They had their 'spies' everywhere, running back and forwards with titbits of information. They'd always lash back at you if they heard you'd started trashing them. Or get someone else to stitch you up somehow. He knew their power. But Reg was good to his sister, wasn't he? Frankie told himself, somewhat unconvincingly.

Word soon got round Bethnal Green that the Sheas were telling everyone they were going to stop the wedding.

'My husband's brother told me, "The Sheas are going to do everything they can to stop it. They think Frances is under Reggie's spell, she's bewitched by him,"' remembered Maureen Flanagan.

Naturally enough, the next time Maureen went round to Vallance Road, she mentioned it to Violet.

'There's bad blood from the Sheas, Vi,' Maureen told her.

'It'll be alright on the day,' was Mrs Kray's response. 'They can't stop the wedding.'

She was spot on. The loss of face for the twins if the big *Hello!*-style wedding didn't happen exactly as they wished didn't bear thinking about. Maureen couldn't help but wonder what Ronnie Kray, let alone Reggie, would do to the Shea family if it didn't happen now. The event itself was going to generate huge amounts of positive publicity for the twins.

'Even though he didn't want it to happen, Ronnie Kray couldn't allow it not to take place,' continued Maureen. 'Imagine what people would be saying about the twins if the wedding didn't happen after all?'

Elsie Shea, however, wasn't the only person to let it be known that she didn't want the wedding to happen. One man, neither family nor criminal, was very definitely against the idea of Frances and Reggie taking their wedding vows. And he made his feelings known to Reggie in no uncertain terms.

Unknown to Frances, Reggie had already booked the church, St James the Great in Bethnal Green. He very much wanted the twins' childhood friend and supporter, Father Hetherington to marry them. Yet when Frances and Reggie went to ask the priest to officiate, they got a shock.

No, said Father Hetherington, he wouldn't be prepared to marry them. In fact, he said, he was hoping they wouldn't go through with it at all. The much younger Father Foster could marry them.

Years later, the author John Pearson talked to Father Hetherington at his Rectory in Ealing, West London after his retirement.

As he wrote in his book about the Krays, *The Cult of Violence*, Pearson had asked Father Hetherington what his reasons were for refusing to marry Reggie and Frances.

'Because they'd simply no idea of what marriage was about,' said the priest. 'Not merely was there not the faintest hope of either of them finding happiness together, but I could see them causing serious harm to one another.'

Reggie respected Father Hetherington, so no matter how much he had wanted him to officiate, he accepted what the priest told him and asked Father Foster to conduct the ceremony.

Yet the wise priest's words were eerily prophetic. How well he understood that this marriage, born mainly out of Reggie's desire to escape his destiny and present himself to the world as a normal, respectable man with a beautiful young wife, was never going to be anything other than a fake, a farce in every way.

Frances was already apprehensive, but she couldn't have known just how accurate Father Hetherington's prediction was. Reggie was lost in delusion. Ronnie wasn't for his twin's marriage in any way. But he knew his other half's vulnerability where their twinship was concerned, felt confident he could always hook him back in, no matter what. That silly cow wasn't going to come between him and Reg.

As for the Sheas, they were helpless now, up against the combined might of the Kray twins' reputation and their ability to manipulate everyone and everything to their own end. They had every reason to feel fearful for their daughter's future.

The day of the wedding, 19 April 1965, was overcast and chilly. The promise of early spring and the sunshine of a few weeks previously seemed to have vanished.

That morning, Maureen Flanagan jumped into her little Mini and drove round to Vallance Road to do Mrs Kray's hair.

Maureen really wanted to go to the wedding, see it all for

herself. But her husband, no fan of the Krays, would never accompany her.

'This was the 1960s and I was married to a man with a ferocious temper,' says Maureen. 'I couldn't get away with sneaking off to the wedding because everyone knew that the wedding was going on and that I knew the Kray family. So I couldn't go behind his back.'

Inside the Vallance Road house, Maureen found the usual pre-wedding flap. Charlie Kray Senior plodded down the stairs, fiddling with his necktie, muttering that he didn't like it. Mrs Kray was in her dressing gown, wanting her hair to be done before donning the wedding outfit. A celebratory glass of sherry was handed to Maureen.

'Mrs Kray said Frances was getting her hair done at home,' she remembered. 'She had a school friend called Pat who was going to get her into the wedding dress and do her hair.

'I sat there with the rollers and portable hood dryer next to me on the table and got busy with Mrs Kray's hair. Charlie – The Old Man – was still moaning about his tie when Ronnie marched in.

'"Oh, so this wedding's going to take place then," he said, half laughing, but mostly sarcastic.

'"Don't start The Old Man off!" snapped Vi.

'You could see her husband was already getting on her nerves,' Maureen went on.

'"She's told me all about the dress," confided Vi. "It's satin, really lovely."

'Apparently it was going to be a long dress, very traditional, very beautiful,' recalled Maureen.

Mrs Kray continued to gossip. The Sheas hadn't wanted the dress, oh no. But Reggie had insisted. This had all gone back to Violet who told Frances, 'Wear what you like. Whatever you like, Reggie'll like.'

Finally, a long spray of hair lacquer and Mrs Kray's immaculate hairdo was in place. Maureen finished the little glass of sherry, packed up her vanity case and started to leave.

'As I was on the way out,' she recalled, 'Charlie Kray was still reassuring his father that the tie looked nice, Ronnie was muttering, "Weddin'? Wot's 'e wanna get married for?"

'"Oh Ronnie, don't start," I remember saying to him at the door. "He loves her. And your mum's happy." Then I drove off.'

The following week, when Maureen went round to do Violet's hair, she showed her the wedding pictures.

'"Ronnie looked fed up all day and all evening, then he left," Vi confided to her.

'"What about if they move to the country and get a house?" ventured Maureen.

'"Oh no, they'll never be apart. The boys will still be working together," Mrs Kray assured her.

'I went through the photos, but to me Frances wasn't the smiling, lovely bride I saw every time someone came into the salon to show me their own wedding pictures.

'Reg was smiling in a couple of photos. But not a lot. Charlie and Mrs Kray were smiling. But she was the least smiling bride I'd ever seen. They were peculiar wedding snaps. To me, she just looked... nervous.'

CHAPTER 7

THE WEDDING OF THE YEAR

Half a century on, we can look at some of those wedding photos and judge for ourselves. There are the images of Frances as a young bride, retained by the National Portrait Gallery in London, taken by the world's most famous photographer, David Bailey, an East End boy whose fame was already soaring sky high in the sixties.

The wedding photos – the only time in his entire career that Bailey photographed a wedding – were Bailey's gift to the couple: he already knew the Krays as fellow East Enders. And it was Bailey's studio images of the twins, taken before the wedding, which went on to play a huge part in projecting their myth as crime icons of the era. ('I liked him [Reg…] Didn't like Ron so much – I avoided him 'cos a slip of the tongue and you'd be fucking dead,' he told the *Independent* newspaper in February 2014.)

The National Portrait Gallery photos showcase a poignant

image of Frances in full close-up. Her big dark eyes are carefully, yet heavily, made up to enhance their pools of liquid beauty, her shy half-smile to the camera innocent yet somehow disarming, the gold-and-diamond pendant around her neck serving to emphasise her purity.

True to form, Bailey captured the essence of Frances at that precise moment: a very pretty, virginal young girl on the threshold of marriage, a truth encapsulated in a split second.

Bailey's wasn't the only camera recording the event, of course. The newspaper photographers and reporters crowded the street outside the red brick Bethnal Green church, primed in advance.

The convoy of special guests climbing out of the Rolls-Royces and Daimlers included sporting names of the sixties, British featherweight champion Terry Spinks and his wife, Lennie Peters (the blind singer), renowned stage director Joan Littlewood, glamorous blonde movie star Diana Dors and, according to the newspaper reports, a number of very big men called 'Big Pat' and 'The Dodger'. A hundred telegrams of congratulation had been sent to the couple, the *Daily Express* reported enthusiastically, including one from Ronnie's good friend, Lord Boothby. (Ronnie's other chum from Westminster, Tom Driberg MP, also turned up to join the other guests celebrating the wedding.) David Bailey arrived at the church in a blue Rolls-Royce. He was wearing a velvet suit.

The nervous bridegroom shunned the hired Daimler waiting outside his childhood home and made the short journey from Vallance Road to church on foot. The bride left Ormsby Street in a maroon Rolls-Royce, a short veil framing her face and perfectly coiffed upswept beehive hairdo. The dress that Reggie so wanted was a stunning confection of ivory satin and guipure lace. The perfect bride.

Inside the church, the bridegroom's side was jam-packed with friends and relatives of the Kray family, Violet and Charlie's wife Dolly both immaculate with sleek hairdos and elegant outfits. On the bride's side, just a handful of people sat there with Elsie and Frank Senior, glum and straight-faced, Elsie in a dark velvet outfit, her sober attire yet another reason for the hypercritical Reg to despise his mother-in-law: how dare she dress dark on his golden day? If it was a deliberate attempt to make a point, it worked.

And the atmosphere? Heavy as lead. Ron's unpredictable nature combined with the well-documented events of the past six months did not exactly make for a laid-back setting.

'It was a curious mixture of celebration and tension,' recalled Cal McCrystal, who was, at the time, part of the *Sunday Times* prestigious 'Insight' team, along with fellow journalist Lewis Chester. They'd been invited to the wedding by the twins because they had interviewed and written about the Krays on a number of occasions, one of the interviews resulting in a legendary piece of *Sunday Times* journalism titled 'The Charitable Life of the Brothers Kray'.

Because the press were, by then, so heavily restricted in what they could write about the twins' activities, Chester's legendary piece had been cleverly worded so that all legal obligations were fulfilled, but the knowing reader could read between the lines, as it were, and understand some of the truth of the Kray twins' notoriety.

'It was all innuendo,' recalled McCrystal. 'Which the twins missed.'

McCrystal noticed that the tension in the Bethnal Green church that day was quite different from the organisational tension you sometimes sense at weddings.

'It was the tension of people who were very uneasy,' he said. 'There was no feeling of gaiety about it all.'

This became very obvious when the organist launched into the traditional marriage hymn ' Love divine all loves excelling'.

Not a single wedding guest joined in.

'No one was singing. It felt like very few of these people had even been inside a church before,' said McCrystal. 'Ronnie, the best man, kept looking over his shoulder from the front pew. Reggie seemed content to just sit and wait for the bride: he looked like a well-groomed waiter, as did Ron. Ron kept shrugging his shoulders with impatience. Kept turning round and glaring at everyone. Which was very disconcerting.'

'Then, because no one was singing along to the hymns, he suddenly yelled out, "SING, FUCK YOU, SING!" Unfortunately that coincided with a break in the organ music. So they all heard it – and tried to obey Ron by making throaty noises.'

Minutes later, Frances entered the church, on the arm of her brother Frank, clutching her posy of blood-red rosebuds. She seemed calm, placid. Frank Junior looked as sleek and groomed as ever, in his well-cut suit and narrow dark tie, if somewhat sombre. In this, at least, Elsie had held sway: Frances's dad would not be the one to give her away.

'To me, she was a very demure lovely looking woman, the white veil, the ivory-coloured dress,' remembered McCrystal.

Then he spotted two familiar faces behind the altar rail: David Bailey with writer Francis Wyndham, holding Bailey's flashlight aloft: 'I hadn't realised they would be there too. In retrospect, of course, having us all there symbolised the twins' love of being "in society".'

There were no dramatic moments in the ceremony itself; it continued in the same muted, slightly sombre vein with the Reverend John Foster officiating as the couple exchanged their vows. (The young priest had recently been called as a defence witness for the twins at the Hew McCowan trial.)

There was no triumphant march down the aisle from the happy couple, flashing big grins to both sides in the 'wow, we've done it' mode of the usual wedding tradition. Husband and wife appeared stilted, self-conscious beyond the church rituals. The best man continued to look exceedingly uncomfortable. More newspaper photos were taken outside the church. There was no joy or sense of celebration. It was a media event, no more, no less.

Then everyone climbed back into the big flash hired cars and headed for the reception at the Glenrae Hotel, Finsbury Park, the same place the twins had been arrested earlier that year.

Here the gloom lifted slightly; there was a palpable sense of relief that the deed had been done, as everyone posed for the obligatory family album photos taken by Bailey. As a party, it was as lavish as any of the twins' usual big bashes, a social potpourri of high and low life (mostly low), as much food and drink as anyone could humanly consume in one evening, and a live band. Later that afternoon the couple were driven off in their hired Daimler. Athens was the chosen honeymoon destination.

Elsie and Frank Senior farewelled their daughter and returned home with heavy hearts: they'd been powerless to stop what they knew was a farce. What sort of life would their daughter face now?

Rita Smith vividly remembered feeling overwhelmed by the crush of so many wedding guests, all of them strangers.

'I went to the reception with my mum and dad for a while, then mum wanted to come home,' she recalled. 'There were a lot of people there I didn't even know, to be honest.'

In fact, few knew it but the potential for wedding-day trouble had not been far away that morning.

Yet it came from an odd direction: a girl from Mile End had been coming round to Vallance Road in the previous weeks, claiming that she had given birth to Reggie's son.

'She would knock on Reggie's door with the child, and the little boy was platinum blond – Reggie's hair, of course, was black,' remembered Rita. Vi would just say, "Who is she?" and tell her he wasn't there.

'On the wedding day, the twins put a couple of minders on the church door, just in case she turned up with the little boy. But she didn't.'

(This was not the only paternity claim in Reggie Kray's history. There was another two years later [see Chapter 8]. Even a few years before he died, a woman claiming to be Reggie's daughter visited him in prison. Her mother, she told him, had had a brief affair with Reggie when she worked at the Double R, yet went on to marry another man, who had raised her as his own. The truth of these stories remains unknown.)

Albert Donoghue was, at the time of the wedding, a member of the Kray Firm and Reggie's right-hand man. Eventually, in 1969, when Ronnie Kray tried to make him the fall guy for the shooting of Frank Mitchell, this led to Donoghue becoming a Crown witness and testifying against the twins. (Donoghue received a two-year prison sentence for admitting to harbouring Mitchell before he was killed.)

'I was Reggie's man,' recalled Donoghue, now in his late seventies and living in an Essex care home. 'We didn't use the word minder or bodyguard then. Where Reggie went, I went. I watched his back, if you like.'

Donoghue missed the wedding itself but as he recalled it, the wedding photos he saw afterwards told him much of the real story. The event, as far as the twins were concerned, was all about their image. The bride was a mere accessory...

'Later, I looked at the photos and I saw everything Frances must have seen: dozens of good reasons to take a lot of pills. Where most people's wedding photos are filled with Mum, Dad, Auntie Mary and other young couples, these were dominated by big flat noses wearing buttonholes.

'The reception was packed wall-to-wall with scar-faced thugs. She could not have missed them. Frances was getting the drift of what was going on, even then. She tried to look happy. She managed a smile. But what's a smile? You can sit in a dentist's chair and open your mouth. And it looks like you're smiling. But you're in agony.'

Only those wedding day photos of Frances and Reggie give any indication of their feelings on that day in April 1965. As Donoghue said, a forced smile is just that. Reggie, for his part, looked nervous on many of the photos. Though this is hardly unusual: on so many photos of Reggie with Frances during their courtship he seemed to have a similarly tense, buttoned-up expression. Or, in some of the nightclub photos he just looked... very inebriated.

But what about their honeymoon? Black-and-white Athens' sightseeing photos at the Acropolis showed an unhappy, uncomfortable couple, completely at odds with their surroundings – and with each other.

Her immaculate beehive hairdo, heavy eye make-up, neat attire, his somewhat incongruous shirt and tie and their troubled facial expressions reveal an unhappy, uncomfortable pair of sightseeing honeymooners. Athens too was a bad choice: the ancient city was rundown, still in the throes of civil and economic unrest. Unlike Spain, which was already gearing up to a giant wave of tourism in the early 1960s, it held little attraction then for tourists or East End couples like Reg and Frances.

The honeymoon couple stayed in an Athens hotel from 20–28 April. Reg went out drinking most nights, often leaving his bride alone in their hotel. A series of diary entries in Frances's own handwriting chronicle some detail of their troubled marriage, presumably written to demonstrate the truth of Reggie's treatment of her and her reasons for wishing to divorce him.

It is a very troubling document, detailed in the following chapter, and it relates to what happened between them after the honeymoon.

However, there is one brief line in her account about that honeymoon week in Athens. It reads: 'honeymoon sex about three'.

Certainly, this could be interpreted as having sex three times – but it could also mean there were three attempts to have sex, given what Frances told others after they had returned from honeymoon.

Frances, at twenty-one, was not in any way a sexually experienced girl. She came from a background where sex before marriage was still frowned upon – and, like many girls then, she wanted to be a virgin on her wedding night. She had been with Reggie on and off for more than six years. But they had never lived together or even shared a bed on their numerous trips away. It had always been separate rooms.

This was the mid-sixties and huge social changes were already underway in 'swinging London', including greater sexual freedoms for some women. Yet in most parts of the UK, including the East End, despite the fashionable short skirts and the immaculate bouffant hairdos, women remained still pretty much where they'd always been: tied to the bonds of family and marriage.

Divorce was complicated and far too expensive for ordinary people. In places like the East End, alcohol and gambling frequently devoured much of the housekeeping money. Women did, mostly, put up and shut up. Ditto for sex. Ditto for domestic violence. All the economic and sexual freedoms now taken for granted today would have been unknown to an inexperienced young girl back then.

Reg, a thirties man to the core, didn't even want Frances to go out to work: it might have implied he couldn't afford to keep her, and dent his image.

The sum total of Frances's sexual experience was limited to foreplay, kissing, cuddling, or 'necking' as it was called then. One of Reggie's early prison letters to her mentioned he had a love bite – presumably from Frances during a prison visit. Later, there might have been times when Reggie pushed the boundaries, persuaded her to bring him to climax through masturbation – 'a hand job' – but given the times and the circumstances, Frances knew little of sex.

Reggie, ten years older, had been around the block, with men and women. Lots of women fancied Reggie. There were frequent one-night stands with women, usually hostesses or prostitutes, before and probably during his courtship of

Frances. And his 'experiments' with men, while covert, had gone on since his teens. Yet none of this means that he was a skilled or considerate lover.

Those early letters from Reggie in prison at the onset of the relationship referred to his affection for her, mentioning cuddling and kissing, so there was obviously normal affection between them at the start, probably heightened by the frustrations of Reggie's incarceration. (As Albert Donoghue pointed out to me: 'Bear in mind that while he was in prison earlier on, he was not in his normal state of mind.') And this was surely true, since the intimacy of those early letters must have deteriorated over time as the relationship changed and Frances started to understand the truth of the situation she was in. The increasing rows and arguments over the years would have changed any genuine affection or warmth she felt at the very beginning, let alone the effect on her of all the very public reports about the twins and their endeavours.

So when it came to consummating the marriage that Reggie had insisted on for so long, all was not as it should have been in the marriage bed. The accounts from those who knew Reggie at the time underline this.

'He'd talk to me about the times when they went to Spain together and I got the impression he did love her very much,' Donoghue recalled. 'But at the same time he told me once that they never consummated the marriage. From the way he talked, he thought it would degrade her. And he'd ask me things like "How do you excite a woman?"'

'I'd say things like "just try to be natural, be yourself, relax." It was difficult to know what to say.'

Micky Fawcett is a retired boxing trainer and author who was a business associate of the Krays in the years between 1957 and 1967. He too said the marriage was never consummated.

In his book *Krayzy Days*, recounting his life and times during those years, he recalled meeting Reggie and Frances just after the Athens honeymoon.

'They both joined me for a drink at the El Morocco. I'd hardly said "hello" before she said in front of him, "Do you know he hasn't laid a finger on me in all the time we've been away?" What do you say in return to something like that?

'Reggie himself didn't sound angry, though, just defeated. "Cor, I'm glad it's you she's told," he said sadly "and no one else".'

Fawcett's account of those years in Krayworld had some other intriguing insights into Reg's relationship with Frances, so he agreed to talk to me at the Mayfair Hotel, in London's Piccadilly.

At our meeting he told me that Frances's remark didn't surprise or shock him at all.

'Once you knew what he was like, the honeymoon, Greece, the David Bailey wedding photos, it was all like... acting,' Fawcett told me. 'I think she said it to humiliate. "Nice holiday? With him? He's fucking useless." That was the gist of it.

'It's a terrible thing to say, I realise it is. But if you knew the level of madness around them, the boundaries that were set... it was just... unusual.'

The comment 'I'm glad she said it to you' was, according to Fawcett, all about Ronnie.

'He wouldn't have wanted Ronnie to hear those words,' he went on. 'Ronnie used to make nasty comments all the time like "You seen 'is bird, Mick? Ain't she got 'orrible legs?" Which wasn't true at all.'

Fawcett told me that Reggie later confided in him that he could have straightforward sex with other women. 'But not Frances,' Fawcett continued. 'He had a bit of a Madonna complex about her, nothing to do with love. In his mind she was a bit of an idol, nothing to do with love between a man and a woman. Somehow he felt she shouldn't indulge in sex. He didn't say it in so many words. And I'd known him to go with other women, hostesses in the West End clubs. But with Frances... it was different.'

Fawcett first met the twins in their billiard hall days, before Reggie started courting Frances. 'I knew there were stories about Reggie being gay. At the billiard hall one day someone said, "You know the twins are gay." I went "WHAT?" Then it sank in. All these younger men around in the billiard hall, of course, they were gay.

'One fella in Bow told me, "Oh yes, so-and-so is Reggie's boyfriend." He didn't want to be known as a gay person, he really didn't want to be gay. But I think it overtook him now and again.'

Before the marriage, Reggie would occasionally ask Micky Fawcett to drive Frances home to Ormsby Street from Vallance Road.

'On one occasion she said to me, "I suppose he's told you that I mustn't talk to anyone. It's ridiculous. All my friends, I'm not supposed to talk to them – because he gets annoyed."'

Micky Fawcett told me about one major incident before the wedding which demonstrated Reggie's fear and paranoia about Frances having anything to do with other men.

One night, a suspicious Reggie had been spying on Frances,

sitting in his car, watching her house. Frances wasn't home and he was very worried. Sure enough, a car drove to her front door late at night and a man dropped Frances off.

Reggie carefully took a note of the car registration. Then he got a dealer friend to identify the owner. Later he told Micky of his suspicions over a drink in the Grave Maurice pub:

'I've got his address,' said Reggie. 'And I wanna do him.'

Micky Fawcett knew what was going on.

'I knew, right away, why Reggie had come to me because he was terrified Ronnie would have found out and driven him mad. The main thing for me was to give him a getout.'

Fawcett promised to sort it out.

'And Reggie let me get on with it. Perhaps, deep down, he wanted only to know that Frances wasn't playing around.'

That same night, Micky was awoken at 5 a.m. by someone knocking on his window. It was Reggie. He couldn't sleep. He wanted Micky to track the man down immediately. Micky persuaded him it was too early and they drove around for a couple of hours. Reggie was still agitated but eventually Micky convinced him it would be better if he dropped him off at a friend's house while Micky went round to the man's address.

'Reggie seemed relieved he didn't need to go himself. His own way of dealing with things would have been less direct than his brother's. But just as violent in the end.'

Micky then went round to the man's house, driven there by a friend. Later he found out that the suspected boyfriend was a car dealer in his mid-twenties. And married.

'You were seen with Reggie Kray's bird,' Micky warned when the man answered his front door.

'He ran back into his house and said, "Tell me through

here", through the letterbox.' recalled Micky. 'He was crying, snivelling, all his nose was running. I'd only said a few words but now you couldn't get any sense out of him. Then I got him to open the door again.

'"It's nearly on you," I said. "Behave yourself in future."'

'I went back to Reggie and assured him that the man driving Frances was the father of a girlfriend, an innocent lift home.

'Reggie said to me: "She ain't pregnant, is she, Mick?"'

'"Wot are you on about, Reg? I've told you, this is wot 'appened."'

'"Are you sure?" said Reggie.'

'"I tell you, this is wot 'appened."'

'And he didn't query it. He was the most sceptical person you ever met who didn't believe anything anyone ever said. But he was worried about what Ronnie would think.'

I asked Micky if he thought there was anything going on between Frances and the married car dealer.

'Definitely. I made up the story I told Reggie, my motive was to quieten Reggie down. And not rock the boat. I knew he would believe what I said. He wouldn't WANT bad news. Or an inquest from Ronnie. She was definitely having some sort of relationship with this guy. I found out later that his wife heard all the commotion and apparently she was told I'd threatened him because he'd been a bit drunk in one of the Kray clubs – a cover-up story. The man definitely had something to hide.'

Micky's story tells us that, despite her fears and nervous behaviour, Frances was not overwhelmingly intimidated by Reggie. She had accepted the attentions of other men before the marriage, surely in the vague hope of finding someone who might be able to release her from the situation somehow.

Her remark to Micky Fawcett about the honeymoon does not indicate someone who was browbeaten or scared of her husband, worried about a reprisal once they were alone. Did she really understand how humiliating such a comment was when addressed to another man? Or was she just too innocent to perceive its impact?

My feeling is she did know it was shaming. Yet the rebel in her, the girl that had told Reggie he'd be better suited to someone else, that he was a nobody away from his own environment, wanted the truth to be out there. Somehow.

Yet the incident with the man giving Frances a lift home took place just before they embarked on the desperately tragic, brief time that was to be their life as a married couple. Here's an outline of what happened once they came back from Athens in those weeks they 'lived together' as man and wife.

Although it is well documented that Reggie rented a furnished luxury apartment for them 'up West' in a big block of flats near London's Marble Arch, and that the couple later moved to a flat underneath Ronnie's flat in Cedra Court, Clapton, Frances's diaries and, much later, her mother Elsie's account of their married life, show that, in fact, they more or less lived like gypsies.

At different times after the wedding they stayed briefly at Vallance Road, in a flat in Chingford (presumably belonging to a friend of Reggie's) and on several occasions, both in London and abroad, Frances was left to stay in hotels alone. As with the honeymoon, the attempt to live as man and wife was a total disaster.

The Marble Arch flat, while luxuriously furnished, left Frances totally isolated. Most days, Reg would go out, leave her in the flat alone, return home to change his clothes, then go out again and return in the wee small hours, very drunk.

Frances had no friends nearby, no job to go to, her entire life was now in the hands of her husband. Very soon, it became obvious that this wouldn't work. Why Reggie decided it would make sense if he and Frances moved into the same block of flats as his twin is baffling: he knew all too well how damaging the undercurrent of animosity between his wife and his twin could be.

Virtually anywhere in London would have been better than Cedra Court. He had the means to pick and choose. But the truth was, Reggie wasn't comfortable anywhere away from his twin. He'd wanted Frances; he'd got her. Now there were three of them in the marriage, a terrified young wife, a jealous, possessive madman who detested the sight of her and an equally intense, obsessive husband. It was enough to send even a stronger woman over the edge.

Yet there was a brief, outward appearance of normality on a social level in this time. Occasionally Frances would accompany Reggie to nightclubs or parties.

But it was the same old routine: the same circle of criminals, minders and Kray hangers-on. Plus a sprinkling of celebrities. There is a *Daily Express* archival photo, taken at El Morocco, days after the couple had returned from honeymoon, which says so much. Reggie, surrounded by well-known celebrities of the day and his proudly beaming mother, are all looking at Frances. She is stony faced, staring ahead bleakly. Reggie merely looks at her sadly, a pained, quizzical expression on his face. Everyone else is smiling. There is the nub of it: Frances had nothing in common with this glamorous bunch – they were not people she could relate to in any way. Nor did she care to make conversation or try to eagerly flatter the celebrities her husband and his twin courted so assiduously. She was no longer the starry-eyed young girl. She was Reggie's missus, his property. Socially she'd clammed up. Not that surprising when you consider that her husband didn't want her talking much to anyone, anyway.

'She was in a situation she couldn't handle,' recalled Freddie Foreman, the 'Godfather' of crime who served ten years in prison for his role in the disposal of the body of Jack 'The Hat' McVitie, and who met Frances many times in the clubland setting.

'She was out of her depth. She used to sit there like a pretty little thing. She could not talk or converse with anyone, it was a different world to what she was used to.'

Foreman too claimed that Reggie was homosexual and thought it unlikely the marriage was consummated.

'He did make the effort to keep her happy. But she was like a trophy to him, someone to have on your arm. I don't think there was any true love there.'

Pampered Frances was, beyond reason. He'd buy her anything she wanted. But she was a prisoner. Sure, she could go shopping whenever she fancied, buy what she liked – as long as someone from the Firm accompanied her.

At the flat in Cedra Court, Reggie made considerable efforts to provide a comfortable home with new furniture and plush carpeting – 'it was beautiful,' Rita Smith remembered when she visited with little Kimmie.

Yet none of this could compensate for the living hell Frances was descending into, the twins' erratic, booze-soaked, criminal way of life.

On the nights when they stayed home at Cedra Court,

Reggie would down his first gin of the evening, leave Frances to the telly and climb the stairs to Ronnie's flat where he'd remain until the wee small hours.

Once in bed, it would be impossible for Frances to sleep without a sleeping pill: the noise from the flat above where Ronnie constantly partied and entertained his friends was unbearable.

Attempting to question or remonstrate with her drunken husband when he finally returned made everything much worse. The rows between them became hideously abusive. What was he doing up there, why was he leaving her all the time? Frances would cry. The answer was always the same: it was her own bloody fault if she was unhappy, she was to blame for everything – her and that mother who hated him, wanted them to be miserable. On and on he'd go, ranting and raving, swearing and shouting, threatening to hurt her, kill her family, until, finally, the taunts would stop and he'd lie down and pass out.

In the past, the rows between them would end with her retreating to her room in Ormsby Street. Now there was nowhere to run.

One night, knowing she hated the sight of blood, Reggie deliberately cut his hand and tormented her by letting the blood drip onto her. It was terrifying emotional abuse for an already nervous and edgy girl.

Reggie must have known, by then, he couldn't have that 'normal' life he so dreamed of, away from Ronnie, as the successful legitimate businessman living in the 'burbs. He couldn't make love to his beautiful young wife for reasons he didn't care to examine, but he still wanted her as his possession, his object of worship, symbol of his success.

The alcohol too played a big part in the equation. It turned Reggie into a monstrous human being, a mass of emotional frustration that could only be expressed in one way – through sadistic, furious, violent rage.

Reggie was one of those people who could drink themselves senseless, yet never wake up the next day with a hangover. No matter how drunk he'd been, how badly he'd scared her with words and threats of violence, in the mornings the demon Reg had vanished. Until the next night…

The late Billy Exley was Ron's bodyguard, a man who also gave evidence against the twins at their trial in 1969. He knew much about the twins and their crimes; he was also at Ron's side at Cedra Court during those weeks when Frances lived there with Reggie.

Exley's friend, Lenny Hamilton, had no reason to be enamoured of the twins: he'd been branded with a red-hot poker by Ronnie Kray in 1962.

Not long after Reggie Kray died in October 2000, the following story appeared in the *East London Advertiser*, 19 October issue:

REG KRAY HAD SEX WITH PROSTITUTE
WHILE IN BED WITH HIS FIRST WIFE

An East End victim of the Kray twins is about to spill the beans on how he says Reggie Kray mistreated his first wife Frances.

Lenny Hamilton, savagely branded with a red hot poker by Ronnie Kray in 1962, claimed Billy Exley, who worked for the Krays, told him of a night out on the town which ended in the bizarre three-in-a-bed episode.

Said Lenny, writing in a new book, *I Was Branded by Ronnie Kray*, 'Reggie and Ronnie returned to the flat in the early hours of the morning. He had left poor Billy Exley behind to make sure that Frances didn't get out of the bedroom and leave the flat.

'Ronnie and his young man retired to Ronnie's bedroom and Reggie, together with a hostess, retired to his bedroom where Frances was lying in bed, out cold from the sleeping tablets they had made her take before they went up West.

'Frances woke up in the morning, unaware of what had been going on in her own bed, horrified at what she was witnessing.'

Lenny went on to tell how she tried to get out of the room to find the door locked.

When she finally did get out Lenny says Billy Exley was forced to watch as Reggie slapped her to calm her down. Eventually Ron came into the room and grabbed Frances as she made a dash for the door.

Billy told Lenny how the twins had got her back into the bedroom and he could hear Ron telling Reg to stuff pills down her throat to keep her quiet, but Billy was in no position to stop the pair, fearing for his own safety.

The shocking incident in this newspaper account, later repeated in *Getting Away with Murder*, a book by Lenny Hamilton and Craig Cabell that recounts stories of several crimes the Krays may have committed but were never convicted for, could have been the trigger that made Frances pack her bags and return to her family at Ormsby Street that summer, but the chronology of events after the wedding is not detailed enough to say for sure.

Once safely back with her family, Frances recounted some of what had been going on. Her husband, she told her mother, was perverted, didn't make love to her at all. On one occasion he'd attempted to take her from behind, as if she were a boy. She felt ashamed, soiled, degraded. She told Elsie she didn't believe any other man would want her now.

This knowledge of the twins' violent inner world, so carefully concealed behind their public façade, propelled Frances into a spiral of shame and fear, not just for her own life, but for those closest to her. It is fair to say that she never really recovered from the shock of what she discovered about her husband and his twin in those brief weeks of married life. Is it really any wonder that, by then, she was more or less dependent on taking pills to help her cope with what she was living through?

CHAPTER 8

SPIRAL

Sunshine and blue skies weren't a panacea for what Frances was going through emotionally. But at least they did briefly remove her from the ugly truth of her marriage. From early June to mid-August 1965 Frances was abroad, first on the Spanish island of Ibiza, then on Spain's southern mainland in the holiday resort of Torremolinos.

These dates are recorded in her diary, though there is no detailed account of her time abroad. She wrote that Reggie accompanied her to the airport before the Ibiza trip, which started on 4 June – and noted that she stayed alone there in hotels for long periods. One can only imagine her terrified state of mind at that time, knowing that at some point she had to return.

The timeline for the events written down in her diary is not chronological, but much of it seems to relate to the immediate post-honeymoon period, the months before Frances decided she couldn't stand living with her new husband and went back to the comparative safety of her family home. After the Spanish trip she briefly tried living with him again, but ran back to her family soon after.

Here is the content of what she wrote in the diary. Exactly when it was written is not clear, though it is most likely to have been penned in 1966, the last full year of Frances's life.

If it is somewhat confusing to read, it still gives painful insights into what went on between the couple and Reggie's tragically abusive behaviour in that brief time when they lived together.

It also confirms that Frances did briefly date other men before the marriage – and highlights much of the tension within the Kray family during Frances's times at Vallance Road. What is very clear from the diary is that what Frances wanted most of all was a divorce, a legal end to the marriage.

Where she mentions 'offence regarding s' this presumably refers to sex – and the incident she told Elsie about, when Reggie attempted anal sex. The word 'offence' was used because she would have seen it in that way, as a shocking act: in those days, anal sex, even between a married couple, was viewed quite differently to the way it is perceived nowadays. (Until the late 1800s in England anal sex or buggery was an offence punishable by hanging.)

DIARY OF DESPAIR

Frances wrote that she had been staying in a dark room with hardly any furniture. Reggie's suits were hanging round the wall. She'd had to take household and kitchen utensils there herself. He had left her there until 4 or 5 a.m. when he would come in drunk from El Morocco. He'd keep a flick knife under his pillow: 'as if something was going to happen'. She was petrified. He was frequently shouting and swearing at her, leaving her there alone. She couldn't stand it any more. So she went away. (Presumably this means to Spain, weeks after the honeymoon).

Reggie had suggested she see a psychiatrist when she came back from Torremolinos in August because her nerves were 'terrible'.

Reggie, she wrote, talked to her 'like a pig' in front of people. He was always arguing with her in front of his family at Vallance Road.

He repeatedly threatened her family, especially Frank and his girlfriend Bubbles 'It will come back on them,' he told her.

Frances wrote that she had told a doctor she would get a divorce for mental cruelty.

She noted 'honeymoon sex about 3', and before she went to Ibiza 'about 2'. Reggie, she wrote, was frequently saying things to deliberately upset her. When they were at the airport, before she flew to Ibiza, he told her she should stay as long as she liked – he didn't care if she stayed there for six weeks.

After she had left him, she wrote that a doctor suggested she go to a solicitor and pretend she'd hired a detective to follow Reggie, and say that there were photos of Reggie in a hotel with a girl, which would thus enable Frances to obtain a divorce on the grounds of adultery. Frances responded by saying she'd tell the truth. The doctor's response, she wrote, was: 'They won't like it if you mention guns and knives' and 'Aren't you frightened?'

Reggie had told her 'there may have been hostesses' at the clubs he visited and now she would have to put up with it. This, he said, was because when she'd broken off with him before the marriage and he visited her at Ormsby Street she had talked to him 'like a friend' telling him she'd been 'out with a boy'. Now, he'd told her, she would have to suffer and listen to him talking about girls. (This was typical Kray twin behaviour, storing up the memory of an insult or an affront, waiting for the right moment to pounce in revenge or recrimination.)

Frances spent one week in a private hospital in October 1965. After she came out she wrote in the diary that Reggie started talking about the clubs he had been to while she was in there, deliberately mentioning this in front of his family, just to provoke her.

Again, after she came out of hospital and they were watching television at Vallance Road, Frances laughed at something funny on television (she thought her laughter seemed very nervy and shaky). Ronnie had looked at her and burst out laughing, saying, 'And Jesus wept', being funny, she said.

On another occasion, after Frances had been sitting in the Vallance Road front room after being in hospital, a friend came to see Reggie, so Frances went in the kitchen. And this was where Ronnie started talking about girls writing the twins letters, and how they were going to take them out, a speech aimed at tormenting her.

One night Violet made a sandwich and Frances left the crusts. When she got in the car to go back to the flat with Reggie, Violet threw the crusts out in the street in front of the car.

On another occasion, Ronnie brandished a sword knife (stick) at her, saying, 'I'll put this through you', then started laughing, turning it all into a joke.

Then the diary becomes a list; presumably these descriptions were the grounds Frances hoped would enable her to divorce Reggie:

'Mental cruelty – never speaking, shouting, swearing, aggravating, provoking. Threats. Habitual drunkenness. Knives and guns. Offence regarding 's' ('s' is underlined).

He'd kept all his clothes at his mother's, had all his food there. Frances was living under extreme strain, she wrote.

Every night at the Marble Arch flat Reggie came back drunk at 2, 3, 4 a.m. Then he'd leave her alone there all day, returning again at 3 a.m. He'd swear and fall all over the place. He'd kept a photograph of a hostess in L'Hirondelle club, which he showed to Frances when she came back from Torremolinos. They went to the club. 'Barely spoke to me – only to her.'

He had left her to stay in hotels alone after her trips to Ibiza and Torremolinos.

At Vallance Road he was swearing or abusing her verbally, frequently making comments like 'shut your mouth'.

Reggie frequently threatened Frances about her brother Frank and the £1,000 Reggie owed him. He also kept telling her 'the same thing will happen to you as will happen to Hannah.'

These last two notes need some clarification.

The £1,000 debt was cash Frank Shea Junior had lent to Reggie who had told him he needed the money for 'legal expenses'. Reggie never returned the money, despite Frankie's many efforts to retrieve it. Reggie told Frances that in asking for the return of the money, Frankie had 'fucked this marriage up over £1,000'.

Hannah was a girl called Hannah (or Anna) Zambodini who had alleged that Reggie was the father of a baby girl born to her in East London in June 1965. She took out a summons for an affiliation order against Reggie and the story made the newspapers in October 1965. The summons was contested by Reggie's solicitors, Sampson and Company, and the case was eventually dismissed. What happened to Hannah remains a mystery.

The diary notes continue:

'Married 19th April 1965.'

'In Ibiza from 4th June – 14th July'. Frances wrote she stayed in a hotel on her own.

From 14 July to 2 August she also stayed in a hotel alone.

'2nd August to 15th August 1965, Torremolinos.'

After Spain, on 19 August, she wrote that she had returned to London and booked into the Alexandra National hotel, Finsbury Park, alone. She stayed there until she went to the Marble Arch flat, after which time she stayed alone in a bed-and-breakfast hotel in Stamford Hill called the Carmel.

Reggie kept a small arsenal by the side of the bed: a gun, a sword, a knife, a chopper and a flick knife.

Following an argument, Frances phoned her brother Frankie, asking him to come and collect her. She mentioned the guns. Ronnie swore at her and started collecting the guns in a laundry bag. He phoned a man called Wally from the Green Dragon, told him to collect the guns, get rid of them.

Reggie never spoke to Frances when Ronnie was in the room. In front of Ronnie and Violet she mentioned something about her looking for a new flat. His response was, 'Shut your mouth.' (As mentioned earlier, this was a common insult he used.)

Before going to the private hospital in October, Frances had told her doctor: 'I must go away somewhere (I had nowhere to go) for a rest.' The doctor had booked the stay in the hospital the very next day. Reggie and a friend had driven Frances there. Her husband was swearing and shouting at Frances in the car, repeating his threats to do the same to her as he'd do to Hannah, the girl in the 'baby claims' case.

Following several days in hospital, Frances returned to her husband at Cedra Court. He came in drunk every night. All his suits were kept at Vallance Road. She 'had to keep on' because she needed the money he'd give her for food – and what she described as 'tablet money'. Reggie ate all his meals at Vallance Road.

He'd bought a rifle in a false name and kept the loaded firearm by the side of their bed. He also locked every door in the flat before going to sleep.

This tyrannical man kept telling her she was ill, and that he had been with other women from the clubs: now she'd have to suffer. Ronnie would torment her if she went to Vallance Road.

Reggie swore and shouted at her constantly. He was frequently drunk, slurring his words, falling all over the place. If she mentioned money, he'd talk about her brother Frankie in a malicious way. He'd stand in front of her, shaking his hands, trying to provoke her.

Frances couldn't stand it any more and decided to leave. As she was packing her case, Reggie told her he would win any divorce case and would bring in character witnesses and others to tell lies against her.

This final section of the diary brings home, in no uncertain terms, the truth of Frances's marriage and explains why an already nervous, anxious young woman became overwhelmed with fear and depression.

The note about 'had to keep on' for food and tablet

money implies that she was already reliant on certain types of medication as well as being financially dependent on Reggie.

Loaded guns. Locked doors. Knives under pillows. Consistent, habitual drunkenness. Threats to Frances and her family. Frequent verbal abuse. Left to stay alone in strange hotel rooms... It is a shocking catalogue of despair – and the debilitating emotional decline she experienced was just weeks after the farce of their wedding.

As Micky Fawcett put it to me in no uncertain terms: 'Bad nerves? Reggie Kray would make anyone's nerves bad. Full grown, successful, confident men would still say that to this day.

'Reggie could never have anything near approaching a normal life with her at all. One day, after they married, I remember him saying, "I'm going to have a night in tonight." But he was saying it with such trepidation; he was usually out every single night.

'This particular night he said, "Oh, I'm buying lots of stuff to take home, crisps, lemonade, it's gonna be so boring." He sounded like a teenager. Even the next day when we saw him he kept going on about "Oh I was wondering where you all were."

'Reggie was the most selfish person you've ever met. Once, Frances said to me, "How would you like to have a gun pulled on you to get your own way?" He would've been threatening to shoot her brother all the time. That was his modus operandi.'

Maureen Flanagan discovered, on her weekly hairdo visits to Violet, that during the weeks after the marriage, Vallance Road was a very tense place.

'Every time Ronnie wanted his twin and Reg said, "I'm

with Frances" that would cause even more rows between the twins,' she explained. 'I got all this from Mrs Kray.

'"Oh I don't think they're talking today," she'd whisper over the cups of tea. And of course, Charlie saw what was going on between the twins and would tell his mother about it.'

'When I did see Frances at Mrs Kray's, she seemed even more nervous. And it was even more obvious how much she disliked Ronnie if he turned up while she was there.

'Her face told you the story. As soon as he came in the door, there was fear, nervousness; she couldn't wait to get out. She'd pick up her bag and say, "Are we goin', Reg?" She never pulled faces. But that fear of Ronnie... after the wedding you saw a nervous girl who was even more nervous.'

'"Take this apple pie home," Mrs Kray insisted one day. But Frances didn't want it.

'"No, I won't take it, it's alright," she'd say in that nervous way. I don't think she wanted to take anything out of that house.

'I did find out from Mrs Kray at one stage that her [Frances's] family were already trying to get her back with them. They loved her, the father, the brother... they just wanted her away from Reg.'

As for the couple's sex life, Maureen noticed that Mrs Kray never said a word.

'Sex was never mentioned in that house. I don't think Mrs Kray was curious, either. She'd have been too scared to ask Frances anyway, in case something was wrong.

'If you asked her how they [Reggie and Frances] were, it was either "Oh they're alright" or "they're not alright." Then one day I heard, "She's left him for good. She's gone back to her family."'

From what is written in Frances's diary, she started seeking psychiatric help for her nervous, troubled state 'after Torremolinos', which is around late August/early September 1965.

Her writing in the diary is not completely legible. She wrote that psychiatric help came from 'the same doctor who gave his brother tablets' and while the doctor's name is not clearly decipherable in the diary note, I was later able to ascertain that the doctor's name was Dr Lewis Clein, a London consultant psychiatrist with a practice in Harley Street, one of the UK's most prestigious addresses for private medical practitioners.

Dr Clein retained his Harley Street practice until 2011 when he retired. He agreed to meet me in his house in London's West End, close to the exclusive thoroughfare of Marylebone High Street.

Recently widowed, as we talked in his kitchen, Clein, eighty-eight, told me he was preparing to sell the house and move to a retirement home in northwest London.

A slight, stooping figure, he did not appear to be very robust and his memory, at times, seemed confused. Yet he was courteous and helpful. I got the impression that any enquiry about his long career in psychiatry, treating troubled or depressed patients, was welcome: his work and his long life were one and the same. While I was there, he took a call from a patient.

Clein said he still had most of his patient records from 1970 onwards. Unfortunately, however, he had not kept his records before that time, so he couldn't refer to his notes on Frances. Yes, he remembered treating Frances and, yes, he had treated

Ronnie Kray as a private patient. Clein had originally worked at Long Grove Hospital in Surrey, where Ron had been treated, yet strangely, he told me that he had not personally treated Ronnie there, despite my understanding that he had originally treated Ronnie at that hospital.

Clein said he had been directed to help Ronnie by a Dr Blasker, whom he didn't know, and who lived on the Isle of Dogs.

According to Clein, Blasker rang one evening and asked him if he could do a home visit, as a psychiatric consultant, to Ronnie Kray. (Blasker had known the twins since their teenage boxing days. He was not a specialist but he always helped the twins out when there were emergencies: that is, when the person involved could not be sent to a public hospital because the nature of their injuries would raise queries with police.)

Clein said he duly visited Ronnie at Vallance Road, saying, 'He didn't need hospitalisation, he was slow and slurred of speech, so I put him on antidepressants. Then later he came to see me at my Harley street surgery. I probably saw him about four times.'

The first time he learned about Frances's nervous state was, said Clein, following an unexpected phone call from Violet Kray.

'She said her other son Reggie was getting married,' the doctor remembered. '"It's not going to work out because they don't get on," she told me. Then she asked me, if anything happened, would I able to see the girl?'

'I told her if her GP arranged a referral, I'd be happy to see her.'

Weeks after this call, Clein said he saw the stories about the wedding in the newspapers.

'Then I got a phone call from Reggie Kray. He told me his new wife was depressed, very up and down. They got the referral from the GP and arranged to come and see me in my Harley Street office. He came with her to the appointment. But he didn't come into the consulting room.'

'She was very low. She said she was sleeping badly. She didn't say very much at all, she seemed very reticent and quiet.'

Clein said that Frances told him she was already taking prescribed tablets for depression from her NHS GP.

'I suggested we change them and wrote out a different prescription for her. I would have prescribed one of the early antidepressants, a medium dose, three times a day.'

Clein suggested that a stay in a private hospital would really help Frances.

'She was cooperative when I suggested a place she could stay in called Greenways in Hampstead, a very old fashioned private hospital with older nurses. She stayed at Greenways for about a week.'

Clein says that he saw Frances at Greenways that week and that she seemed better. He suggested she remain there for another two or three weeks.

'But she wanted to get out. So she left. Then she had another appointment booked with me. But it was cancelled. I never saw her again after that week in the hospital.

'I thought she was a severe depressive. For Reggie's part, I got the impression he felt she was not getting the right attention through the NHS, which was why they had contacted me.'

My research afterwards backed up what Clein told me. Later on, I discovered a bill for Greenways Nursing Home in Hampstead, dated 30 October 1965, for the week 22–29 October. The bill was addressed to Mrs Kray.

Greenways had been located in a house in Fellows Road, Hampstead and was well known in sixties London as a nursing home-cum-private hospital. (Enid Blyton died there in November 1968. It was demolished some time ago and is now an upmarket apartment block.)

Here are the details of the bill, paid on 31 October, 1965. It was for £47.18s.6d (forty-seven pounds, eighteen shillings and sixpence). In today's terms this sum of money is equivalent to just under £900, money that an ordinary family like the Sheas would not have been able to drum up, so it is fair to assume the Greenways hospital bill was paid by Reggie.

There were a number of small items of money on the bill, including £1 for phone calls, £1.11s.6d for tea for visitors, and 5s for newspapers. There were sums for items purchased from the chemist totalling £4.3s.6d. The two biggest items on the bill were the room charge of £32.11s and a charge for 'special nurses' on 29–31 of £9.6s.

When Frances returned to Ormsby Street for good in the late autumn of 1965, she'd been married for seven months. Much of that time had been spent living apart from her husband. The Sheas, not surprisingly, forbade Reggie from even entering their house.

He had no choice but to accept that the terrified and nervous woman he'd claimed as his bride could no longer live with him and that the best place for her was with her family.

Yet just as before, he still could not bring himself to stay away for good, to leave her to get better. Or allow Frances to have her own life. As traumatic as those weeks after the marriage had been for her, the suffering woman was still unable to disassociate herself from Reggie completely. The truth was, he would not let her out of his life.

Now she existed in a sort of limbo: on regular medication to calm her down, in theory, at least, able to do as she pleased, to see friends and go out and about.

But of course, she was now a married woman with a gangster husband, a man who still insisted he played a role in her life in 'looking after her'. So much damage had already been done to Frances's fragile state of mind through that brief exposure to the twins' inner world, yet in leaving Reggie physically, she remained a 'marked' woman: she was still seen as 'Reggie's girl'.

It was at this point that their tortured on/off relationship moved into its strangest, most bizarre phase.

In the early evenings, at around 6 p.m., Reggie would go round to Ormsby Street, remain on the pavement outside the house and talk to Frances, who would stand at the open window of her bedroom. It would have been romantic, had it not been so tragic.

Albert Donoghue told me that he often accompanied Reggie on these visits. 'She'd look out of the window and Reggie would poke an envelope through the letterbox containing money for her. I never saw her come down to answer the door,' he recalled.

'I thought it was all very sad. "I've put it in the letter box," he'd tell her and she'd just stand there and say, "Okay".'

Then Reggie would get back into the car and be driven off, back to his smoke-filled clubs, his twin, the hostesses, the minders – the life he couldn't relinquish for the love of Frances.

At thirty-two, as much as Reggie had dared to fantasise about leading a normal life, he was incapable of being anything other than one half of a criminal and violent duo, dominated by both his need for his twin and the need to protect Ronnie from his most destructive impulses.

Rather than searching inside himself to understand why Frances, so fragile emotionally, had been driven to breaking point following her exposure to his crazy and scary world, he continued, as before, to heap blame on the Sheas for the breakdown of the marriage.

They'd interfered, he'd thunder to himself in his brooding drunken rages. He'd show that old cow Elsie what Reggie Kray did to people like her.

The stories about what he did demonstrate how deluded Reggie must have been about the end of the marriage. He sent anonymous letters to Frank Senior, saying his wife was sleeping with other men. He wrote to the men Elsie worked with, claiming she was anyone's for the asking. He even got someone to go round to the Shea house in the dead of night and damage the front of the family's Mini car. Reg, yet again, was hell-bent on hitting back. Yet the Sheas had done nothing other than try to protect their beloved daughter.

There is no rational explanation for any of this. Nor would there be any rational explanation for what lay ahead.

For by then, Ronnie Kray's illness was poised to send him completely round the bend. And despite all Reggie's efforts over time to save them both from the consequences of Ron's wilder outbursts, the whole house of cards, the artifice of the Kray reputation, the shocking pointlessness of their crimes and the end of their 'immunity' from the law loomed ahead. All would come crashing down in spectacular fashion within two years.

With hindsight, it is still a harsh truth that the most undeserving victim of all the Krays' activities was the girl

Reggie claimed to love and worship above all else. He couldn't love her in the normal way of man to woman, yet even now, with the marriage in tatters, he was determined to keep his hold on her. Was it this attempt to continue to possess her that drove Frances further down into depression and despair?

Trevor Turner is a leading consultant psychiatrist who has worked for many years in the East End of London.

He told me that no matter how nervous or fragile Frances's state of mind might have been before they married, someone like Reggie would have only made her mental state worse through his possessive behaviour.

'It's well known in our business that that kind of possessive, morbid behaviour is a common generator of depression in others. From a psychological point of view, morbid jealousy of a partner can only make that person even more anxious – because the behaviour of the jealous partner is so unreasonable,' he explained.

'She was an anxious soul in a very strange, uncontrolled marriage, terrorised and trapped and because she was not very robust, it was assumed she was "ill".

'A good doctor would have tried to obtain some sort of corroborative history, i.e. from someone close to her, in order to understand what she was dealing with in her day-to-day life.'

We cannot know for sure if any of the doctors Frances saw attempted to obtain this kind of history. From her diary it seemed as if when she did confide in one doctor, he did not exactly encourage her in her idea to seek escape via divorce, given the violent reputation of the twins.

This is understandable in a sense, not just because of the potential for violence, but because divorce was complicated and expensive in 1965 – the changes to the divorce laws and the 'no fault' laws did not come into force until 1969 – and, at the end of the day, a doctor is not a legal adviser. Yet this reality, of the doctors who were treating Frances not attempting to find out more from those closest to her, does reveal how isolated she was. Yes, everyone around her knew what the Krays were capable of. Her family loved her, no question. But all those in her immediate circle were powerless to help her recover from the damage that had been done to her state of mind.

There is also the fact that any kind of mental illness or nervous breakdown was less well understood in those days. There had been major breakthroughs in the treatment of mental illness, indeed something of a revolution in psychiatric care, as a result of the introduction of certain drugs in the fifties and sixties. It was this factor, Trevor Turner told me, that would have led to Frances's doctors prescribing both antidepressants and tranquillisers for her as a means of dealing with her depression and fear.

'The tranquillisers are a group of drugs that calm you down,' he explained. 'The antidepressants were given if the doctors saw depression as the problem. In those days too, for some people they prescribed combination drugs, a little bit of a mild tranquilliser attached to an antidepressant to calm someone down – and boost them up at the same time. At the time, everyone was very excited that these drugs might work for all sorts of problems.'

But why did Frances continue to communicate with Reggie after all that had happened? There are complicated reasons. For a start, she'd known him virtually since childhood. He'd shown her things, taken her to exciting, exotic places that were way beyond the experience of any other young girl in that environment. Consider too that there had always been a certain intimacy between them, forged at the beginning through his time in prison, when he would have been at his most vulnerable, reaching out to her from captivity.

Frances had, in a sense, defied her parents, married him against their wishes. So there was already a huge conflict which must have also pained her, left her feeling guilty, because she loved her family. She didn't want to be at war with them. Yet she was trapped. She wasn't capable of moving on, going to live in another part of the city, picking up the pieces of her life: financially she wouldn't have been able to support herself, and emotionally she was too frail to make such a huge leap of faith.

Frances, for all her beauty, wasn't a party girl or someone who'd artfully use men as a means of getting what she wanted, and Reggie recognised this. It was the combination of Frances's beauty and innocence, quite different from the other women he had around him, that had drawn him in at the beginning. And, of course, if she did attempt to 'escape' there was always the threat – which Frances believed – that the Kray network could seek anyone out, no matter where they went. Let alone what they could do to their family.

Conversely, nice Reg, the polite, caring, considerate man who wanted to bring the moon to her doorstep when sober, was still turning up at Ormsby Street nightly – and he was the only man who had ever been in her life.

Both of them had strong family loyalties – a hallmark of East End life back then – and neither was remotely capable of breaking away from those ties. So despite all the turmoil that had gone down between them, they wound up in this strange place of emotional dependency, neither together nor quite apart. And that is precisely where they remained...

CHAPTER 9

THE GIRL IN THE RED JACKET

By the beginning of 1966, Ronnie Kray was convinced that the twins remained invincible. Reggie wasn't quite so delusional: their new the club, El Morocco, was doing well. Their protection rackets still brought in the cash. The various frauds they got involved with were mostly lucrative.

Yet Ronnie's illness, as usual, created a terrible unpredictability. The drugs he took couldn't keep him stable. As winter ended, he went into a deep, black depression. It got so bad he returned to live at Vallance Road so that Violet could keep an eye on him.

This might have been helpful – had it not been for a chance remark from one of Ronnie's associates who was visiting him at Vallance Road.

The man was probably trying to curry favour with Ron. That was how it went with the twins, tiny morsels, titbits of information were passed on to them all the time; a verbal

Twitter feed where the consequences could be lethal. On hearing that a minor East End villain called George Cornell had been seen in a local pub, the Blind Beggar in Whitechapel High Street, a horrific scenario ensued.

Effectively, George Cornell was an old adversary of Ron's from many years earlier. On one occasion, Cornell had beaten Ronnie up very badly, something Ron would never forget. Nor had he overlooked a more recent story told him by another henchman, which was that Cornell had been overheard calling Ronnie 'a fat pouf'.

Paranoid and hyperactive, the news that Cornell was close by sent Ronnie into a frenzy. In his crazed mind he was consumed by the fear that Cornell was out to kill him – so he decided that he'd better sort him out once and for all.

Within a short space of time he'd retrieved his 9mm German army Luger automatic from its hiding place under the floorboards. Then he and Reggie went for a drink at the Lion Public House in Stepney. As they left the pub, Ronnie propelled two of his minders, Ian Barrie and John 'Scotch Jack' Dickson into a car en route to the Whitechapel Road and in the direction of the Blind Beggar. Once outside the pub, Ron alighted, told the others he would only be a few minutes and asked Ian Barrie to go into the pub with him.

It was early evening, 9 March, and the Blind Beggar was half empty. Cornell was seated at the bar, his first pint of the night on the counter before him.

And it was all over in a matter of minutes.

Ian Barrie strode into the pub, firing a warning shot at the pub ceiling. Behind him, holding his gun, came Ronnie. He marched up to Cornell and shot him at point-blank range, directly into his forehead. As the victim tumbled to the floor, Barrie and Ron marched out and into the waiting car and were driven off into the night; a completely senseless crime.

When Ron, on a distressingly manic high from the killing, told his twin what he'd done, Reg went potty. All his hard work had been for nothing. His worst fears were coming true: his brother had committed the ultimate crime, which would drive everything they'd achieved away from them. And it would directly propel them into a prison cell for life. (Had Ronnie killed Cornell a year or two beforehand he'd have faced the hangman's noose – the death penalty for murder was only abolished in England in November 1965.)

Later, when they all continued drinking in a pub in nearby Walthamstow, a news item came on about the shooting in the Blind Beggar: the man who had been shot had died on the way to hospital.

'That's good,' Ron said. 'Dead men can't speak.'

Yet when Reggie had stopped cursing his brother, he still did what he always did: a well-organised mop-up job.

He told Violet that if the police came to the house, to say nothing. He organised a local safe house for Ron to lie low in and got him there, with a minder to keep an eye on him. Then he made sure that all the witnesses in the pub knew exactly what would happen to them if they opened their mouths about what they'd seen.

If he was already troubled by his obsession with Frances, his compulsion to remain in control of her life, even as her doorstep Romeo, the killing of Cornell seriously compounded all Reggie's woes and fears. The Sheas, he reasoned, had already done their best to wreck his marriage. Now Ron had lost control and he would have to look out for him even more carefully or he'd drag Reg down with him. The madman was now in charge of the asylum.

This was a pointless murder carried out by a homicidal schizophrenic. It wasn't even a brutal attack in a darkened East London street. It had been played out on a stage – in full view of the pub's staff and customers, witnesses to the senseless slaying. It could have been an open-and-shut case as far as the law was concerned. Everyone in the East End heard what had happened, the rumours and the stories spread like wildfire. Yet the witnesses, too terrified of Kray retribution to open their mouths, could not tell the police the truth about how, in a half-empty pub, George Cornell lay dying from a gunshot wound on the floor. They were sorry but they knew nothing.

On 22 March, just under two weeks after the murder of George Cornell, Frances visited a firm of solicitors called Lowe & Company on Kingsland High Street, Dalston.

The purpose of the visit was to legally change her married surname from 'Kray' back to her maiden name of 'Shea' by deed poll.

I believe these two dates in March are connected. Frances and her parents would have heard all the gossip and stories about what Ron had done in the Blind Beggar. Being married to a criminal was bad enough, but being the wife of a man whose twin had committed murder – and seemingly got off scot-free – put everything on a different level. At least, Elsie would have argued, Frances would no longer be a Kray. Their name, therefore their reputation, would be rescued.

Once she'd sorted this out, Frances made it known to Reggie that she wanted a legal end to the marriage. The marriage had not been consummated, therefore there were grounds for an annulment. Typically, on hearing this, Reg resorted to devious tactics. Okay, he said, he would handle the petition through his solicitors. He'd talk to them tomorrow.

Of course, he did nothing to push this forward as she wished he would. Reggie Kray's marriage annulled? For non-consummation? No way. Bad for the image. He didn't even dare to think what Ronnie's reaction would be.

Yet the death of George Cornell, while not directly connected to Reggie, told the Shea family, in no uncertain terms, that what they were dealing with had now gone way beyond anyone's control, including the law. The name change was merely a sad attempt to disassociate themselves from it all, to save the family from being besmirched by the twins' reputation.

In the end, alas, this didn't work: Reggie Kray was far too cunning, as future events would demonstrate.

There were other consequences as a result of the Cornell killing. That summer, there was a noticeable decline in the twins' fortunes. As much as Ronnie loved reliving the moment when he shot Cornell – there are ugly stories that he told people he reached orgasm when he pulled the trigger – and while he had convinced himself that his status as a gangster was now elevated by the murder, not everyone that did business with the twins saw it the same way. He'd pushed the boundaries way too far.

Some of the twins' valuable 'minding' contracts with club owners ended abruptly – with a big payoff, of course. Other business started to drain away.

Ever mindful of their reputation, Ron started to scheme, to dream up ways to retrieve their standing, show themselves to the world as a force for good again. Yet again, his fantasy world took over. And in the midst of all this, Reggie ran between the two situations, trying to cope with Ronnie's mania and worrying about the health of his estranged wife.

Despite all his efforts – he'd even persuaded her to take a short weekend trip with him, that spring, to Devon, where they visited the twins' old friend Frank Mitchell in Dartmoor prison – Frances remained, as she had been for some time, extremely nervous. There were bad headaches and frequent spells of bleak depression. She was now more or less dependent on her medication. The smallest thing could upset her, have her reaching for her packet of pills, legally prescribed by the doctors and now a consistent feature in her life. She was in a bad way.

This visit to Mitchell, or 'The Mad Axeman' as the press eventually dubbed him, took place partly out of Reg's loyalty to a fellow crim but also because Ron had begun to draw up a plan designed to restore themselves in the world's eyes as good guys.

Put simply, the plan was to help Mitchell escape from Dartmoor, get him into hiding in London and then, via the huge publicity their involvement in his escape would attract, their efforts would convince the authorities to release Mitchell. The former convict would then be free – and the world would know the twins could do virtually anything they wanted. It would enhance their prestige, give them even more power.

The crazy plan, which preoccupied Ron throughout 1966, did eventually culminate in a very public and almost laughably easy escape from Dartmoor. However, it went badly wrong after that – resulting in the killing of Frank Mitchell. Once in hiding, Mitchell had proved difficult to control. Tragically, this resulted in his 'disappearance', by order of the twins, on Christmas Eve 1966.

The police were never able to prove, beyond doubt, the full details of Mitchell's slaying. The body was never found. In 1996 Freddie Foreman admitted in his biography, *Respect*, that he and another gunman, Alfie Gerrard, had killed Mitchell, as a favour to the twins. In 2000 he repeated his confession in a TV documentary.

Because Foreman had already been acquitted of the deaths of both Mitchell and Tommy 'Ginger' Marks, in the sixties, under the former double jeopardy rule (an English law that meant at that time that no one could be tried twice for the same crime) he was not prosecuted for the Mitchell crime, nor was there sufficient evidence to prosecute him for perjury.

But all this lay ahead. Frances's problems had clearly worsened dramatically. In June 1966, she was admitted to a psychiatric ward at the then Hackney Hospital in Homerton High Street. (The Hackney, which was closed down in 1995, was one of the largest NHS general hospitals in London at the time.) Frances had already seen a psychiatrist at the Hackney Hospital the year before as an outpatient. But now the psychiatrist had decided it would be better for her if she was treated there as an inpatient.

It is not clear whether this was because Frances had already experienced some sort of breakdown prior to admission, or whether she had talked of attempting suicide in one of her visits to the psychiatrist at the hospital's outpatients department. But she ended up staying in the hospital's psychiatric ward from June until September 1966.

Michael, or 'Mick', Taylor is a sixty-nine-year-old divorced pensioner who grew up in London's East End and still lives there. Known locally as 'The Sartorialist' because of the way he always smartly tricks himself out, he is one of the area's more colourful characters, a living reminder of 'the old days' of the district.

We had coffee together in the now ultra-fashionable Brick Lane where he told me his story of the time he too was a young psychiatric patient at the Hackney Hospital during that World Cup victory summer of 1966.

He told me, in some detail, how he found himself falling for a lovely young woman who was being treated on the same ward.

'I was 21 at the time and I'd had a nervous breakdown,' he recalled. 'I'd suddenly cracked up after a family bereavement. They diagnosed me with a nervous disability. I didn't remember much about how I got there, but I wound up in the Hackney hospital for sixteen weeks.

'You were in this huge long ward, with about twenty people on it, men at one end, women at the other. One morning, not long after I'd got there, I was lying on my bed and a girl came over, very smartly dressed lady. Immaculate. At first glance, I thought she was one of the doctors – because of the way she dressed and spoke to me. She was so nice.

'She asked me about how I came to be there and said she was the same as me. She told me, "If you do what they tell you, you'll get better." She told me she'd already been there for over a week.'

That was the start of Mick's friendship with Frances. 'When she went back to her bed, I went to see the matron, who had an office on our floor. She told me, "That young lady is Reggie Kray's wife. I thought I'd better tell you."'

Hospital friendships tend to develop quite quickly and

this was no exception. They were both around the same age, from local working-class backgrounds, in the hospital for similar reasons.

They were not in a locked or secure ward situation: the psychiatric patients in this ward were free to go outside the hospital if they wished, the only proviso being that they had to return on time for their medication and their meals. (In those days, the Mental Health Act of 1959 permitted considerable discretion on the part of the hospital consultants as to how patients were managed, and changes to the Act, focusing on patients' rights, were not introduced until 1983.)

The Matron's comments didn't trouble Michael. 'I wasn't really frightened by knowing Reggie was her husband.' he explained. 'The same day, we went for a long walk outside and she started to talk to me about her life. She told me she was never in love in her life. He never had the time for her, he was always out, drinking, clubbing. She told me she would wake up in the morning when she was with him and find a gun or a hammer lying under the mattress.

'She said she was scared something might happen to her because of the life they were living. It was the uncertainty. And there was no end to it, arguments, violence. Reggie wasn't violent to her. But she said Ronnie was always threatening her, telling Reg to get rid of her.

'Reggie treated her well. She could have anything she wanted. She never went to work; in a way he had her entire life. But she couldn't take Ronnie. Him and Reg had to be together all the time, they were a fighting force.'

During those weeks in the hospital, Taylor said they were both given shock treatment (ECT, electro-convulsive therapy) as well as drug treatments four times a day.

'They'd give us drugs like Valium. The drugs made you docile. You saw a psychiatrist every two weeks. I had to sit in front of a group of people who would interview me, ask me questions.

'I had shock treatment twice. I didn't like it. You didn't really know yourself for a couple of hours until the effect wore off. My hair was pretty long then and her hair was long and shiny. A kind of glue was used when they put the electrodes on your head, so that afterwards part of your hair was stuck together. She managed to get it off. She really cared about herself, her appearance.

'One week I remember her having it twice, then once the following week, but I think she had it more than that, over five or six weeks. She said it made her forget about the life she was living. She was so scared.'

Mick Taylor also recalled that Frances had confided that 'nothing had ever happened with Reggie, they never consummated the marriage'.

'I felt so sorry for her. She was a good-looking girl, small, cuddly, warm. I can still see her now, wearing a bright red jacket with a tartan skirt with black slingbacks, quite high. The shoes cost a lot of money. All her clothes were immaculate.

'She told me she was going to go in for a divorce; she was going to sort that out. The marriage was over. There was never any love there.'

She told him, Taylor explained, that she wasn't scared of Reggie but of Ronnie.

'Why he married her, I don't rightly know. She said every time they went out as a couple they were never actually together. He had to go here, there, she would be sitting there with people around her. But never her husband. Everywhere she went she'd have minders, people driving her around. At home she was either with a minder or someone else, family.

'She told me she was scared of Mrs Kray. She could never do anything without her knowing. Wherever she went people would point, "There's Reggie's wife".'

That summer, the pair wandered around the area during the day, enjoying each other's company away from the hospital ward.

'We'd go for a walk across Hackney Marshes for a couple of hours. We even went to the Spread Eagle pub next door but the guv'nor of the pub, once he found out who she was, told us to stop coming. I wanted to take her to meet my family, but they were also too scared to even meet her.

'Her mum would come to see her every other night for an hour or so. Her mum was very quiet, but she had a fierce look on her face. Her dad, Frank, was a quiet man too. Her brother and his girlfriend came to visit too; sometimes they'd come on their own, without each other. I got on well with them, they seemed like very nice people.

'But I could see her mother didn't like me, I guess because she saw how friendly we were.'

On weekends they were sometimes allowed to go back home if they wished. Mick recalled the twins visiting Frances on two occasions.

'The first time they came, they talked to Frances downstairs, away from the ward. The second time, she spotted them walking into the ward from the other end and then she went a bit haywire. I remember her pushing Ronnie out of the way: "Go away!" Then she started crying. But Ronnie was Reggie and Reggie was Ronnie. You couldn't divide them. Ronnie made sure of that.'

All the staff at the hospital were aware of the friendship. 'They did warn me, "Don't do anything stupid or get involved in any way, Michael. Behave yourself," they said.

'And I did. I knew I had to do that from the very beginning. I was scared of the Krays. But I was a patient in Hackney Hospital. They certainly didn't make themselves busy when they came in – they came in like gentlemen. As far as Reg was concerned, I was a mental case. They couldn't touch me. Or her.'

As their friendship developed, Frances confided that suicide had been in her thoughts.

'But she said she didn't have the guts to do it. Reg had taken her to a Harley Street specialist but she said the drugs he was giving her were making her worse.

'When she told them this at the hospital, they didn't want to know. She told me the drugs the West End doctor gave her made her high, then low, then depressed. She suffered a lot, in a way. The drugs were too powerful, mucking her head up.'

For all this, Mick Taylor vividly remembered the happiness of their short time together that summer.

'She'd buy me the odd gift, a tie, a handkerchief. Someone would always bring her whatever she needed in cash. I'd buy her the odd meal, one day we went to Blooms in Whitechapel. Another time it was Lyon's Tea Shop, near Aldgate Station.

'She was quiet but she wasn't a stupid girl. When you talked about things, she knew what she was talking about. Part of her was quite religious, there was a church at the back of the hospital, we used to go and sit there sometimes.

'When you went out, she always walked on the inside as we went down the road. As a cockney, you were taught certain things as a boy, how to behave, chivalry towards women. We respected each other.'

He told me the relationship gradually developed into displays of physical affection. Yet he was acutely conscious of where the lines were drawn.

'There was a bond between us. She made me happy.

'I do remember the day I first kissed her, on the grass at Hackney Marshes.

'"I'm glad I met you," I said, then we kissed. She said, "I'm glad I met you too."

'She needed that affection. It didn't go further than kissing and cuddling. I suppose it could have happened but I thought if I had done anything it would have been dangerous, she wasn't divorced.

'She said that if anything happened to him, she would have her freedom. She did have plans in her mind. We even talked about moving out of London, where no one knew us, things like that. But she never got to do anything. It never happened.'

A little after three months later, both were discharged from the hospital.

'She went home and I went to stay at my brother's place at the Guinness Trust, behind Moorfields Eye Hospital,' Mick continued. 'I missed her. Times like that in your life, you don't forget. People knew about our friendship, yes. But I kept out of harm's way afterwards, went to work for the council, doing highway repairs.'

The news of what happened to Frances, less than a year later, came as a devastating blow when he read about it in the newspaper.

'I couldn't believe it at first. But when something like that happens, you have a sense that it's meant to happen. Knowing her, in a way, made me grow up. You start to realise what's right and what's wrong – and be honest with yourself. For me, it shook me into getting back on track. I stopped taking the medication and got on with my life.

'She would have made me a good wife. I do know that.'

The discovery that Frances had received shock treatment on several occasions that summer should be viewed in the context of the times. More commonly used to treat depression then, today it is only used in extreme cases, where all else has failed. Its use declined over the years as new drug treatments were introduced and were shown to be more effective and with fewer side effects.

'ECT has been demonised because it was overused; some people did get chronic memory loss afterwards,' explained psychiatrist Trevor Turner. 'Also, they used to give it without modifying drugs, which resulted in shaking, foaming at the mouth, very scary reactions – and people have retained that powerful image of it. And the idea of having electricity shot through your brain feels pretty barbarous. So it has a bad press. It was more its nature, rather than side effects, that generated its demise.

'It sounds like she wasn't getting better on two or three different types of medications, so a course of ECT had a fifty-fifty chance of helping her. What they'd have been hoping for is to get her sufficiently un-depressed not to need the drugs.

'One side effect would be loss of memory around the time the person had it. But it would come back.'

Michael Taylor's account of Frances reveals a person who clearly understood her situation and was cooperative with the doctors who were treating her because she still wanted or hoped to get better.

The long stay in Hackney Hospital was, in many ways, a refuge from what she was struggling to deal with, and her comment about the shock treatment making her 'forget' the life she was living is illuminating. Not only had she admitted to Mick Taylor that she was already contemplating suicide as a way out, but also that it was obvious to her that the treatment for her depression offered various ways of 'forgetting'. For good.

Yet the young woman who came out of hospital that autumn just before her twenty-third birthday was, sadly, nothing like the beautiful bride of David Bailey's photos.

'She did lose a lot of weight after she came out of Hackney Hospital,' remembered Rita Smith. 'I saw her in the car and, looking at her, you could tell she wasn't getting better. She was far away.'

Maureen Flanagan remembered seeing Frances briefly at Vallance Road that autumn. On the day in question, Reggie was nowhere to be seen. 'Either she'd just popped in to say hello,' she recalled. 'Or maybe Violet had been in touch, asked her round. She didn't look like the girl I'd met a few years before. She looked drawn, like someone who had just given up. It was all too much for her. She could never be scruffy or untidy, but she had no make-up on, pale, white as a ghost, like a little will-o'-the-wisp: not really there.

'After she'd gone I said to Vi, "She doesn't look like she's with us."

'"I thought that," said Vi. She looked weak, like she should be in hospital.'

The sad truth was that despite the efforts of the medical

profession to help Frances, really, nothing had changed at all. She was still trapped in the Kray web, shunned by many out of ignorance and fear, still haunted by those weeks when she'd been chillingly exposed to the sordid truth about Reggie's way of life.

As for the twins, rumours now persisted that the police were poised to arrest them for Cornell's murder. At one point the murdered man's widow, Olive, had been round to Fort Vallance at night and smashed the windows, screaming at the top of her voice that Ronnie had killed her husband, much to Violet's disgust: as if her boy would do anything like that, she tutted. Such stories were common currency in the pubs and drinking clubs of Bethnal Green and the East End. They soon got back to Ormsby Street.

The next thing everyone heard was that the twins had flown the coop, to Tangier, Morocco.

As John Pearson recorded in *The Profession of Violence*: 'Ronnie enjoyed the Arab boys, Reggie invited out a hostess from the Latin Quarter Club in London. During her fortnight with him he never once referred to Frances or the East End.'

But this sunny sojourn was cut short. The twins' notoriety now trailed behind them everywhere.

'The chief of Moroccan police arrived in person at their hotel to inform them they were undesirable aliens,' said Pearson. 'Two seats were booked for them on the next plane back to London,'

When my research later unearthed a short, handwritten letter addressed to Frances dated 17 October 1966, posted in Tottenham, London, another tragic piece of the jigsaw puzzle surfaced.

The note, from someone with a Greek-sounding surname,

indicated that Frances was buying street drugs. Whatever Frances was hearing or being told about Reggie via the local whispers and the rumours at that time, they would only have served to exacerbate her fears, her terror. The unhappy young woman was now embarking on a perilous road towards self-destruction.

> Sorry I didn't meet you last Saturday. If you want those pills, I'll see you this Saturday, 22nd October. I'll get them this Friday. I will meet you outside the Odeon Cinema at 3pm. Be there.
> PS: If you want to answer back, write to me. Please answer if you are not coming.

The same day the note was posted, 17 October, Frances was admitted to St Leonard's Hospital in Nuttall Street, Kingsland Road, as a result of an overdose of barbiturates she had taken at Ormsby Street.

Frank Senior had found her only just alive, and called the ambulance in time. Fortunately, St Leonard's was just a few minutes away from the house.

On 20 October, her consultant at the hospital, Dr N Jones, discharged her from Parkinson Ward and she went back to Ormsby Street. It was obvious the incident had not been a mere 'cry for help'. She had meant to kill herself. According to John Pearson in *The Cult of Violence*, she said afterwards: 'I've been defiled. I'm useless. What is there left for me to live for? I deserve to die.'

Whether she'd deliberately tried to obtain the street drugs for a planned suicide attempt and managed to source them elsewhere remains unknown. But as Trevor Turner pointed out: 'You can't stop someone buying street drugs. Most psychiatrists are quite streetwise; you have to be aware of the world as it is. So if you are prescribing drugs, even in very small amounts, in the end people can always get more.'

Reggie, on hearing the news of Frances's attempted suicide, had rushed round to see her at St Leonard's. No, he was told firmly by hospital staff, he couldn't see his wife right now. She was far too frail.

Off he went into the night, raining verbal blows on Frances's parents again and again. Like a spoilt child whose favourite toy was being denied him, he was driven back to Vallance Road where he reached for the gin bottle, ranted, cursed and heaped his rage, yet again, on the Sheas, his wife's innocent family.

The truth was, tragedy and retribution were now about to engulf everyone.

But the only retribution ahead would be that of the law.

CHAPTER 10

GRIEF

Ron Kray went into hiding in a flat in north London towards the end of 1966. He had been asked to appear in court as a witness for the prosecution in a police corruption case – a case, ironically, he had engineered – but he refused.

Barricaded in the flat, curtains tightly drawn, with plenty of booze and medication and his men ferrying in teenage boys at his behest, Ron's unpredictable illness took over, yet again. Another crisis. Ron seemed even worse than before this time. The last thing Reg wanted was for their mother to even see her son in this state.

After the ordered slaying of Frank Mitchell just before Christmas 1966, Ron had become increasingly paranoid that his enemies – namely Mitchell's friends and those of George Cornell – were now out to get him.

He had shockingly vivid nightmares about Cornell's last seconds of life. But in the dreams it was Ron's head that took the bullet and caused the subsequent explosion of blood and brain.

Drunk and barely coherent, in his semi-literate scrawl he compiled lists of all his 'enemies' who deserved to die, who needed to be taken out. Raving and delirious, at one stage he attempted suicide, slashing his wrists, only to be saved by Reg, who contacted Dr Blasker. His twin, warned Blasker, was a very sick man. He should be in a secure hospital.

Reg couldn't even contemplate that. By February 1967, the initial press outcry over the disappearance of Frank Mitchell seemed to have calmed down. Even the search for his body seemed to have abated. It was a terrible struggle, but Reggie finally convinced Ronnie to see a new psychiatrist, smuggled him into a car and managed to get him to meet the man in London. It worked. A change of drugs and a move to a different hideaway, this time in Chelsea, seemed to do the trick: the nightmares stopped. Crisis over. For now.

Yet at Ormsby Street, calamity had struck for a second time that winter. On 30 January 1967, Frances had barricaded herself in the front room, turned on the gas fire and taken substantial quantities of barbiturate pills. Again, Frank Senior found her in the nick of time and managed to quickly get her into casualty at St Leonard's Hospital.

This time she remained there for eight days. The diagnosis of her illness was barbiturate poisoning. Consultant Dr Jones discharged her from the hospital's Tanner Ward on 7 February 1967. There had been two suicide attempts in four months – the Sheas were virtually at their wits' end with concern. They felt utterly helpless.

When Frances came home from St Leonard's she was mostly quiet and fairly unresponsive. No, she was okay, she assured them – when just looking at her, so thin and pale, it was obvious she was anything but okay. What would happen now?

At that point, Frankie Junior stepped in: he was now living close by with Bubbles and their daughter in a brand new flat in a multistorey tower block, Wimbourne Court, on Wimbourne Street on the Wenlock Estate, just a mile away. He could see how bad things were for everyone. Why didn't Frances come to live in his flat? he suggested. She adored his daughter; surely the move would be good for her?

The young couple would keep a watchful eye on his sister, he promised his parents. At the very least, it would take some of the day-to-day worry off their shoulders. And Elsie wouldn't have to keep dealing with the neighbours' whispers and nudges every time Reggie Kray walked down the street or his car appeared near their house.

By this time, Frank Shea was twenty-seven. He'd grown up since those far-off days at the billiard hall when he'd been so chuffed to be seen driving Reg around in the big flash cars. He was a dad now. He'd had his problems with the law but he was still managing to establish himself as a haulage contractor. His friendship with Reggie had turned very sour over the £1,000 loan that Reggie had never repaid. He knew, because Frances had told him, that the loan had caused fights and rows between Reg and Frances.

Nonetheless, his sister's welfare was a priority and like their mum and dad he was desperate for her to pick up somehow, to get better. How vividly he remembered the bright, sparky, inquisitive teenager she'd been; he couldn't stand to think of the way she'd changed in a few years into a passive, near lifeless shadow of herself.

He kind of understood the lows, the depressions. He too got down sometimes; it was a bit of a family trait, though their dad didn't seem to suffer from it. Yet it was time Mum and Dad had some sort of break from all the worry. They were in their fifties now, getting on. The house at Ormsby Street was down for demolition in a redevelopment programme. They'd be rehoused soon, to a new home built by the council. If only they could all help Franny get better, try to make her see that she still had some sort of future, life could be better for everyone.

If Frances didn't believe that for one minute, she still went through the motions of living as winter gave way to spring. Her old passport had expired, so she got a new temporary twelve-month one, issued on 20 March 1967. She hadn't been abroad since those trips immediately after the honeymoon as she'd been too ill. A winter sunshine trip now would give her a lovely boost; it was just what she needed.

On 27 March, Frances's passport shows she took £50 – 'foreign exchange for travel expenses' – abroad with her. (In the sixties, strict currency controls in Britain meant that anyone travelling abroad had to formally declare any cash they were taking with them, up to a limit of £50.)

The holiday with friends, from 27 March to 8 April, a ten-day cruise around the sunny Canary Islands starting at Las Palmas, was her last trip to Spain. Tickets would soon be purchased for another trip, to the island of Ibiza. But there would be two empty seats on the plane.

What went through Frances's mind in those weeks after that last trip?

She might have been a bit happier away from Ormsby Street with all its associations with the past. But any uplift she felt from the change in environment would have been brief: given what was now a fixation in her mind, that drugs would help her escape for good, she would have already been quietly determined to do what she believed she had to do, once the opportunity arose.

Over the years many people have claimed that it was Reg who fed her drugs, Reg who supplied them; that Reg was the culprit in getting her addicted to pills that could calm her down – or kill her. That theory has some truth in it, but there is more to take into account.

The pills, by then, were not restricted in their availability via the criminal world. Reg may have initially given Frances tranquillisers or barbiturates, yet by the mid-sixties they were fast becoming quite commonly used.

A GP would legally prescribe them for 'bad nerves', in modest doses. And the illegal street trade in any drug of choice was positively thriving for those seeking recreational highs induced by medication. Drugs such as purple hearts, black bombers, speed (amphetamine), Mandies (Mandrax, a barbiturate drug with several formulations) or Quaaludes, known as 'ludes' (another form of barbiturate, a sedative hypnotic drug), were not difficult to obtain on the streets of London. It was where the mid-sixties cultural explosion of sex, drugs and rock 'n' roll had already burst forth.

Certainly, if Frances was regularly using both prescribed and illegal street drugs, dependence would have formed. But as Trevor Turner pointed out, it is impossible to be sure: 'Some drugs, like Mandrax, had a considerable tendency to produce dependence because of the extra 'buzz' they gave; people became addicted to it very quickly,' he said. 'But by and large, addiction to any drug is dominated by the individual's metabolism.'

Without any specific knowledge of the drugs Frances took or exactly when she took them, it's far too simplistic to say, 'Reggie got her addicted'.

On the topic of addiction, it was no secret that both twins were totally addicted to alcohol. Pills too were used all the time, though Ron had little choice: without drugs he was a crazed lunatic, a danger to himself and everyone around him.

Reg would openly take handfuls of tranquillisers such as Librium and wash them down with gin or beer. But deliberate intent on his part to 'get Frances hooked' as part of any conscious desire to possess cannot be easily directed at Reggie: his crimes were many, but his desire to help her, pull her away from the abyss, seemed outwardly genuine. He was possessive beyond reason. But losing her for good, which now seemed to be a possibility, was still unthinkable as far as he was concerned.

This desire to help was demonstrated to me by Dr Lewis Clein's recollection, during our interview, of a phone call from Reggie, which came out of the blue many months after Clein had last seen Frances.

'He wanted me to arrange for her to go back to Greenways,' he recalled. 'They had split up, he said. She was with her parents. But he was prepared to pay the bill for her to go to Greenways again.'

Clein says he duly rang the Sheas on the number Reggie had given him. 'They flatly refused to allow me to see her because of the link with the Krays. They didn't want anything to do with him.'

The doctor's memory of the precise timing of this call is not clear, though he says it was not long before Frances died. According to what Frances had told Michael Taylor during her time at Hackney Hospital, the decision to abandon further private treatment with Clein at Greenways could have been hers alone – because, as she made it clear to Michael, she didn't like the effect of the drugs the private psychiatrist had prescribed. The Sheas could have known this. But of course, by then, they wouldn't have tolerated Reg's intervention in any way.

Yet Reggie, who was happy to swap one private doctor for another in his quest to help his twin, may well have convinced himself that private medicine might just make the difference to Frances's treatment. In everything, he was supremely determined to have 'the best' available: cars, holidays, clothes, lawyers, furniture, country houses... you name it, he had it. Private medicine and Harley Street specialists, he'd have reasoned, were far superior to anything available for free on the NHS. Everything could be bought – especially when the currency was fear.

But the one thing that couldn't be bought was a return to happiness or peace of mind for Frances. Reg must have funded Frances's trip to the Canaries; the Sheas would have been unable to stop this. Yet in the last few weeks of her life it certainly seemed, to Reg at least, that they'd retrieved some of their old intimacy, what they'd once shared as a younger courting couple. For, incredibly, in those last weeks they had started seeing quite a bit of each other again.

Ron continued to remain in hiding. He'd endlessly goad Reg about seeing his ex-wife – the twins always had an uncanny, quite psychic ability to know what the other one was getting up to, even when apart. However the physical distance from the East End to Chelsea, plus the fact that Ron couldn't go out and about at all, meant that Ron's constant taunts about Frances had less effect.

The atmosphere at Wimbourne Court when Reggie visited was slightly less oppressive than that of Ormsby Street, though the issue over the loan from Frankie Junior had driven a distinct wedge between the two men.

But while Frances seemed outwardly to accept having Reggie back in her life, one might pause to question her motivation.

Did she just go along with it to keep the peace? Had she learned, by bitter experience, to dissemble, pretend to Reggie that all was well while hiding her real feelings?

Reggie's motivation was surely partly driven by what was now happening to him and Ronnie as the net of the law started to close in on them.

He knew all too well that getting back together with Frances, finding that normal, happy married life they'd often talked of, far away from the East End and Ronnie, was surely his last chance of freedom from the bonds of twinship.

He knew that after Cornell's murder, and the crazy ordered killing of Frank Mitchell, the time would come when they'd be behind bars. He also knew that his twin's illness was getting worse. He believed he still had it in him to be a legitimate businessman. He could, he convinced himself, make amends with Frances, prove to her that he wasn't Evil Reg at all – but the same caring guy who still loved her as much as ever. They'd find another place together, he'd make everything up to her, he promised.

A cynic might also say that a reunion with his pretty wife would also prove highly positive for the twins' public relations machine, especially if they did go down for some time.

Whether Frances was convinced by all Reggie's promises remains doubtful. She was weak, thin, quite passive. But she was as intelligent as she'd always been. She'd heard it all before many times. And she'd noticed that the promises to change always seemed to intensify when he was away from Ron's influence, as he had been at the beginning of their relationship. Yet he did seem to be genuine, she told a friend. He was certainly different. He reminded her of the younger Reg who'd been so pleasant and attentive to her. Was she merely playing lip service to his renewed pleas for one more chance? And was Reg merely acting the part of the husband hoping for reconciliation because he knew the net was closing in on him?

I don't believe Frances now shared Reg's dream of a future together. It was surely comforting, in her unhappy existence, to see him as keen as ever and to do some of the things they'd enjoyed in the past, the drives to the country, the two of them far away from the East End – and Ronnie.

In all probability, Frances was too diminished by everything she'd experienced to push him away or make big demands. She was exhausted. It was easier to just pretend.

Frances Shea, by this time, had chosen her path. The knowledge that there was only one way to banish her torment and fear for ever was now stuck fast in her mind. It just wouldn't go away.

The calendar said it was almost summer, but the English weather, as usual, had proved unreliable. The days were getting longer, yet May that year was a disappointingly cool, dull month in London. Apart from one brief spell of sunshine, it remained chilly and rainy.

Reg, ever aware of how the Mediterranean sunshine lifted his Frankie's spirits, suggested a second honeymoon at the end of June. Just them, away from it all in Ibiza. Frances loved the sleepy, pine-scented Spanish island with its near deserted beaches and laid-back old town. Yes, she said, they could do that.

On 5 June Frances went for an appointment at the Hackney Hospital with the psychiatric consultant, Dr Julius Silverstone. He thought she seemed a bit brighter. She told him she was going on holiday with her ex-husband and asked him for some tablets for the flight, which he duly prescribed. The following day, she saw Reg and they booked the tickets for Ibiza at a local travel agent. Later, they farewelled each other at her brother's flat and Reg went home.

It was her brother Frankie who found her. That morning of 7 June, he took his sister a cup of tea, as he usually did, carefully placing it on the bedside table.

She seemed to be still sleeping peacefully, so he went out to work. Yet something, he couldn't quite explain what, sent him back to check on his sister around lunchtime. She was just as he'd left her earlier. The tea was stone cold.

'Oh no, she's gone and done it again,' he whispered to himself as he stood over the bed, fervently hoping for evidence of some sign of life. But as he touched her hand, now cold, he realised the truth. There was a strange little half-smile on his sister's face, a smile, almost of triumph, that was to haunt him down the years. To Frankie, it was as if she was saying, 'I'm happy now'. His beautiful sister Franny was dead. She'd found her way out.

Frankie called the doctor, who came and confirmed what he already knew and contacted the police. He then called his dad who drove round straight away. At first glance, Frank Senior thought his daughter was just sleeping. But by now she was stone cold. Rigor mortis was already setting in. Franny was gone. She'd taken a huge number of sleeping pills. 'Those bastards the Krays have finished her off,' said Frank Senior to his son.

After his dad had driven off to break the terrible news to his wife, Frankie asked a friend to go round to Vallance Road, to summon Reg.

According to Rita Smith, Reg had already experienced a premonition of something terrible happening to Frances the night before and had even driven round to Wimbourne Court in a panic around dawn. He didn't ring the bell, however, realising that everyone might still be asleep.

'He had that feeling that something was wrong,' recalled Rita. 'The day before he'd said she was really down. She'd coloured her hair, put some stuff on it and she couldn't get it off. Reggie even went to the chemist to get something to brush it out.'

Yet despite Reg's efforts to cheer Frances up that night, when he left her he later told Rita she seemed distant, not very communicative. At the time, immediately after she died, some people wanted to believe it was this small thing, a bad hair day, that had tipped Frances over the edge: she was a very appearance-conscious girl, almost to the point of neurosis. Maybe it was an accident, and she just took one pill too many? She couldn't have planned it, many argued. They were looking forward to going away, weren't they?

These were false hopes. Frances had been merely biding her time, pretending to Reg about the holiday, knowing full well she'd never be going anywhere with him again.

How did she get the drugs that killed her? The doctors had insisted that though Frances could be prescribed certain drugs, she should not be permitted to keep any drugs in her possession.

'She had sleeping pills but they were kept away from her, just to be given to her when needed. But she found them. The whole lot,' recalled Rita Smith.

As Trevor Turner pointed out, all the instructions and efforts of the doctors treating a suicidal person outside a hospital setting have their limitations: a truly determined person will find a way to get their hands on the drugs that can kill them, if they wish to.

Yet now, faced with the shock of their loss, the two opposing factions in her life, rather than becoming united in their grief, linked by their loss, were driven even further along the path of hatred and vengeance.

Reggie, upon seeing Frances lying there, lifeless, lost to him for good, was overwhelmed with grief. He drank himself into oblivion that afternoon and spent that same night on the floor beside her body, weeping bitter tears – and wallowing in his undying hatred for the Sheas. They had done this terrible thing. He wanted to kill them.

Back at Ormsby Street, the family's pain must have been unfathomable. Even with the knowledge of the previous suicide attempts, they'd never quite managed to truly believe it could come to this: as far as they were concerned, Reggie Kray was the monstrous killer of their daughter, a man beyond evil.

What happened next in June 1967 is a measure of Reg's dogged determination to possess Frances Shea to the grave and beyond. It also shows contempt for Frances's loved ones at what was surely the worst time of their lives.

After Frances's body had been moved to the mortuary

where, as her husband and next of kin, he was required to identify it, Reggie didn't waste a minute.

There were plenty of histrionics, with Reggie weeping and pleading with his darling Frankie to come back to him over and over again, an incredibly theatrical display of grief he would repeat, day after day, even after her body was moved to a silk-lined coffin in the funeral parlour at Hayes & English in Hoxton Street, N1. Despite all this, the practical, devious Reg went into action.

He drove round to Ormsby Street and Wimbourne House and demanded every single item belonging to Frances. Her engagement ring. All her jewellery. All the letters between them. Photos. Her bank book. Her collection of little dolls from their trips abroad. A silver dressing table set he'd bought her. Her clothes, underwear. Even her make-up. Everything.

Here we see the same Reg the organiser, the businesslike twin who always did a first-class mopping up job after one of the Kray's calamitous crimes, the same Reg who'd successfully engineered the silence of the entire East End after the disastrous Cornell slaying. Cunning Reg, the planner who thought ahead, knew the law, understood perfectly he was entitled to everything as Frances's legal next of kin. The same Reg who'd strung Frances along on the annulment of their marriage – until it was too late.

There was no pity or concern for the family of the girl he claimed to love, at a time when they desperately needed the smallest crumb of comfort they could salvage from their wrecked lives. His savage ransacking of Elsie and Frank Shea's daughter's life, right down to the last hair grip, was yet another example of Kray terrorism, rule by fear.

But it was also an act of sheer calculation, lest anything in her belongings might betray his image and incriminate Reggie as the monster controller he surely was at that moment. The Sheas needed something to hang on to, no matter how small, in the early days of their grief, something to briefly assuage the sorrow that would never really leave them for the rest of their lives.

What Reggie Kray gave them as a grieving son-in-law was as violent and crushing as if he'd taken a brick and smashed it right in their faces. Though as we will see, despite his raid on her possessions, he didn't quite manage to get his hands on everything.

Until Frances died, it was relatively simple to understand, even to find a modicum of sympathy, for the conflict in Reggie Kray's emotions: his desire for Frances and a different, normal life versus the overwhelming need to remain with his crazy twin brother – who hated Frances's very existence and scared her witless.

Yet at this juncture, when all Reggie's fantasies for their future were finally destroyed, you have to question the motivation of a man who, in the midst of such tragedy, so chillingly sets out to put his own interests before anything else.

This also strips bare the Kray myth, persistent to this very day, that the twins were ultimately a force for good.

The ransacking of Frances's bedroom, the plundering of the remnants of her short life, were never the actions of a caring, generous or thoughtful man. Respect is a word that crops up again and again in the Kray lexicon. It's almost a mantra within the world they inhabited – even today the word has profound connotations in the criminal world. Where was the respect for Frances and her family in this?

Six days after Frances's death, an inquest was held at St

Pancras Coroner's Court on 13 June. Here is the report of the inquest from the local paper, the *Hackney Gazette*, dated Friday 16 June 1967:

MRS KRAY TOOK DRUGS OVERDOSE

At a time when she had been planning a holiday with her husband, Mrs Frances Elsie Shea (otherwise Kray), wife of Mr Reginald Kray, a company director, took an overdose of drugs at her brother's home, 34 Wimbourne Court, Wimbourne Street, Shoreditch, it was disclosed at Tuesday's St Pancras inquest.

Recording a verdict that she had died from barbiturate poisoning and had 'killed herself' the Coroner, Mr Ian Milne, said she had suffered a personality disorder.

'Her marriage was on the rocks, although there seems to have been rising hopes of a reconciliation' said Mr Milne.

'Barbiturates can be bought almost as easily as sweets on the London streets and she has clearly taken an enormous overdose. I am satisfied it was self-administered.'

Her brother, Mr Frank Shea, a haulage contractor, said she had lived at Ormsby Street, Shoreditch, but for the past three months had been living with him. He said she had reverted to her maiden name by deed poll, but she had been 'hoping her marriage would come right.' She used to practise typing and shorthand to get her old skill back. He was not worried about her in any way.

Mr Shea said she did have tablets prescribed by

her doctor. He agreed with the Coroner that he had at one time searched her handbag to see if she had got hold of more from somewhere else. He also agreed that his wife had some sleeping tablets and that she had 'missed some'.

Mr Shea said that her husband had been to see her and she and Mr Kray had been discussing plans for a holiday. Everything was quite all right, and there was absolutely nothing to indicate she might harm herself.

On the Wednesday morning (June 7) he took her a cup of tea and he thought she was just waking up. It was about 10 a.m. His wife was still in the flat. He went out and returned about 2 o'clock and noticed the tea was still there. He called a doctor who certified she was dead.

Dr Julius Silverstone, consultant psychiatrist at Hackney Hospital, said he had known Mrs Kray as a patient since January this year (1967) but she had first attended a psychiatrist in 1965 for a while as an outpatient. She was seen in 1966 by his predecessor and it was thought advisable to bring her into the hospital as an inpatient. She stayed in the hospital and had a 'variety of treatments'.

'I think she was [sic] largely a personality problem,' said Dr Silverstone.

He said that in October last year ('66) she was taken to St Leonard's Hospital, as a result of an overdose of tablets, and again in January this year. It was diagnosed as barbiturate poisoning but she was found in a gas-filled room.

Replying to the Coroner, he said it was 'very

difficult to say' whether or not they were genuine suicide attempts. She was certainly a very distressed young woman. He last saw her on June 5 and she was talking about plans for a holiday. He gave her some tablets, which she asked for, for the plane flight.

P.C. Geoffrey Tomlin said he found Mrs Kray wearing pyjamas. The cup of tea was still there, he added.

Dr N Patel, pathologist, stated that there were no signs of violence or injury and no evidence of alcohol.

Other newspapers reported the story. *The Times* reported that 'Mr Reginald Kray was in court at the inquest but did not give evidence.'

His twin, of course, remained in hiding.

According to Rita Smith, Reggie was shocked to learn at the inquest that Frances's suicide attempts went back much further than he'd known: 'He found out she had suffered from depression and attempted to kill herself when she was about 13. He didn't know before that.'

Unfortunately, archival records of the inquest are not available. In a sense, this hidden history of depression – there was no reference to it in any other aspect of my research – makes it clear that Frances was already far too vulnerable a young girl to be able to handle the violent world she'd unwittingly stepped into – and remained trapped in.

As with the wedding, the Sheas' wishes were cast aside when it came to Frances's funeral. Her brother attempted to start making the arrangements at English's Funeral Parlour but Reggie intervened.

No, she couldn't have a quiet, small family funeral: as his

wife she'd have a big, lavish funeral befitting her celebrity status. No, she could not be buried under her own name, the name she'd changed legally. She was a Kray. He'd be organising the headstone and it would say she was a Kray. And she was to be buried in the satin and lace wedding gown which he'd purchased. He was her husband and he'd bury her the way he wanted. As he told John Pearson afterwards: 'I'd given her the East End's wedding of the year. Now I was giving her the East End's funeral of the year.'

The lavish, extravagant East End Cockney funeral is, of course, as much an expression of self-assertion as a tradition in that part of London. It goes back a long way, to the nineteenth century, where working-class funerals meant horse-drawn hearses, coffins with brass knobs and mourners dressed in black silk. In due course, an over-the-top display of flowers became de rigueur too.

Frances's funeral was as ostentatious as Reggie wished. At the time, the story went round that the funeral cost ran to £2,000. (Today's equivalent of that sum is around £30,000.) There were enormous floral displays from their underworld contacts and members of the Kray firm, complete with condolence cards, dwarfing the more modest wreaths from Frances's family. Reggie ordered huge floral wreaths, one in a heart shape with red roses and white carnations going through the middle, the biggest one being a six-foot tall wreath spelling out her name. Ron, still hiding from the law, sent a huge bunch of carnations.

Albert Donoghue recalled his distasteful task at the cemetery before the mourners arrived: 'I had to go and check all the bouquets, see who had sent flowers and then tell Reggie who'd been missing. He'd remember that. It was sick.'

For the Sheas, while the funeral turned out to be everything they didn't want – an extravagant gangster funeral – there had been one small victory in the midst of their grief.

After the funeral, Elsie told people that she had secretly visited the undertakers and convinced them to let her put a little slip and a pair of tights onto Frances underneath the wedding dress. She also claimed that she had managed to remove the wedding ring from Frances's finger and replace it with a little ring Frances had kept since childhood.

Reg's old friend Father Hetherington conducted the funeral service at St James the Great, the same church where the marriage had taken place.

After the service, the mourners, mostly culled from the Kray's world, where celebrity met underworld, were transported in ten huge black limousines for the journey to Chingford Mount Cemetery where Reg had purchased a large burial plot, his intention to be buried there with Frances, along with all the other members of the Kray family.

At the cemetery, police even mingled with the mourners, in the vain hope that Ronnie might appear, much to Reggie's disgust. At the grave, as he watched his wife's coffin lowered into the earth, Reggie wept. Everyone else watched in silence. It was a classic Hollywood performance, a ritual demonstrated to show the world how Reggie Kray had loved and lost his wife.

As Albert Donoghue commented: 'He was a good actor. If Frances was mentioned afterwards, he'd start to cry. It was either remorse or acting.'

Yet within a few months, as the Shea family struggled with their loss, the grief-stricken husband would be finding comfort in the arms of a twenty-three-year-old woman. And a man answering to the name of McVitie would be meeting a grisly end...

CHAPTER 11

AFTERWARDS

Gin. Bottle after bottle of Gordon's, poured continuously down Reggie's throat. Medicine, if you like, gulped down in a fruitless attempt to help him handle what had happened. There were also handfuls of Valium taken with the gin in a pointless attempt to calm himself down. A tidal wave of intoxication, night after night, anything to alleviate the pain – and crush the truth, which he couldn't acknowledge, of his own responsibility for Frances's downfall.

He'd always been the rational twin. Yet now there seemed no reason at all in his behaviour: consequently there were two madmen giving orders to the men in the Firm, drawing up hate lists, behaving unpredictably. Very soon Reggie looked haggard and drawn. Haunted.

Just a week after Frances's funeral, now virtually consumed by paranoia, Reggie Kray decided it was time to get out there and wreak revenge on the Shea family. He'd start, he thundered, with Frankie Shea. The row over the unpaid debt of £1,000 that Frankie had lent Reggie still rankled. He'd sort him out once and for all.

He despatched one of the men around him, Tony Lambrianou, to drive him to a pub in Hoxton where he knew Frankie drank regularly.

'He had a gun on him and I realised he was thinking about shooting Frankie Shea,' recalled Lambrianou, in his book, *Inside the Firm* (Lambrianou died in 2004).

Tony Lambrianou said he found himself in a difficult position, having known Frankie since childhood. 'I understood his [Reggie's] feelings, especially since other people were putting a lot of poison in, sticking up Frances's name while knowing it was a sore point. At the same time I saw the other side of it all and I could never have harmed Frankie Shea; could never have seen him shot.'

Inside the pub, Frankie was drinking with his mates, unaware of how close he was to Reggie's paranoid rage – and the gun.

Tony Lambrianou parked the car opposite the pub and started talking to Reggie, hoping he could get him to see reason. 'In my heart of hearts, I was almost certain that Reggie could not have hurt Frankie,' he wrote. 'If he'd come face to face with him, he'd have been more likely to break down, because every time he saw him, he saw Frances; or maybe he might even have given him a few quid rather than do anything to him. But when Reggie was in a funny mood, you could never be completely sure.

'I said to him, "Look Reggie, you don't mean it. Come on. You don't mean it." And as we talked, I knew that the moment of danger had passed. Reggie calmed down; he was rational again.'

On another occasion not long after Frances's death, Tony Lambrianou wrote that he ran into Frankie Shea in a West End club. 'He said, "Am I all right? I know you and Chris are very strong with the twins now."

'I said, "Frank, we go back a long way and I'd never do anything to harm you. I'd be insulted if you thought I would."'

Kray minder and enforcer Ronnie Hart saw the state Reggie was in at very close range. He'd been living alongside it right from the time Frances died. Hart was the twins' cousin, a blonde, good-looking, former merchant navy sailor. He'd relished being part of the Firm, had opted to get involved with it for kicks, for the sheer thrill of living dangerously.

Ronnie Hart, in fact, played a key role in the twins' downfall. Yet in those weeks immediately after Frances's death, he went everywhere with Reggie as his driver. He'd been with Reggie when he'd gone to the mortuary to identify her body and after the funeral he would drive Reggie each week out to the suburbs to the cemetery at Chingford Mount.

'The minds of the twins were, of course, completely warped and inhuman,' said Hart in 1969. 'In his peculiar way he was devoted to Frances and he was convinced – probably because of his ego – that she really loved him and that after she left him, she only stayed away at the instigation of her parents.

'On every trip to the cemetery, Reggie would sob. He spent £20 on fresh flowers for the grave every Saturday. He became so upset he was incapable of changing the flowers he'd bring. I had to do the job. All he could do was kneel in front of the grave and cry. He bought a windmill that stood about three feet high, a working model made in a plastic material which looked like stone.

'He said, "This will do until I get the headstone made." The headstone was to be made in Italy from Italian marble.'

The expensive, specially made headstone bearing the name Frances Elsie Kray was to be a permanent reminder for the Sheas of Reggie's complete rejection of their wishes, a visible affront to Frances's memory and, even more painfully, a denial of what had been her own wish to be buried as Frances Shea.

On the anniversary of Frances's twenty-fourth birthday, 23 September, 1967, Hart drove Reggie to the graveside. This time, they were accompanied by Violet and her sister May. Elsie and Frank Senior were already there.

'Mr and Mrs Shea put two black vases down, one on either side of the grave, and on each was a label. One read: "To my beloved sister: from Frank, for your birthday" and the other read: "To our darling daughter, remembering you on your birthday",' recalled Hart.

'While the parents were putting flowers on the grave, we all stood back by our car.

'Mrs Shea broke down and cried. She came across to Reggie and spat at him.

'She said, "You killed my daughter, you bastard, and if you spend a thousand pounds a week on flowers it won't do any good because we will never forgive you and neither will she."

'Then they walked away.'

At the time, Reggie said nothing.

'The following Saturday I took him to the cemetery, he pulled the flowers out of the pots Frances's parents had left and savagely screwed them up in his hands. "I don't want their stinking flowers on my wife's grave," he said.

'"I would love to have choked her last week when she said that to me but I daren't because of Frances."

'He then moved the two pots into bushes where they could not be seen,' concluded Hart.

'When she died it was like the world had come to an end,' remembered Rita Smith. 'We didn't know what to do. He looked absolutely terrible. One of his mates said, "He's worrying me, Reet. He's drinking himself silly. He doesn't care if he lives or dies."'

Throughout the East End, the story of Frances and how she died was an endless topic of speculation. Some believed it wasn't suicide at all. Ronnie had murdered her, they claimed, forced the pills down her throat, though there was no foundation in this whatsoever, since Ron remained in hiding at that time.

Others claimed they'd both 'done her in' themselves, hatched a plot between them to kill her because she was threatening to go to the police. Most people, however, knew that Elsie and Frank believed Reggie and Reggie alone carried much of the responsibility for Frances's self destruction. All these stories, of course, eventually found their way back to Reggie. Which made him even more deranged.

'After she died, we all thought it would send Reggie over the edge,' recalled Maureen Flanagan. 'Their brother Charlie always said that people kept telling him in pubs that Reggie had scared this young, beautiful girl out of her life with his lifestyle.'

Tormented, drunk nearly all the time, and more under the influence of his twin than at any time before, Reggie now started to take out his rage, his anger, on virtually any random target.

Ronnie, who came out of hiding that July, merely added fuel to the fire. He didn't stop reminding Reggie that he hadn't yet done what he'd done that night in the Blind Beggar pub.

Reggie had to kill, he told him over and over again. Did he call himself a man? Or was he just soft? Did he want to be a cissy for the rest of his life? Only murder by Reggie's hand, he insisted, would seal their bond, reinforce their legend as killer twins.

By now, Reggie was teetering on the edge of breakdown. Ron, helpful as ever, told him a man called Frederick, a small-time criminal, had been rude about Frances. That was it. Reggie went round to the man's house and shot him in the leg. He knifed another man for some half-imagined slight. Both men survived their attacks. Neither took their grievances to the law, of course.

Business was ticking over but it wasn't that good. The twins changed tack: they got involved in peddling purple hearts, took over fruit machines in the West End, even briefly took a cut from others involved in the pornography business. Word got back to them that a Detective Inspector from Scotland Yard's Flying Squad was in the East End, talking to people about George Cornell.

For the Kray twins this was to be their final summer of discontent, their last as free men. Given Ron's illness and Reggie's own mental instability, the summer gave way to a terrible autumn of blood, gore and the crazily botched murder of 'one of their own': Jack 'The Hat' McVitie (the nickname was used because McVitie always wore a hat to conceal his baldness).

There are many accounts of how small-time crook Jack 'The Hat' McVitie met a violent end at the hands of the twins in a basement flat at 65, Evering Road, Stoke Newington on

29 October 1967. Few tally precisely, though like the Cornell killing, there were many witnesses to the slaying.

Jack 'The Hat' was well known around the East End, a fighter and a bit of a ladies' man. He'd recently got involved with the Krays in the purple hearts business, yet there was bad blood between McVitie and Ronnie in the weeks before the murder. Ron had given McVitie £100, as a down payment for the killing of businessman Leslie Payne, a key Kray associate Ronnie was convinced had now shopped them to the law (this information turned out to be pretty accurate).

McVitie, who was far from a professional hood, bungled the killing of Payne. The man's wife had come to the front door of their home and told him that Payne wasn't there – so McVitie just drove off. This was not exactly the handiwork of a dedicated hitman.

Yet with his mission unfulfilled, he had not troubled himself to repay the £100 'deposit' Ron had handed him to do the killing. With Ron on the warpath for the slight, Reggie had stepped in, even smoothed things over in the wake of Ronnie's wrath. Even more bizarrely, he reputedly lent McVitie some money when he'd pleaded poverty. Somewhat stupidly, however, McVitie, a habitual drunk and pill popper, didn't repay the kindness: he was later overheard in the Regency Club, in his cups, threatening to shoot the twins.

This, of course, was not to be tolerated, and set in motion a chain of events which culminated with McVitie being lured, at midnight, to the Evering Road flat on the promise of a party where the twins were both drunk, Reggie high as a kite on booze and pills, and awaiting his arrival. The 'party' ended with McVitie's mutilated corpse, wrapped in a bedspread, being dumped in a parked car, an old Ford

Zephyr belonging to McVitie, in south London. Police never found the corpse.

Freddie Foreman, writing in his autobiography, *Freddie Foreman: The Godfather of British Crime*, served ten years for his role in the murder of McVitie, though he had taken no part in the killing itself.

'The Lambrianou brothers and Ronnie Bender dumped the body on my doorstep in Bermondsey,' he wrote. Later Foreman transferred McVitie's corpse to a van and disposed of the Ford Zephyr in a wrecker's yard.

He then wrote: 'I drove his body down to the coast with a back-up motor minding me off. We had a friend who wrapped him up in chicken wire attached to weights... our contacts were now called in to help out again.' According to Foreman, just like the body of Frank Mitchell, McVitie's body was duly buried 'far out at sea'.

Ronnie Hart's description of how the twins murdered McVitie was to save him from at least twenty years behind bars, a huge betrayal, which shocked all those who were involved with the Krays at the time. (Hart, now deceased, is reported to have attempted suicide after the Kray trial and then emigrated to Australia with his wife, Vicky.)

Many others in the Firm were to ultimately betray the twins and break the wall of silence around them at their Old Bailey trial. Yet Hart's initial court account of the murder, first given to Bow Street Magistrates' Court in 1968, told the public, in no uncertain terms, what the Kray twins were really capable of. Repeated even more sensationally when the twins' case was finally sent for trial at the Criminal Court at the Old Bailey in January 1969, it was a chilling eye-witness account of the depths to which the twins had sunk in those last months of their freedom. Here is that first ever account. It shocked everyone: it was the first time the public was able to learn, in detail, the blood-drenched truth about the twins. The following account is from *The Times* newspaper, 16 October 1968:

Nearly a year after the murder, on October 16, 1968, Ronnie Hart told Bow Street Magistrates' Court that he saw Reggie stab Jack the Hat to death while his twin held him from behind saying 'do him, Reg'.

Hart told the court that he was present at the Evering Road flat that October night when a drunken McVitie arrived at the flat with four other men.

'Soon after arrival there was a scuffle between Mr McVitie and the Kray twins.

'I saw Reggie's hand trapped under McVitie's arm – he had a gun in his hand. McVitie was holding Reggie Kray's hand over his arm – Reggie was trying to get his hand from under his arm.

'At one stage McVitie attempted to run from the room but Reggie Kray grabbed him, made him sit down.'

During the scuffle, Ron Hart said Reggie Kray had attempted to shoot McVitie with a black gun. But each time he pulled the trigger it failed to fire. McVitie was sitting facing a window as Reggie Kray stood in front of him.

'Reggie then held the gun against McVitie and tried to shoot him again. He was holding the gun a foot or two from McVitie's face. The gun didn't work.

'Then McVitie tried to jump through the window.

He broke the window and we pulled him back. Then we started to hit him and he kept saying, "stop it".

'Ronnie Kray got him in a lock from behind. Reggie got a knife from a shelf and stuck it into McVitie's face. McVitie was still saying, "stop it".

'Reggie stuck the knife into his stomach and side. He stabbed him more than once.

'Ronnie Kray was telling him to kill him. I don't know how many times he said it. "Kill him Reg".'

When Hart was asked of any reason why Reggie Kray would want to kill McVitie, he told the court: 'Ronnie was taunting him all the time. He said it was time Reggie done his. I heard him say this on more than one occasion. Every time they had a row, Ron would say, 'I've done one, it's about time you did yours.'

This account, of course, and the phrase itself 'I've done mine, you do yours', linked the twins to both the McVitie and Cornell murders and meant the two cases could eventually be heard together. (There was a separate trial for the murder of Frank Mitchell, where Freddie Foreman and the twins were acquitted of his murder.)

The court statement by Hart demonstrated all too clearly Ronnie's power over the weaker Reggie, his goading, his jeering, his determination to make his twin his partner in the ultimate of crimes. This evil power, unleashed on his 'other half' would go on to form an important part of the legend of the Krays over the years.

Reggie initially denied his part in the murder. He insisted it was Hart who stabbed McVitie to death, though he confessed to the murder much later in a book. Yet even two years before he died, when he was seeking parole, Reggie Kray still insisted he didn't feel guilt for this murder.

At that time in 1998, Reggie had put in a formal application for parole. Consultant psychiatrist Trevor Turner was then asked by Reggie's solicitors to meet with Reggie and prepare a psychiatric report on his mental state. Turner talked to Reggie at length. His report concluded that Reggie's mental state was stable and he was not, in any way, a risk to the community should he be released.

'He was perfectly coherent, no sign of being depressed, paranoid or demented,' recalled Turner.

When it came to the question of the McVitie murder, Reggie's response to Trevor Turner was along the lines of 'if I hadn't killed him, he would have killed me,' added Turner.

'He put it in a perfectly coherent way: "I could say I'm sorry, but I'm not".'

A few days before he died in 2000, as his life ebbed away with cancer, in his last few days of freedom, Reggie Kray conducted a deathbed interview broadcast on the BBC.

In the interview he again showed no remorse for McVitie's death, saying he was 'a vexation to the spirit' and on that night of the murder he had a lot of frustration in him 'and anger, probably more than any other night of my life'.

There was only one thing fuelling that anger and frustration: his tortured grief and anger at the loss of Frances, a factor which could have been taken into account by Reggie's defence team and which could possibly have earned him a lesser prison sentence in 1969.

There was, of course, no way that Reggie Kray would have given his brief the go-ahead to use this grief as part of his defence at the time. It would have destroyed his hard-man image, and set him apart from his twin. Yet even when you consider Ronnie's role in McVitie's death as a significant contributory factor, you still have to ask yourself: Would Jack McVitie have met such a nasty end had it not been for the combination of Reggie's grief and Ronnie's taunts?

Dick Hobbs certainly believes the McVitie killing was a consequence of Frances's death: 'That particular episode seems to have been largely driven by Reggie Kray's grief and the increased amounts of drink and drugs he was taking as a result of that grief. His behaviour became more violent and unpredictable after her suicide. Had she not done so, it might have delayed the twins' demise.'

Chris Lambrianou (Tony's brother), who served fifteen years in prison for his role in the disposal of McVitie's body, also believed it was this unpredictability that drove the events leading up to the murder. He described the crime as 'a tragedy of errors', going on to say:

'Reggie had no intention of killing anyone that night. I honestly don't think it was meant to happen. They'd fallen out with him and Ronnie was making all sorts of threats but just a week before, they'd been sitting talking to Jack in the Regency like good mates. There was no suspicion that this was going to happen.'

Yet the 'now it's your turn Reg' killing of Jack McVitie was, in essence, the beginning of the end of the Kray madness. The moment encapsulated an era when, as Ronnie Kray, described it, they were 'the bosses of London', and it was reaching its endgame. Because the on-off police investigation into their activities was now ready to swing back into action with a vengeance. The Krays had to be stopped.

After the McVitie murder, as Ronnie Bender and Tony

and Chris Lambrianou were left to mop up the blood, and to clear the flat of all evidence and dump the body, the twins had left London.

Ronnie Hart drove them first to Cambridge, then to the Suffolk village of Lavenham, where they visited an old friend and enjoyed the peace and quiet of their favourite place, the English countryside.

At the same time there were already big developments underway at Scotland Yard: Nipper Read's superiors had given him permission to launch a high-priority investigation into the twins.

It was to be a totally secret operation, run undercover with a fourteen-strong team of men working outside Scotland Yard from a police building, Tintagel House, on the River Thames's Albert Embankment.

Around Christmas 1967 Read told his superiors he believed he could catch the Krays. Yet he understood all too well that the men who would bring them down and give evidence against them were criminals.

The price of these men's evidence, for the police, would be high. It could mean the police having to look away from these men's other crimes, a bitter pill to swallow for the police hierarchy.

Yet with some reluctance, the police bosses agreed. The hunt to trap the Krays was on. And as the investigation grew and witnesses gradually started to talk, they were given a guarantee: their evidence would not be used until the Krays were finally locked up. From the police perspective, the trade-off, a first in the Met's long history, made the entire exercise far more risky. But the risk was worth taking. As 'Nipper' Read admitted later: 'It was the only way.'

By the New Year, Fort Vallance had been abandoned, one of the last houses in the street to be demolished in the slum-clearance programme. Charlie and Violet were allocated a new local-authority flat in a high-rise building, Braithwaite House in Clerkenwell, about a mile away. But the twins decided it was a good idea to move their parents to the country. In February 1968, they bought a country house (in Violet's name, with a huge mortgage) in the Suffolk village of Bildeston, near Sudbury.

The twins' last months of freedom were spent playing country squires on the weekends and in their parents' flat on the ninth floor of the high-rise building overlooking the City during the week. Their spies kept them well informed. Reports came through to them all the time that Read and his men were on their heels, yet they were both delusional: Ron, of course, relishing a new enemy, wanted Read's head on a platter. He even went out and bought two boa constrictor snakes from the famous Knightsbridge department store, Harrods, and named them Read and Gerrard, after the two detectives who were now his main adversaries. David Bailey took photos of the twins with the snakes.

As for Reggie, he was convinced the key witnesses to the murders would not dare betray them and speak out.

He was so wrong: Leslie Payne, terrified by the whispers of repeated threats he and his family were facing after the McVitie killing, finally agreed to conduct a series of interviews with Nipper Read. He and he alone had helped the twins make a lot of money and buy into Esmeralda's Barn. So he knew an awful lot about what the twins and the Firm had been doing for the last twelve years. Details. Names. Times. Places. It was a breakthrough the police desperately needed.

AFTERWARDS

By this time, Reggie had recovered somewhat from his tormented grief and found a new girlfriend, a twenty-three-year-old called Carol Thompson. Chris Lambrianou described Carol as 'very pretty, a nice ordinary girl, nothing flashy, just a decent girl'.

According to John Pearson in his book, *The Cult of Violence*, in the weeks before the police net closed in on the twins, Carol had briefly confided in him about her relationship with Reggie.

Just like Frances, she found the endless drinking and the fact they were never alone very difficult to handle. She told Pearson she and Reggie were having 'bitter arguments just as he had had with Frances'.

'Carol told me he was often on the edge of violence,' recalled Pearson. 'She said, "So I used to tell him: hit me if you want to, show me what a brave man you are." But of course he never hit me.'

It was less than a year since Frances had died. By taking up with Carol, who briefly tried living with him but finally gave up, it seems Reggie was still pursuing the same impossible dream of a normal life away from the nightmare world of betrayal and lifetime imprisonment he was now facing.

At precisely 6 a.m. on the morning of 8 May 1968, Nipper Read's team of detectives finally pounced. One group, headed by Read, arrested the twins at 12 Braithwaite House; others went to the homes of the leading players in the Firm to arrest them in a meticulously planned operation. They found Reggie in bed in the flat with a girl called June. Ron was in the next room with a young man. No resistance was made at all when Nipper Read, their Number One enemy, finally slipped the handcuffs on the pair.

Ron is reported to have said, 'Alright, Mr Read. I'll come quietly. But I've got to have my pills.'

The news of the Krays' arrest galvanised everyone. Could this really mean the end of their reign? Would they go down for a long stretch? After all, they'd been arrested before and wound up triumphant.

At 95 Geffrye Street, just a stone's throw from their former home in Ormsby Street, now scheduled for demolition, the news of the twins' arrest reached Elsie and Frank that same day.

The couple were doing their best to adjust to life in their newly built two-bedroom flat, recently allocated to them by the local authority, a home with all the conveniences they'd lacked for so long. Hearing about the Krays' arrest seemed to come right out of the blue – even the East End rumour mill hadn't known very much about the details of Read's top secret operation to bring the twins down once and for all.

And Elsie Shea didn't waste a minute. She'd been praying for this day for a long time. Without even considering the eventual outcome of the news, Elsie decided it was time she made that phone call. She rang the superintendent's office at Chingford Mount Cemetery. Could they please tell her what the procedure was for having her daughter's remains removed from her grave at Chingford Mount to a resting place elsewhere? Did she have to fill in a form? Fine. Could they please send it to her as soon as possible?

'They'll never get off this time,' she told her husband.

'They've got to let us do it.'

CHAPTER 12

THE LAST LETTER

That phone call to the cemetery in May 1968 marked the beginning of Elsie Shea's quest to have Frances's remains removed from the Kray plot and buried elsewhere in her own name, the name she had so determinedly changed back to Shea in the year before she died.

A note of that phone call was the first entry I discovered in the Home Office file for 1968 that covers Elsie's formal application to move Frances's body from Chingford Mount, a file first released in 2004.

The file contains a detailed history of Elsie's attempts to remove Frances's remains from 'Kray corner'.

Its contents are set out below. They are important because they include Elsie's version of the trajectory of Frances's relationship with Reggie, though some of the smaller details written in the file are incorrect and it seems Elsie herself was unable to clarify certain aspects of the story.

Yet what I also discovered amidst the papers in the Home Office file were some other documents, letters I never expected to find. This unexpected discovery revealed a great deal about Frances and her state of mind around the time of her death.

A week or so after her initial call to the superintendent at the cemetery, Elsie received a form to fill in. She duly sent the form off on 14 May 1968. But it was not until 31 March 1969 that Elsie was able to phone the Home Office officials to discuss her application.

This gap of several months was, of course, because she was waiting for the outcome of the Krays' arrest and the final, much-publicised hearing of their case at the Central Criminal Court at London's Old Bailey.

The Krays' trial at the Old Bailey had started on 7 January 1969. It lasted for thirty-nine days, a 'show trial for the sixties', the longest and most expensive criminal trial to be held in London at the time.

It ended on 8 March 1969. The twins each received sentences of life imprisonment, recommended by Mr Justice Melford Stevenson to be not less than thirty years without parole, for the murders of Jack McVitie and George Cornell.

Elsie's phone call to the Home Office was generated by this news. Now, she reasoned, the authorities would be more sympathetic to her request. Reggie Kray was a convicted murderer, locked up, probably for good. He'd been given the longest prison sentence legally permitted.

The Home Office file on Elsie's application, written by Home Office official, R. Varney, reads as follows:

'She was concerned that the mere filling in of a form would

not sufficiently convey what she felt to be the strength of her case.

'Mrs Kray explained that her daughter's marriage to Reggie Kray was "in the process of being annulled at the time she took her own life and that a memorial stone was now being erected over the grave showing her daughter's married name and not the maiden name in which she had expressed her wish to be buried."

'She indicated there was no prospect of her feeling herself able to approach Reggie Kray and I was left with the impression there was no chance of him giving consent to the removal.'

R. Varney did not encourage Mrs Shea in the belief an interview at the Home Office would serve any useful purpose. Yet an interview was arranged at the Home Office, Romney House, Westminster, for 9 April 1969.

A note taken from this meeting at Romney House explains that Elsie brought her partially completed application forms and a number of other papers with her. It further states:

> Mrs Shea seemed to be a sensible sort of person, no more emotional than the circumstances warranted and to be genuinely motivated by concern for the good name of her family and desire to execute the wishes of her daughter.
>
> At the same time she seemed not to be very clear about some of the details of the events she described and said much of what she said about her daughter's married life was reconstructed after the event.
>
> 'Married in May 1965 at age twenty-one having been friendly with him since sixteen.' [The marriage took place in April 1965 but this error may have

been Elsie's incorrect recall of events, as was the statement that Frances was sixteen when first going out with Reggie.]

The marriage was never really much of a reality. After a week's honeymoon in Athens, Reggie Kray sent her to live with his mother. For the rest of her married life she stayed variously with her own family, alone in hotels and in flats provided by Kray, in hospitals and occasionally with women friends of the Krays, on trips abroad but never, apparently, together with Kray.

Her history through this time seems to have been one of growing addiction to drugs.

In March 1966 she changed her surname by deed poll to Shea. It was apparently around this time she formed the intention of pressing for an annulment of the marriage on the grounds of non-consummation.

According to Mrs Shea, Reggie Kray persuaded Frances to allow him to make the petition instead which, in her anxiety for the success of the annulment, she was willing to do. Kray then used every means to delay the process, which only arrived at the stage where it was ready to go to courts just before she died. And was therefore never completed.

Frances killed herself 7th June 1967 at her brother's home. It was her third attempt.

The death was reported to the coroner and the inquest was held, Mrs Shea thought, at Hackney [it was Clerkenwell]. Death certificate issued in the name of Frances Elsie Shea, otherwise Kray.

Frank's initial negotiation with undertakers Hayes

and English of 148 Hoxton Street N1 was interrupted according to Mrs Shea by the arrival of Reggie Kray with a priest whom Mrs Shea described as 'crooked' who later gave evidence at his trial.

Kray then made all the arrangements for the funeral including distribution of the booklets to accompany the service – in the name of Frances Elsie Kray.

Mrs Kray was not sure what denomination of religious rite the ceremony was accompanied – or whether her daughter was buried in consecrated ground.

She said the Krays ignored her at the funeral and evidently felt it to be a source of grievance that a friend of the Krays came after the ceremony to remove the names of donors from the funeral wreaths.

Elsie told the Home Office that the flowers her family placed on the grave had regularly been removed. She had seen the headstone Kray intended to erect over the grave costing £500 which was felt to be offensive and hypocritical, i.e. 'in loving memory of my darling wife Frances Elsie Kray' with verse. Mrs Shea seemed to be under the impression that the words on the headstone were conceived out of spite for her family and that she and her husband were upset to be seen visiting the grave linking them with a murderer.

Asked about her husband, Elsie said he shared her concern that his daughter's grave should not bear the Kray name but was not entirely happy with the idea of removing her body. She said he was very upset by the whole business and was not well enough to come to the Home Office with her.

It was not clear that Elsie's overriding concern

was the headstone, i.e. that it should bear the name by which she (Frances) was now legally known and which she believed at the time she wrote her last letter would be the name which would go on her grave.

If the headstone could be changed, Elsie told the Home Office, she would no longer wish to remove the body. She had not written to Kray to ask for his consent: she said it was inconceivable he would agree.

Kray was both legally the next of kin and he owned the freehold rights to the plot. It was explained that the scope of the Home Office was limited in view of Reggie Kray's objections and the objection of the burial authority for Chingford Mount. Elsie did not own the grave, therefore her rights were limited.

However, she told the Home Office, 'It was our daughter's dying wish that she should be buried in our name. She wrote a note to this effect shortly before taking phenobarbitone tablets. My husband and I are desperately anxious that this should be so.'

The file also revealed Home Office correspondence with the Registrar of the Abney Park Cemetery, the burial authority for Chingford Mount Cemetery. They, in turn, confirmed on 31 July 1969 that Reggie Kray was the owner of the grave: he was said to have purchased the freehold rights. The grave contained only the remains of Frances Shea – but there was room for three more burials. The ground was not consecrated. Abney Park Registrar Martin Clark reaffirmed that the burial authority would not allow the grave to be opened without Reggie Kray's consent: it was written into the cemetery regulations that the grave could not be opened without the owner's permission.

THE LAST LETTER

On 30 July 1969 the file noted that the public relations branch of the Home Office had suggested that Mrs Shea be invited to visit again and suggest that she defer her application for a year or more 'in the hope that RK's views may have mellowed by this time'.

They went on to say: 'The case for deferring the decision is surely that one would not wish to see a strong story in the newspapers about this at a time when sympathy for Mrs Shea is likely to be at a maximum.'

(The public relations people also suggested closing the file IF the Home Office could say in a letter and/or in an interview that under the law the Home Secretary had no power to act.)

The file also contains a Home Office letter sent to Elsie on 14 August 1969 saying that the Secretary of State could not help in this matter.

Another letter, dated 11 August 1969 from Reggie Kray's solicitors at the time, Sampson & Co at 11–13 St Bride Street, Ludgate Circus, London, EC4, confirmed that:

- Reggie Kray had full rights over the grave.
- The burial authority would not allow the grave to be opened without his consent.
- The only person with any authority to alter the headstone wording was the owner, Reggie Kray.

Furthermore, Sampson & Co wrote that Kray 'takes the very strongest possible objection that the remains of his late wife be removed from her grave or that any alteration be made to her memorial'.

'He is aware that during a period of separation resulting

from a matrimonial dispute his wife purported to change her name, but they were afterwards reconciled.'

The Home Office file also contains correspondence they had received from the Prison Department of the Home Office.

On 29 May 1969 the Prison Department wrote that beside being responsible for his security (in Brixton prison at the time), 'Kray poses a considerable control problem to prison staff and if we can help it we should avoid anything likely to make the control problem worse and it would appear that the matter of the grave and the removal of his wife's remains is a very delicate subject.'

So there it was. The authorities had played 'pass the parcel' and Elsie's request to them was rejected.

Reggie, always the organiser, had been very canny in his purchase of the freehold to the burial plot.

Perhaps he had done so on the advice of his solicitors; maybe he already understood it would give him absolute control over Frances's remains and that of his family. The authorities in the Prison Department were far too scared of Reggie's temper to do anything about it and, in the end, the Home Office concluded that even Frances's suicide 'was not enough to justify departure from the accepted principle that he had to give his consent'.

'It is a great pity but I cannot see any other decision is possible. The fact that a person has been sentenced for so serious an offence as murder, does not make him an outlaw, deprived of all other rights,' wrote the senior Home Office official overseeing the case.

Reading the file, I reflected that after this rejection, it would be very difficult for anyone in Elsie's situation not to feel profoundly bitter about the hand she had been dealt by authority.

Certainly, the Sheas came from a place where authority itself was paid scant respect. Yet this blow would have defeated anyone's belief in justice, the fair play the British are so renowned for.

But the yellowing file, its paper worn thin by time, also contained a few single sheets of photocopied paper, carefully folded up in the centre of the file, yet with no accompanying note or description at all.

These, I realised, after I had examined the contents, had been the papers Elsie had taken with her to the Home Office, to prove to the officials that it had been Frances's last wish to be buried in her own name. Frances's mother had clung to these tragic little documents, all photocopies, in the vain hope they would convince officialdom to help her.

These documents consist of four photocopied sheets of paper, all undated, seemingly written at different times, though the handwriting on two of them is much more legible than the remaining two.

One of the two legible notes is obviously a suicide note, addressed to Frances's family. From its contents it looks like it was written just before she died. The other, shorter, legible note is clearly directed at Reggie and takes the form of a goodbye, 'get out of my life' note.

The handwriting is stronger, clearer in this note and the tone is angry, rather than passive or defeatist. It doesn't read as anything like a suicide note.

The remaining two notes are difficult to decipher. But what can be deciphered is indeed proof that Frances did believe that by changing her name legally, she could be buried as Frances Shea.

It was an enormous shock to find these poignant notes,

ignored for so long, an eerie moment in what had already been a long quest for insights into Frances's story.

Here was Frances's voice, her last attempt at self-expression. And proof, if you like, of her determination to end the horror of the last two years for good. Showing these tragic letters to the Home Office officials had made no impact whatsoever on the outcome of Elsie's application. But it seems these were notes that the Sheas, in the confusion and grief of the days after Frances died, had somehow managed to conceal from Reggie's grasp.

Reggie Kray made it widely known that he was troubled by the fact that he never saw any suicide note after Frances died. In 1990 he wrote a book called *Born Fighter*. In his account of Frances's death at Wimbourne Court he wrote of arriving at the flat and being told that she had committed suicide.

Then he wrote: 'There was no last note anywhere in sight, which I found hard to believe because on the last two attempts, she had left notes. I was suspicious of my father-in-law... I thought he might have picked up a letter or a note.'

The originals of the notes could have been handed to police by her family after Frances died – but they were not mentioned in any reports of her inquest. It's possible that the less legible photocopied notes in the file could have been the notes Reggie mentioned about her previous attempts. Reggie, of course, desperately wanted them all – because he wouldn't want anyone else to read their contents. But in keeping these copies, at least, it seems the Sheas had achieved one small sad victory over their foe.

Here is the first legible letter. On the back of it, Frances had written:

'To my family.

'P.S. Dr Clein and him killed me'

At the top of the letter she had written:

'I love you forever until the end of time. All my things – to Frances [her niece] and my necklace to Frances.'

Dear Mum and Dad and Frankie

I'm sorry I've had to do it so this way but do me one favour don't grief [*sic*] too much over me after all, it's useless now and you have the baby to compensate for me.

I was dying in any case [underlined] you know when it comes there's nothing any doctor can do for you then.

I wish it wasn't me that had to bring disaster on the family – if I'd have had the guts I would have drowned myself – it all happened since I had that relapse xxxxx xxxxx [not legible] and I've had to keep on as long as possible for your sake. I'm sorry. I've told Bubbles some of the xxxxxx [not legible] things that have happened to me. Please don't grief [*sic*] for me – it's been a hard enough job for me to keep alive these last 7 weeks that's why I've always been so fidgety. Please forgive me as my last wish. I couldn't go on any longer and you know I'm not the person to give in if there's any chance of survival which there wasn't. Please love me always think there's always Frances to [this word difficult to read but looks like compensate].

Please forgive me

Love and xxx

Frances.

This looks like it was the final suicide letter; Frances mentions 'these last 7 weeks' which would have roughly been the period since her return from the last holiday in April.

Below is the most legible letter. It is written on a separate sheet of paper, possibly torn from a notebook, most likely written at another time because the writing itself is clearer, less shaky and well punctuated.

However, it is the last phrase that is so chillingly prophetic. This letter reads:

> Your low breed, sickly mouth ugly face sicken me.
> If I remember words of this effect from your mouth
> "F----- OLD BATTLEAXE" which are only suitable
> for your type of creatures. CRAWL BACK TO THE
> GUTTER. Get some ... 'F------ OLD B/AXE' to be a
> scrubber for you. Find a dumb blond, old, slave for
> yourself.
> Get a ROBOT – a stupid woman void of humanity.
> I'm finished with you forever and don't come
> crawling back gutter snipe. [These last six words are
> underlined] Have the decency to let me live my type
> of life and you can stink in yours unless you want a
> ghost to haunt you.

Of the remaining two pieces of photocopied paper, the writing is difficult to read and the photocopying much fainter. But here is what can be transcribed from the notes which run into two separate pages.

> ... ..suffering [underlined] any more and its best for
> you all to get over me. I wish Fate had been a bit

kinder to me and that I could have regained my peace of mind [underlined] and my strength [underlined] and my spirit [underlined] so that I would have proved to you all my love for you.

This is followed by several illegible lines and then it reads:

I can't [underlined] take anything any more. Please use all my money to help you for a holiday or fresh life somewhere else and tell Frankie to sell the ring and necklace to pay his debt. I would just like to have red roses on my grave to express my love because I'm incapable of showing it. It's better for me to take my own life than make you all ill [these last three words underlined] having a burden like me on you. I just haven't any strength or peace or anything to fight the impossible. At least I know I can have the name Shea on my grave because it's been changed by deed poll ... he can't get the money because it is in the name of Shea.

Ends: Please don't hate me for this: it's because I can't help it ..Frances xxxxxx

These notes reveal Frances's feelings, her guilt towards her family for her actions, the sincerity of her love for them and her concerns for them about money, particularly Reggie's unpaid debt to Frankie.

The ring and the necklace mentioned were originally gifts from Reggie to Frances, retrieved by him in the raid on her possessions in the immediate aftermath of her death. Rita

Smith told me that Reggie gave away certain items of Frances's jewellery to members of his family afterwards.

As for the phrase 'he can't get the money because it is in the name of Shea' this is likely to refer to a savings account passbook which Frances kept in her name. The note makes it clear that she knew her family needed the money: my understanding is that the little passbook was taken away by Reggie when he removed all Frances's belongings from the Shea home and Wimbourne Court. Here again, Rita Smith told me that Elsie had asked for the passbook and Reggie had responded by saying words to the effect of 'it can rot'.

I made contact with 'Bubbles', or Lily Shea as she was known at the time, since Frances's letter makes it clear she had confided in her, but she refused my request for an interview.

She confirmed that she was Frankie Shea's girlfriend for ten years (though she was known as Lily Shea, the pair never formally married) and that Frances's problems had started after the marriage to Reggie. Her recall of those times was obviously far too painful to discuss with me.

The PS on the back of the first suicide note was also puzzling, given that Clein's involvement in Frances's treatment had ended in 1965, eighteen months before her death.

When I sat in Lewis Clein's kitchen and asked him what he thought Frances meant by saying, 'Dr Clein and him killed me', he reacted quite calmly.

'Maybe it's because I let her go back home from the clinic,' he said, referring to her insistence that she leave Greenways, rather than prolong her stay.

This was a somewhat odd response. But later I understood that in Clein's profession, suicide notes from patients who die from an overdose go with the territory.

A professional psychiatrist, as Trevor Turner explained, sees suicide somewhat differently from the rest of us. 'It's one of the things a psychiatrist has to deal with,' he said.

'Some depressive conditions are so intractable that suicide is literally unavoidable. In Frances's case the combination of her depression, the cruel environment of Reggie and Ronnie, her limited response to treatment and her early history, before Reggie, of some depressive/personality issues as well would have combined to create a very resistant to treatment condition.'

The consultant psychiatrist who had treated Frances at Hackney Hospital and had been called at her inquest, Dr Julius Silverstone (known now as Dr Trevor Silverstone), is a leading expert on drug treatment in psychiatry. Highly respected in his field, he has now retired to New Zealand. He refused my request to be interviewed about Frances's story.

However, these are professionals, with sensitive confidentiality issues around their patients, and while their insights can be helpful perhaps it is the written word, the individual's 'voice' that tells us more after they've gone.

After absorbing the contents of these letters, I could only reach one conclusion: despite all the speculation and rumour around her death, Frances Shea died by her own hand of her own volition.

The drugs she had been taking over some time may have clouded her vision, blurred her perspective, but it is clear that Frances was determined to deploy them to end her pain for good.

She knew she was trapped. Her life was no longer her own. Expensive sunshine holidays, diamond rings, promise after promise from Reggie, would make no difference whatsoever. She alone knew, from those nightmare weeks 'living' with him, how Reggie operated, the way the Krays ran their lives with whispers and spies relaying snippets of information back to them 24/7.

Even if Reggie had been locked up for years, she'd have known he'd still make sure she was trapped within his orbit, relentlessly manipulating her to visit him, write to him, keep the ideal of the loving relationship alive.

It would have been impossible for her to form another relationship with anyone. He'd have continued to have had her watched, made sure that anyone who ventured too close was 'sorted out'. It would never have stopped.

As Albert Donoghue commented, all those years later: 'She had no future. She knew that.'

Despite all the blame heaped upon Reggie, his lifestyle and his possessiveness, my belief is it would have been the finality of Frances's death, the end of it all by her own choice, that would have sent Reggie into the emotional spiral that impacted so strongly on his actions afterwards and the murder of McVitie.

There was always guilt, mostly denied by Reggie at the time, but I'm pretty sure the overwhelming sense that he could no longer have any control over Frances was what pushed him close to madness.

The Kray twins were all about control; that was their raison d'être. They manipulated everyone around them – and they didn't stop doing this until the end of their days.

By removing Reggie's control of her for good, Frances finally defeated him in one sense. That, I believe, was at the heart of what Reggie couldn't handle.

But what about the Shea family? They too had been utterly defeated by the Krays. Their attempts to retrieve some dignity for Frances's memory were rejected in the face of officialdom.

Elsie and Frank had to live with the knowledge that not only had they lost a beloved daughter, but everyone around them knew the details of their tragedy, what had happened to their lives.

They weren't a sophisticated middle- or upper-class couple who could leave the country, settle in some sunny Mediterranean hideaway, far away from the whispers. They were just working-class Londoners who'd come through a war, raised their kids and hoped for something better. Now they just had to keep living their lives somehow, and come to terms, if that were possible, with their history – and, just like they had in the grimmest depths of wartime, get on with it.

They tried their best. Elsie eventually got her wish, and by the seventies Frank Senior had finally settled into a 'proper' job, as a clerk with the London Electricity Board. At the time, utility companies like the LEB were owned by the public sector, which entitled Frank Senior to a regular salary, paid holidays and, when he retired at sixty-five, a small pension. It wasn't much but it was a helpful addition to their state pensions when Elsie stopped working at the clothing factory when she too reached retirement age.

So by the early seventies, like millions of other British pensioners, the couple started to take advantage of the cheap travel now widely available: two-week winter sunshine package holidays in Spain were taken for many years. They tended to stay put during the summers.

But of course, Elsie could never ever get over her anger at what Reggie had done. The bitterness and the pain were always with her. As is sometimes the case with bereaved people, she would frequently talk about Frances as if she were still alive, still the pretty teenager carefully painting her nails in the upstairs bedroom at Ormsby Street.

It helped a little bit, having a different flat in Geffrye Street. But the memories would still come flooding back all the time. What made it even worse, of course, were the endless reminders of Kray notoriety, every time the Sheas picked up a tabloid newspaper and saw yet another story or photo about the twins.

Frank Senior, alas, didn't live long enough to read about the demise of the Krays. He died in Homerton Hospital following a heart attack in March 1987 at age seventy-five.

Elsie survived him by fourteen years, dying in 2002 at the age of eighty-five. Her final years, after Frank Senior died, remained uneventful, though she would have known about Ronnie's very public death and funeral in March 1995, followed by Reggie's in October 2000. Seeing – or being told about – the newspaper photos of Reggie kissing Frances's grave at Ronnie's funeral would have been yet another reminder too far for a frail seventy-something widow.

As for Frances's brother, Frankie, he remained as he always had, living in north London, immaculately dressed, highly personable, running a variety of businesses.

At age twenty-nine, he had fallen for Barbara Keane, a twenty-four-year-old widow with a two-year-old daughter, Jane. The couple married at St Etheldreda's Church, off Holborn Circus, in central London in August 1969. Later, Barbara gave birth to a son, also named Frank, and the family moved to a house in Etheldene Avenue, Muswell Hill.

For many years, through the seventies and eighties, life was good. Frank had secondhand car sites in Camden Town and

Islington and at one stage he opened a children's wear shop. Like his mother, the echoes of the past remained with him. He couldn't obliterate what had happened to his sister – and his part in it all. But it was easier to pick up a drink and party than it was to sit around going over it all endlessly in his mind.

He kept up a good front. He tried to be a good dad. No one saw the torment Frankie lived with or heard him talk about the family's pain. Only when he visited his mother, listened to her talking about his sister, again and again, did he really have to face the worst details of their painful past. And that was only for a few hours.

In the late eighties, disaster struck. Frankie lost a great deal of money in various financial endeavours. The house in Muswell Hill was sold. With the children gone, he and Barbara moved to a flat in Islington.

In the summer of 1999, Frankie was approaching sixty. Always a heavy social drinker, he'd started to binge, got stuck into the drinking as never before, and he eventually reached a disastrous breaking point. Frankie Shea crashed and burned. He had a breakdown. In a state of total distress, he wound up in rehab.

Rehab for drug and alcohol problems is a much-touted solution, yet it doesn't always work. For some, it is a kind of 'bandage': they stop, dry out and then, at some point, the bandage comes off and they start again. But for Frankie, rehab did work. Getting into the daily counselling sessions, talking about his excesses, his mistakes, his life, once he started, he couldn't stop. He'd carried too much pain around with him for too many years. He'd tried to blot it out with alcohol, but now he was much older. If he was to survive, he realised, to come to terms with who he was, the drinking had to go. For good.

In August 2000, Barbara died unexpectedly at the age of fifty-five. It was a testing time for Frankie but he stuck fast to his vow to never touch booze again.

By now, he was starting to be a regular at Alcoholics Anonymous meetings. He'd get up and 'share', talk about how drinking had affected his life, how he'd realised that sobriety had saved him and that the support he was getting from AA helped him cope, to get through the bad days without picking up a drink. The more he stayed sober, the more he could handle the reality of his past. At one point, he went to talk to young offenders in prison. He wanted the message to get through: 'Don't do what I did.'

But he didn't quite share everything. Because now that Frankie Shea had started facing the world soberly each day, he had no other choice but to look his innermost demon right in the eye.

And that demon was the secret he'd carried, the real reason behind much of the pain he'd been living with for over half his life. Over the New Year holiday in 2002, he spent a lot of time thinking. The Krays were dead now. His family had suffered enough through the years since Franny went. But he was beginning to wonder, was he right to keep what he knew to himself? And then, out of the blue, the phone rang.

It was a young reporter from a local paper. There was a new TV documentary coming out about the Krays. Would he answer a few questions about what he knew?

'Yes,' he said with some hesitation.

'I'll answer a few questions.'

CHAPTER 13

AN ENDING

Here is the story that appeared in the *East London Advertiser* on 18 January, 2002.

'I SPURNED GAY REG, SO HE WED MY SISTER IN REVENGE'

Reggie Kray's former brother in law has revealed the East End gangster married his sister because he spurned his gay advances. Frankie – who used to work as a driver for Reggie and his twin Ronnie before they were caged for murder said:

'That geezer married my sister because he was in love with me.

'I was one of those baby faced kids I suppose.'

'He did the worst thing any man could ever do to get his revenge at not being able to get hold of me and that's what it's all about.'

Dismissing claims by Reggie's former gay lover in prison, Bradley Allardyce, that Ronnie had murdered Frances by forcing pills down her throat, Frankie said:

'We know she committed suicide but Reggie was the instigator of it all as far as I'm concerned.'

He claimed Frances was so desperate to get away from Reggie that she changed her name back to Shea by deed poll, adding: 'That's how much she wanted to be away from that a***hole.'

'She married him to keep the peace because he threatened to kill me and my father.'

Frankie said his 85-year-old mum was still living with the memory of what happened to her daughter.

Elsie Shea died the same year the story was published. The comment about the threats to kill her family certainly coincides with what Frances wrote in her diary after the honeymoon, though as Frankie told it to the local paper, he believed Reggie made these threats before they wed. After finding this story in the newspaper archive, it was obvious I had to find Frankie Shea, see if he would talk to me, help put the final pieces to the jigsaw puzzle in place.

But where was he?

I was frequently told he still lived in north London, still drank in certain pubs, was definitely around. He'd been spotted in various places at different times. Yet ultimately all my enquiries drew a blank. People in the East End who barely knew him were happy to talk about him; he'd become a bit of an enigma, even a 'celebrity' in the story of his sister and the Kray twins.

AN ENDING

I discovered I wasn't the only writer seeking him out. Then, along the showbiz grapevine, I learned that key filmmakers had taken great interest in Frankie's story, inviting him to meetings and discussing ideas with him.

Frankie Shea listened to the filmmakers, shook hands and said he'd think about it. And that was it. Whatever his feelings, there wasn't any further sign of a public declaration of Frankie Shea's version of what happened to his sister, other than that brief outburst in 2002.

Perhaps, I mused, after voicing his long held feelings in the local paper story, he had read and heard too much about the Kray twins to ever believe he'd be given a fair hearing. Especially when many of his contemporaries from those days were still around, now mostly retired from the misdeeds of their past, but still out there, gossiping and swapping endless stories about the old days, in the same old haunts.

But getting sober had changed Frankie's world for good. That same year he spoke out, he decided it was time to get out of London and find a more tranquil existence in rural Essex.

Within months he'd met an attractive divorcee, Deborah Hawkins, and the pair soon became an item. Frank loved the quieter pace of the countryside and village life, after all the years in London. This, he decided, was exactly what he needed. Finally, in December 2010, after eight years together, the couple got married.

Eight months later, Frankie Shea was gone.

He'd committed suicide.

With an overdose of drugs.

From the *Herts & Essex Observer*, Tuesday 14 May 2013.

A brother-in-law of infamous London gangster Reggie Kray killed himself by taking a massive overdose of liquid morphine to end the agony of cancer a coroner has ruled.

Frank Shea, 71, took the lethal measure and an inquest at Chelmsford on May 13 probed the issue of whether his death was the result of an assisted suicide.

But Essex deputy assistant coroner, Lorna Tagliavini, ruled it was not and that Mr Shea had needed no help to take the drug and recorded that he took his own life.

She said: 'He had sufficient mobility and strength in his limbs to take the bottles from where they were stored in his bedroom, open them and swallow the contents without requiring or being given any assistance by another.'

She added she was aware of the difficult decisions the paramedics, doctor and family had to make, but said the professionals had sought advice from more senior colleagues. There was no 'one size fits all' guidelines for the professionals, but individual decisions had to be made for individual circumstances, she said.

Frank Shea died on August 5, 2011 from an overdose of morphine.

He had emptied four or five bottles of prescribed Oramorph and drunk 3,300mg of the liquid. He had been diagnosed with cancer of the larynx in April that year and his wife Deborah, 50, told the inquest: 'He was just waiting for death. Everyone knew he was just counting down the days.'

He had refused any surgery and told family

members, his GP and palliative care nurses he did not want to be resuscitated.

Mrs Shea told the hearing: 'I think suicide was his intention. He refused treatment from the off. He had no quality of life because he would not have an operation.

'It was a case where we were waiting. I think now, looking back, what he did was incredibly brave. He just knew each day he was getting worse and worse and he decided to take matters into his own hands. I think in his mind he thought by the time I found him in the morning it would be over.'

She found him collapsed in bed about 8.30am on 5 August and the empty medicine bottles were on the floor. Paramedics gave him all the antidote they had available from two ambulances, but then Mrs Shea pleaded with them to stop treatment and let him die at home as he wished. She knew he would not have wanted to be revived.

She told the court: 'I told the doctor, "I don't want them to do it" and she said, "Let them try." She didn't feel it was going to make any difference.'

The paramedics, in liaison with his GP Dr Juliet Rayner, who had the ultimate responsibility, decided to stop treatment. Mr Shea died about 11pm that night.

Police had attended both in the morning and after his death. Detective Inspector Alan Pitcher told the coroner police initially had concerns that it was 'a potential assisted suicide'.

He said that there was no living will, but from

numerous notes and poems in Mr Shea's handwriting he gauged that 'they were of a man in a desperate place.'

Mr Shea was able to move about and feed himself, the prescribed bottles were in his bedroom and the decision to stop further treatment had been on medical advice, added the inspector.

'After I had conducted my investigation I was happy there were no criminal offences. It was a very sad situation,' he said.

Questioned by the coroner about why she thought police attended, Dr Rayner told the hearing: 'I was confident neither Debbie nor I had tried to assist Frank's suicide.'

Expert medical witness Dr Stephen Metcalfe told the hearing Mr Shea had taken 'a massive overdose' some hours before he was found by his wife.

He said any further treatment would have been fruitless and continued: 'I believe he had permanent brain damage and would have died anyway. I believe the right decision was made to stop treatment.'

He admitted that such decisions where consent is given on behalf of someone else were 'a grey area' but the patient's wellbeing should always come first.

Finally discovering the tragic end Frankie Shea's life had taken, and the bleak irony of him choosing to take exactly the same path his sister did all those years ago, was yet another shocking point in my research.

And it was obvious that the brief story in the East London paper revealed long-buried guilt for what happened in his sister's tragic marriage, guilt and remorse that left him in emotional turmoil for much of his adult life.

In those years while Frances was still alive, he'd only ever mentioned the secret incident to one person – and that was his mum, Elsie, though it's not known how much of it Elsie repeated to her husband – or her daughter. But how could the Sheas discuss it openly in conversation? Back then, it wasn't exactly the kind of thing you talked about with everyone, was it? A gay overture? From Reggie Kray? Frankie wouldn't have been the only one to wish to keep such a thing under wraps back then.

Of course Frankie had been a tad naïve in those teenage Regal billiard-hall days when he'd been so flattered by the attention the Krays had started to pay him. They'd made such a huge impression on him, six years older, slickly dressed, well-known 'faces' in the area, plenty of money, drinks across the bar all night and, of course, they let him drive the expensive cars.

To a car-crazy Hoxton kid in the fifties this was Dreamland, driving motors you could never afford in a million years.

He was a mug, really, Frankie told himself. He'd been completely taken in by their flash aura, their charisma. They were quasi-glamorous figures then – and in a raw, dank place like the fifties East End, glamour was an awesome commodity. Only film stars and royals had glamour.

One night, when they'd all been drinking too much, he'd gone with Reggie back to the house in Vallance Road. He'd passed out. Until he'd woken up abruptly with a start – to find Reggie Kray attempting oral sex on him.

In sheer blind panic, he'd started shouting and screaming. It was loud enough for Charlie Senior and one of Reggie's uncles to hear him yelling and, thankfully, step in and pull the inebriated Reggie away in disgust.

Charlie Senior already knew about the twins' youthful homosexual escapades and couldn't disguise his dislike of what they were doing, though Violet remained tolerant of homosexuality throughout her life.

Ashamed and fearful, the teenage Frankie had quickly dived for his stuff and bolted through the front door, out into the street.

The incident had quickly sobered him up: for young Frankie it was probably the biggest shock of his life. Where he came from, people never really talked about homosexuality openly, just the odd whisper and nudge. Yes, he'd known that it existed; even at school you'd hear scornful, mocking talk about 'nancy boys' and what they did to each other.

Not long after he'd started going to the billiard hall, one of the blokes he vaguely knew had made comments about Ronnie Kray and poofs to him one night, but he'd shrugged them off, thinking 'So what?'

So for Frankie, the discovery that Reggie Kray, someone he'd kind of looked up to, wanted to do those things to him, shocked and terrified him at the same time. This was a man with a reputation for a killer punch. His twin was renowned for his love of the knife. What was going to happen now, when he saw him again?

Nothing happened.

The next time he saw Frankie in the billiard hall, Reggie acted as if the whole thing had been a dream. The drinks still came across the bar. Would Frankie drive him somewhere tomorrow?

Frankie was relieved, for a bit. Reggie had got the message.

But was it going to happen again? He could hardly refuse to go anywhere with Reggie, what with driving for him. He needed the cash then, anyway.

So he playacted, continued to go along with the so-called friendship, being pals with Reggie Kray but managing to steer himself away from the big drinking sessions with them, all the going round to Vallance Road afterwards, not too difficult once Frankie had a girlfriend.

And then, without warning, Reggie was taking Frances out. Weeks later, he was talking about them getting married. His dad seemed to think it was okay but Frankie didn't. Yet he didn't dare talk about what he knew. He couldn't.

Much of the guilt that plagued and tormented Frankie Shea for many years of his life stemmed from the fact that even though he'd blurted out something to his mum about Reggie, he'd done nothing at all to warn his sister properly, sit down with her, do the serious big brother talk, to steer her away from Reggie right from the start. Why did he never try to do that? he asked himself time after time. There were opportunities galore, especially at the beginning, when Reggie was in prison and Franny was sitting up in her room, writing to him all the time. It wasn't as if they weren't close, he loved his baby sister and she always loved him right back.

But he'd been so scared at the time, worried about himself. He'd even made a brief attempt to get away from the Kray scene, when he moved to another part of London. It didn't last. He came back to Hoxton after a few months.

Maybe Reggie had guessed that this 'vanishing' was because of him – they always wanted to know where so-and-so was, what so-and-so was doing – but curiously, nothing had been said, probably because by then, it was widely accepted that Frances was 'Reggie's girl'.

So he'd remained friends with Reggie, all buddy buddy, even when he stopped driving for them, because that was the only way with them, whatever you felt or thought. And you didn't dare say anything to anyone around them, they'd go straight back to the twins and dob you in.

It was sickening, how he'd kept quiet, walked Frances down the aisle, knowing all this. He'd hated himself for it, even though long before she'd died, the so-called 'friendship' had been well and truly over. That £1,000 debt Reggie never repaid saw to that. But of course, he'd simply used it to scare Frances even more, every time she mentioned it.

In Frankie Shea's mind, there was never any doubt about it: Reggie had started courting Frances as an act of pure revenge, a means of getting back at him, Frankie, for that drunken rejection.

The Krays could be incredibly generous, in the East End way. But they were totally unforgiving when it came to getting their own back if they'd been upset by someone. No one rejected a Kray twin without retribution. Reggie fancied two good-looking teenagers, both called Frankie. If he couldn't have one, he'd make sure he had the other...

Frankie had also struggled with the knowledge that he, not his mum or dad, was the one that could have done something. He could have warned his sister about exactly what she was dealing with long before he accompanied her down the aisle – and towards her early death. Yet he'd stayed silent.

Should anyone blame Frankie Shea for his inability to step in, to try to 'rescue' Frances from her fate? It's debatable. In that era, telling anyone that Reggie Kray really wanted him, not his sister, was unimaginable; they were such different times.

Now, of course, someone making a gay overture is hardly a big deal, a person's sexuality is no longer a matter of shame or concealment. In the fifties, men could go to prison for being gay, but who'd have had the bottle in those days to go to the police and say 'Reggie Kray tried to give me a blow job?' And what copper would have taken action, anyway?

In the end, despite all the pain the Sheas had lived with for all those years, it's not difficult to understand why Frankie Shea kept quiet about what he knew. And why he didn't grab the opportunity to attack Reggie Kray in a major blaze of publicity once Reggie was safely beneath the earth.

Essentially, Frank Shea was 'old school': he'd kept the same East End values he'd grown up with. And silence, virtually unknown now in the twenty-first-century world of kiss-and-sell, was a big part of that long vanished world. He'd also had his mum to consider. But even after Elsie had gone, after the story appeared in the paper, he'd known there was no real merit in making a huge noise about it all. It wouldn't change anything.

When you consider the stories and deals the Krays were happy to cut with the media over thirty years, in exchange for cash and further notoriety (though to be fair, their reputation as hard men meant more to them than any amount of money), there's a certain kind of dignity in Frankie Shea's decision to remain silent about his story, rather than sell it off to the media as a commodity once the Kray twins had died. The past was the past and once he'd quit drinking and moved away from the East End, Frank Shea found great personal contentment in the later years of his life. He'd wanted the world to know the truth about his sister. But perhaps he felt it was a story that could only be told after he'd gone.

And so I finally reached a concluding point in the story of Frances Shea. She'd eerily predicted Reggie's destiny if he didn't let her go and indeed became the ghost that continued to haunt him.

He had all the time in the world during his thirty-odd years of incarceration to ponder his youth, his mistakes: there were terrible breakdowns and suicide attempts during those years in prison, though he would always present the face of the defiant yet avuncular gangster to the media when required to.

In January 1990, London Weekend Television, as it was then known, screened a documentary film entitled *Still Krays After All These Years* as part of their prestigious current affairs series, *The London Programme*.

The film focused on the twins' business activities in prison after two decades and was screened prior to the launch of the biographical movie of their story, *The Krays*.

Journalist and documentary filmmaker John Parrish told me his story of working on that documentary – and his memories of both twins on interviewing them. His meetings with them for the documentary underline the very different impressions the twins could create, face to face. He told me:

> Born in the East End and raised there until we moved to Essex when I was six, I'd had close ties to the East End my whole life. Most of my family lived there and as a kid and student most of my Saturday and holiday jobs had been there. I'd worked on a Brick Lane market stall for years. My grandfather was an

East End car dealer; my father had a car parts shop in the East End.

Growing up I'd heard family stories about the Kray twins. When the twins were starting out, they'd attempted to put the squeeze on my grandfather. Apparently, granddad, a big tough man, had sent them away with a flea in their ear.

In the late eighties, the Krays were becoming popular East End icons. There had always been people who regarded them as latter-day Robin Hoods, but now it seemed there was an all-out effort to rehabilitate their reputation, turn the Kray name into a brand.

Ronnie's affairs were mostly handled by his then-wife, Kate, a Rolls-Royce-driving blonde who happened to live in the same pleasant Kent village my grandparents had retired to.

I interviewed Charlie, the twins' older brother and other assorted characters, some living in squalor, others in palatial circumstances. I quickly learned that though the twins were safely behind bars, they still commanded respect and induced fear.

Some of their old friends and foes flatly refused to speak to me. I lost count of the doors slammed in my face when I tried contacting people in their old neighbourhood. Time and time again I heard that though the twins might be locked up "they've still got friends on the outside". This fear was very real.

The other thing I heard constantly was that the twins only harmed their own, meaning fellow gangsters. When they ruled East London nobody feared crimes like rape and burglary because the twins 'policed' the area and would hand out their own violent form of justice if they caught anyone misbehaving on their manor.

'Women and children were safe on the streets then,' I was repeatedly told.

This, I knew, was absolute romanticised nonsense. I went through the archives of local papers and found plenty of references to all kinds of horrific crimes. Memorably, one day I found a story on the front page of a local newspaper about a rape, while on the back page there was a story about the twins presenting a cheque to a local boxing gym. So much for women and children being safe.

As I saw it, the twins were not latter-day Robin Hoods. They were a couple of thugs who preyed upon people. I saw them as parasites and the people who mythologised and revered them as fools. Nothing since has changed my mind. Not even meeting them.

Through my research, I got word: Reggie wanted to meet me. My documentary wasn't exactly going to be complimentary, though it seemed Reggie had got it into his head that it would be. Either that or he just couldn't resist the opportunity to try and charm another member of the media.

At Lewes Prison, Reggie was led into the visiting room, a big smile on his face. I remember being surprised at how old he looked – he was then around fifty-seven – and that he was a man of about average size, though barrel-chested and bristling with repressed energy.

AN ENDING

He shook my hand with the usual bone-crunching gangster grip, greeted me warmly. 'I'm really grateful to you for giving me the opportunity to have my side of the story out there,' he said.

I didn't mention that what I was actually doing was exploring how two killers could effectively be involved in a business from behind bars that was re-branding them as Robin Hoods who loved their dear old mum.

Reggie was earnest, avuncular, smiled and laughed a lot.

If I hadn't known he'd stabbed Jack 'The Hat' McVitie to death, I would have been completely fooled. He chatted openly about how he hoped the sale of paintings and books would bankroll a campaign to get him and Ronnie free.

There was no sense of menace from Reggie.

Through my work I'd met a few killers and they usually made me feel uneasy. Reggie didn't. He could have been an elderly East End relation. Later, he sent me a signed book and a letter, thanking me again for the opportunity to tell his story.

Then I met Ronnie.

I've never met anyone since who struck me as so evil.

The meeting was at Broadmoor, the hospital for the criminally insane. I went with Kate, Ronnie's wife at the time. Beforehand she warned me not to interrupt Ronnie and that he could come across as menacing. No kidding!

We sat at a very small table in the visiting room and Ronnie came in. I noticed Peter Sutcliffe, the infamous Yorkshire Ripper, behind him. Ronnie was wearing a suit, an incongruous look in that place.

Ronnie sat across the table from me and hissed, 'You're late!'

Those were his first words. No preamble, no greeting. His tongue flicked across his lips and his black eyes bored right into me. All of a sudden that table seemed very small. I could easily see Ronnie leaping over it and tearing at my throat and I had no doubt if I said the wrong thing he might be inclined to do so.

This man radiated evil.

As I said, I'd met killers before. I'd even gone undercover and met paedophiles.

But Ronnie Kray was in a class of his own.

Looking into his eyes was like looking into the eyes of a lizard. They were dark, expressionless and cold. I'd never met anyone before or since who was so malevolent.

We chatted about the documentary but Ronnie was hard to make conversation with. Kate kept prompting him to talk but he seemed distracted, disinterested. When he did speak he was softly spoken, almost girlish. Like his twin, he wasn't a particularly big man or physically intimidating. But he was scary in a way that Sutcliffe, sitting nearby, a serial killer of nightmare proportions, simply wasn't. Ronnie was bloody frightening. Sutcliffe was not.

I believed then, and still do, that while Reggie saw extreme violence as just the way business was done in the East End, Ronnie actually enjoyed it.

AN ENDING

Maureen Flanagan, loyal to the family, visited the twins in prison throughout their lives. Violet Kray made her promise to continue to visit them just before she died in hospital in August 1982, age seventy-two.

'Reggie would only talk about Frances if I was on my own, never if there was another visitor there,' Maureen told me. 'I'd take flowers to Violet's grave and he'd ask when I was going and made me promise I'd put roses on Frances's grave. The card was always the same: "To Frances, you are with me for always, Reg".

'In all the years I visited, Ronnie never mentioned her. Not once.'

Carol-Anne Kelly is an attractive blonde sixtysomething Londoner who met Reggie Kray in Parkhurst prison in the eighties. At the time she was visiting her former husband. She told me: 'I was in the visiting room and Reggie came over and introduced himself. The first thing he said to me was, "You remind me of my late wife Frances, your mannerisms are the same, the way you use your hands to express yourself."'

Later, after divorcing, Carol-Anne corresponded with Reggie and visited him for a few years. He frequently confided in her but she ended the friendship when she realised he was getting far too serious about their relationship.

'He said he was scared of going to hell for what he had done in his life – and that given the chance, he'd have done things differently.

'He said Frances was the most pure thing in his life and that part of him blamed his brother for what happened. It was a threesome, not a twosome.

'"When you come from a very tight knit family, it's very hard for other people to come in," he said.

'I didn't see a monster. I saw a man who regretted everything,' Carol-Anne told me.

Purity. It's not a word you can easily connect with the Kray twins, is it? But from all that I had learned, Frances Shea died as she had lived in her brief marriage, a virgin bride.

She was certainly innocent of the world when Reggie met her as a schoolgirl. But by the time Frances decided to kill herself many years later, she'd seen and experienced far too much that was utterly shaming for a young girl who was already emotionally fragile: that very innocence itself, so appealing to Reggie, was brutally corrupted by her exposure to Reggie's world.

Whether Reggie could not consummate the marriage because he preferred male sexual partners or because he simply could not bring himself to damage or defile that purity in any way has to remain an unanswered question. Most likely, it was a combination of both. Yet he succeeded in defiling Frances mentally, totally destroying her peace of mind – without any physical expression of love.

At the final count, the veil of sentimentality that Reggie Kray nurtured through his life around Frances is the last thing left to consider, some sense of his true motivation.

He insisted that she should be buried in her wedding dress and had this poetic inscription by William Shakespeare engraved on her grave: 'If I could write the beauty of your eyes/ And in fresh numbers number all your graces/ the age to come would say "this poet lies"/ such heavenly touches ne'er touched earthly faces'. These gestures do not seem, at first glance, to be anything other than hugely sentimental ways to mark the passing of a much-loved woman.

Or are they?

AN ENDING

Consider the insistence that Frances had to be buried as a virgin bride: pure, untouched. There is dramatic symbolism in that: virginity before marriage is no longer an ideal in much of Western culture today, yet it still carried some meaning in Britain half a century ago.

Yet the idea of the virgin bride, pure and untouched forever IN THE TOMB would have had immense appeal to Reggie: it was *his* bride, *his* tomb. Again, this was about total control, the same control he exercised so thoroughly by scooping up all her possessions – and even buying the freehold to the plot on which she was buried.

But surely the Shakespeare sonnet on her memorial stone is a relatively innocuous, fitting tribute to Frances's beauty?

It is. But only at first glance.

Until you realise that William Shakespeare wrote the sonnet, 'Sonnet 17', as an ode to procreation, to having children (as he did the preceding sixteen).

Knowing how much time Reggie Kray put into reading poetry, the Bible and so much else in prison, he'd have surely known about the history of that particular Shakespeare sonnet – and for whom it had been written.

The sonnet, you see, had not been penned by Shakespeare for a much-loved woman at all.

It had been written as an ode, a dedication to someone who had inspired the writer.

An ode to an exceptionally beautiful young man...